IMAGES
of America

LEGENDS OF HOLLYWOOD FOREVER CEMETERY

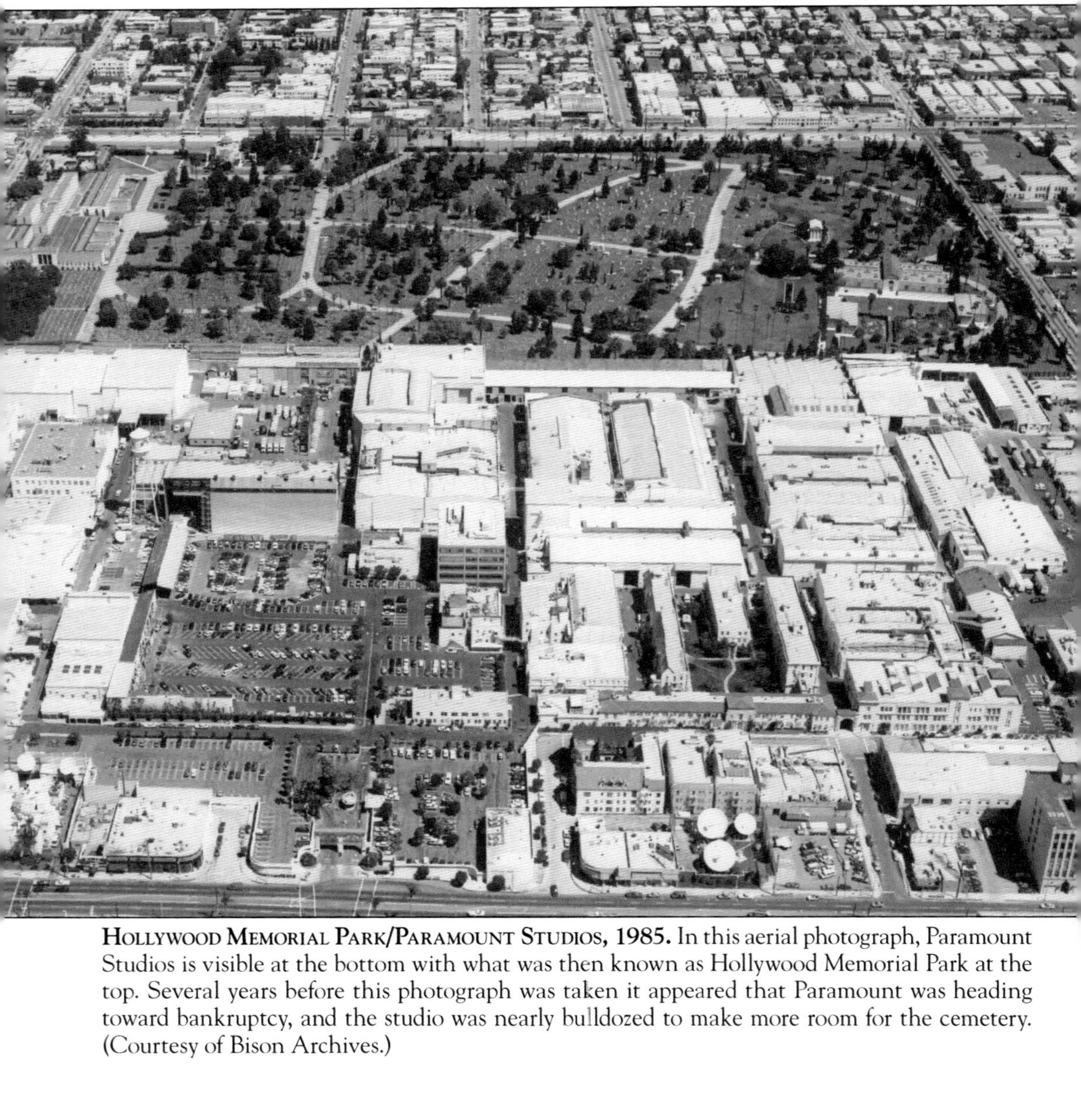

Hollywood Memorial Park/Paramount Studios, 1985. In this aerial photograph, Paramount Studios is visible at the bottom with what was then known as Hollywood Memorial Park at the top. Several years before this photograph was taken it appeared that Paramount was heading toward bankruptcy, and the studio was nearly bulldozed to make more room for the cemetery. (Courtesy of Bison Archives.)

On the Cover: Hollywood Forever Cemetery, 2016. One of the most historic spots in America, if not the world, Hollywood Forever Cemetery contains the graves of hundreds of people who left their mark on the world of entertainment. Pictured here is the grave of Johnny Ramone, the guitarist for the Ramones. His statue has become a gathering spot in Hollywood for lovers of rock 'n' roll, just as Jim Morrison's grave in Paris still attracts flocks of fans to Pere Lechaise Cemetery. (Photograph by Kim Stephens.)

IMAGES
of America

Legends of Hollywood Forever Cemetery

E.J. Stephens and Kim Stephens

ARCADIA
PUBLISHING

ISBN 978-1-4671-2586-4

Published by Arcadia Publishing
Charleston, South Carolina

Printed in the United States of America

Library of Congress Control Number: 2017942078

For all general information, please contact Arcadia Publishing:
Telephone 843-853-2070
Fax 843-853-0044
E-mail sales@arcadiapublishing.com
For customer service and orders:
Toll-Free 1-888-313-2665

Visit us on the Internet at www.arcadiapublishing.com

Dedicated to Tyler Cassity and his staff at Hollywood Forever, who have breathed new "life" into the old boneyard.

Contents

ACKNOWLEDGMENTS

The authors would like to thank everyone at Arcadia Publishing for their hard work, especially editor Stacia Bannerman.

Heartfelt thanks go out to Tyler Cassity and his staff at Hollywood Forever Cemetery for resuscitating a decrepit graveyard and transforming it into a place to celebrate life. We would also like to thank fellow taphophiles Karie A. Bible and Steve Goldstein for sharing their passion and love of Hollywood Forever. Thanks to the good people at findagrave.com for doing a lot of the heavy lifting. And a sincere thank-you to our friend Marc Wanamaker for being such a fountain of knowledge about Hollywood history and for making his treasure trove of Bison Archives images available to us.

We are button-popping proud of our children, Mariah and Dylan. We love you to the moon and back! We are grateful every day for our parents, Dick de Geus and Pherbia Stephens. And to Kim's amazing mother, Lorey de Geus, who we lost during the writing of this book, we want you to know that you will be forever loved, forever remembered, and forever missed. We will carry you in our hearts all of our days.

The authors would like to thank our dear friends (in alphabetical order, to avoid the perception of favoritism) Arthur, Herb, Liane, Michelle, Renard, Sam, and Sean ("the Disnerds") for their loyalty and friendship through thick and thin. Passion!

Kim would like to thank Caylyn Reeves (Is she from *Frozen*?) for keeping her sane during her day job. For the same reason, E.J. wishes to thank Erica Tomlinson, Jonathon Auxier, and LaFonda Perez.

And a shout-out goes to all the great Dia De Los Muertos celebrants at Hollywood Forever who help make it the most fun night of the year.

We strive throughout for location accuracy, but if any errors are found, please write us at deadwrite@yahoo.com.

All images courtesy of Marc Wanamaker/Bison Archives, unless otherwise credited.

INTRODUCTION

A turn takes you off Santa Monica Boulevard—once a stretch of legendary Route 66—and away from the world of the living. Just past the gates, you coast to a stop under a shady tree. Stepping outside, you lock the doors, even though it doesn't feel like you need to. Although surrounded by thousands of people, the only sounds you hear are the rustling of the leaves, the splash of a fountain, and the honking of geese on a distant pond.

The necropolis you have just entered is the Hollywood Forever Cemetery, a city of the dead with a six-figure population. You have come here to disappear off the Los Angeles grid—to slow the pace for awhile. You have also come to get unobstructed views of some of Tinseltown's most iconic landmarks: the 50-foot letters of the Hollywood Sign, the Griffith Observatory, and the Paramount Studios water tower. But mostly, you have come to commune with dozens of souls you never actually met, yet befriended during the hours they spent entertaining you from the stage, screen, or radio.

The first group of friends are found a short walk away, near the chapel. You enter a building with two floors of post office box–sized niches, each containing the cremains of a passed life. Downstairs, you pass by silent-era stars Bebe Daniels and her husband, Ben Lyon, the man who changed Norma Jeane Baker's name to Marilyn Monroe. Agnes Ayres, another silent star, is nearby. Upstairs is Jerry Siegel, half of the team that created Superman, and his wife, Joanne, who was the model for the first Lois Lane.

Along another passage, you pause to say hello to Ford Sterling, once one of the world's most famous silent comedians, and Elmo Lincoln, cinema's first Tarzan. Continuing on to another building, you greet Joan Hackett, whose epitaph tells you to "Go Away—I'm Asleep." Clifton Webb, and possibly his ghost, is nearby, as is Renee Adoree, a delightful talent who has been forgotten by all but those who love silent film.

Farther along, you pause by Mildred Harris, Charlie Chaplin's first wife. She is near Paramount cofounder Jesse L. Lasky and director Victor Fleming, who, during 1939, directed both *Gone with the Wind* and *The Wizard of Oz*. Ahead in a different building is Edgar Ulmer, a director who could guild cinematic gold from dirt-cheap Poverty Row budgets. The Ritz Brothers are close by, as is Nelson Riddle.

Outdoors, you stroll past the great Paul Muni toward Mel Blanc, a man whose thousand voices, all now silent, will entertain Warner Bros. cartoon fans forever. Waving to Carl "Alfalfa" Switzer, you pause to pay a visit to Charles Middleton, whose portrayal of Ming the Merciless terrified legions of young *Flash Gordon* fans everywhere during the 1930s. Close by is Alan Crosland, director of *The Jazz Singer*, the film that essentially ended the silent era. To the right is silent star Karl Dane, a tragic Tinseltown figure, who took his own life after losing his silent film career, thanks largely to Crosland's work. In a nearby building adjacent to the Paramount lot is gangster Bugsy Siegel, who left behind both Las Vegas—which he helped create—and undoubtedly scores of bodies.

Ahead in the distance are Douglas Fairbanks's *père et fils*. Across the way by the lake is Johnny Ramone, the rarest of individualists: a punk rocker who was a conservative Republican. Nearby is Fay Wray, forever remembered as the love interest of King Kong. Continuing around the lake, you stop to offer pleasantries to director John Huston and Johnny Ramone's bandmate Dee Dee. You greet Maila Nurmi, better known as Vampira, ironically watched over by Darren McGavin, who as the title character in *Kolchak: The Night Stalker*, hunted down vampires during the 1970s. McGavin is himself shadowed by fashion cop Mr. Blackwell.

Nearby is Col. Griffith J. Griffith, the man who donated to Los Angeles the huge park that now bears his name, yet went from hero to pariah after shooting his wife in the face. Looking up from Colonel Griffith's grave toward the Hollywood hills, you can see the observatory that is named after him. Continuing on, you find Cecil B. DeMille, the man largely responsible for the industry that lured many of the other Hollywood Forever residents to Southern California. Steps away you say hello to Florence Lawrence, the world's first movie star, before retracing your steps to say good day to, "Would you believe," Don Adams—Maxwell Smart himself.

Later, you rest on a bench that serves as the gravestone for Tyrone Power. It is situated near Marion Davies, the mistress of William Randolph Hearst, who Orson Welles so scathingly satirized in *Citizen Kane*. Charlie Chaplin's mother is close by, as is Virginia Rappe, the starlet who died after a party hosted by Roscoe "Fatty" Arbuckle, ending both Fatty's career and Hollywood's era of innocence.

Canadian geese chase you past Nelson Eddy and the universally despised Harry Cohn, head of Columbia Pictures. You greet Mickey Rooney and give a knowing nod to Toto, Dorothy's dog from *The Wizard of Oz*, before entering through the brass doors of an imposing granite-faced mausoleum. Inside, you stop to say hello to director William Desmond Taylor, whose still unsolved murder, coupled with the Arbuckle scandal that same year, prompted millions of moviegoers to demand that Hollywood clean up its act.

Peter Lorre, immortalized in such classic films as *Casablanca* and *The Maltese Falcon*, is here, as is the amazing Eleanor Powell, a dancer so talented that she intimidated Fred Astaire. Close to Barbara La Marr, another of the silent era's cautionary tales, is Elmer Berger, the guy who invented the rearview mirror. Peter Finch is here as well; he won an Oscar for his performance in *Network*, declaring, "I'm mad as hell and I'm not going to take this anymore!"

This brings you to Rudolph Valentino, the "great lover" of the silent screen, another cinematic friend who died decades before you were born.

Hollywood Forever Cemetery, known to taphophiles everywhere as "H4E," is a final resting place like no other. While many cemeteries boast a famous "permanent resident" or two among their internments, H4E has an embarrassment of riches, as it were, including some of the most recognized figures in entertainment history. Names like Rudolph Valentino, Douglas Fairbanks, and Cecile B. DeMille are still familiar to much of the world's population, even those who have never seen any of their films.

Nestled on 60 acres in the heart of Hollywood, H4E is, in essence, American film's early history writ large. It was founded among the citrus groves and vineyards of the Eden-esque village of Hollywood at the close of the 19th century. In those days, alcohol and "movies"—as the pioneers who worked in the flickers, not the films themselves, were then known—were both unwelcome.

What was then known as Hollywood Cemetery was originally intended as the eternal home for the pioneers of this bucolic community, like city founders Harvey H. and Daeida Wilcox. By 1910, the first moviemakers had arrived and the formerly dry independent town of Hollywood was annexed by the city of Los Angeles. Other producers quickly followed, and by the end of the decade, Hollywood was churning out the majority of the world's films.

Thanks to the universal appeal of silent film, dozens of actors quickly became recognizable to the world's huddled nickelodeon masses. Many of these early cinematic pioneers lived, worked, played, partied, and eventually died in Hollywood. As the only burial ground in town, Hollywood Cemetery became their primary internment spot. Found here are the graves of many of these early actors, producers, directors, writers, and crewmembers whose names—and often the films they made—have been lost to history.

At the start of the 1920s, the cemetery sold off half of its acreage. Eventually, the Paramount and RKO studios were built on this plot of land once intended for the dead. Part of the remaining property was set aside as Beth Olam Cemetery, a burial place for those of the Jewish faith.

In 1927, silent-screen lover Rudolph Valentino was interred in the Great Mausoleum, in what was intended to be a temporary crypt. Nearly 90 years later he is still here, and every year on August 23, the day he died, a Valentino celebration is held in the mausoleum by his fans, nearly all of whom were born after his death.

In 1939, a shyster named Jules Roth bought the cemetery, renamed it Hollywood Memorial Park, and spent the next several decades running it into the ground (pun intended), draining the cemetery's maintenance funds to pay for his lavish lifestyle. What had been "the cemetery of the stars" quickly lost its luster, with more celebrities choosing to spend the rest of eternity in one of the nearby Forest Lawn cemeteries.

Stumbling along for years, the cemetery made headlines for the occasional luminary burial, like the 1959 internment of Cecil B. DeMille. But the grass literally was greener in other area cemeteries, and Hollywood Memorial was relegated to second-tier celebrity status.

Plagued by scandalous ownership, the cemetery fell into decrepitude; it made more money from families removing their loved ones rather than on new internments. For decades, the mismanaged burial grounds steadily crept toward ruin with leaky roofs inside the mausoleums and weed-choked graves outside. By the end of the 20th century, there was even talk of locking the gates of the historic cemetery for good.

Enter young Midwestern brothers Tyler and Brent Cassity. In 1998, they purchased the cemetery and rechristened it Hollywood Forever. This new generation of forward-thinking cemeterians have since invested millions in repairs and added video memorials called "LifeStories" on their website, where visitors can learn more about the former lives housed here. Unlike LA's Forest Lawn cemeteries, which are tight-lipped about the stars inside their gates, the Cassitys capitalized on H4E's celebrity heritage to bring the cemetery back to life (again, pun intended).

During its early decades, the cemetery had been segregated, allowing only white burials. In 1952, African American Hattie McDaniel, who famously played Mammy in *Gone with the Wind*, was refused internment. One of the first acts of the Cassity brothers was to offer to rebury McDaniel's remains at H4E to right an old wrong. (Her family chose not to exhume her body, and instead, a cenotaph—a grave without a body—was placed near the lake in McDaniel's honor.)

Cemeteries were once considered parks meant for use by the living as well as the dead. This all eventually changed, and the two became separate domains. The new owners have worked hard to pierce the veil and make H4E a place to go in Southern California—and not just on Memorial Day.

Today, a visit to Hollywood Forever Cemetery is a look at Hollywood's past and present in a parklike setting. Not only are there thousands of monuments, each representing a life, but also a family of peacocks, flocks of geese, and dozens of stray cats (cared for by volunteers) that have made the grounds their home.

You may be thinking, "Sure, Hollywood Forever sounds like a great place and all, but who wants to visit a cemetery?"

Well, the answer is lots of people—some to pay their respects, others to enjoy the solitude, and still more to take one of Karie A. Bible's wonderful tours. More come during warm summer weekends, hordes in fact, to picnic on the Fairbanks lawn while watching classic films projected on the side of the Cathedral Mausoleum.

Additionally, H4E has become the must-see spot in Southern California around Halloween when the cemetery hosts the premier Dia De Los Muertos (Day of the Dead) festival in the Southland. Dia De Los Muertos, which originated in Mexico, is based on the belief that a loved one is not truly dead until forgotten. During the festival, the living get to honor the dead by elaborately decorating graves with altars, mementos, and photographs of the deceased. Women wear brightly colored costumes and carry marigolds, which are thought to attract the souls of the dead. Families gather around the graves of their descendants, often with their faces painted like skulls to make the departed feel more welcome should they decide to return and take part in the fun.

In an era of film flight, the entertainment industry appears to be slipping away from its home of the last century, and the question everybody seems to be asking around LA these days is "Is Hollywood forever?"

Time will tell, but it is comforting to know that whatever happens with the ever-evolving entertainment industry, Hollywood Forever Cemetery will remain, and with its current ownership in place, there are no longer any lingering fears that the living public will be barred from its gates.

Where some see only stones, others hear stories, making H4E a mecca for "tombstone tourists" from around the world. Just like its surrounding city, Hollywood Forever is a place of memories and cautionary tales.

Hollywood was built on storytelling, and as long as there is a Hollywood Forever Cemetery, there will be memories to relive and stories to tell.

E.J. and Kim Stephens
Newhall, California
May 2017

One

Chapel Columbarium, Colonnade, and Mausoleum

The Chapel Columbarium holds the cremains of thousands of people, including those of several celebrities. Here, either displayed in urns or hidden behind bronze plaques, are the final resting places of the beautiful Ann Sheridan, Hollywood's "Oomph Girl," and silent film stars like Agnes Ayres, Bebe Daniels, Ben Lyon, and Edna Flugrath.

Also here is Elmo Lincoln, the first man to play Tarzan on-screen, who is near Ford Sterling, once the chief Keystone Cop. Frank Woods, the man who co-wrote the script for *The Birth of a Nation*, is here, and so is cinematographer Gregg Toland, whose most famous work was for *Citizen Kane*. Silent star Louise Fazenda is not interred here, but there is a statue she modelled for inside the columbarium that was brought here to celebrate the opening of the building in the 1920s.

One of Australia's greatest athletes is in the columbarium, along with counter-culture figure Tomata du Plenty. Also in the columbarium is developer Hobart Whitley, a "Sooner" who rushed into Oklahoma and helped found hundreds of towns in the West—including Hollywood.

Also present are lots of folks who once worked for fellow H4E internee Cecile B. DeMille. Among them is Ann Bauchens, DeMille's editor for over four decades, and Jeanie McPherson, who penned over 30 of DeMille's screenplays. Jesse L. Lasky Jr., son of the cofounder of Paramount Pictures, is also here. Cecile B. DeMille was once one of his father's partners, and Lasky Jr. later wrote many of DeMille's scripts.

Hollywood Forever Cemetery contains hundreds of hard-luck stories about the tarnished side of Tinseltown. Many of these tales are told here. Included in this group is the aforementioned Agnes Ayres, who in short order lost her career, her fortune, and her health. Jerry Siegel, one of the two men who brought Superman to life but shared little of the fruits of his labor, is here as well. Also in the columbarium is Lana Clarkson, the B-movie "scream queen" who only reached household-name status after she was shot by Phil Spector.

While all cemeteries house victims of accidents, scandal, suicide, and murder, Hollywood Forever's residents seem overly represented by tragedy.

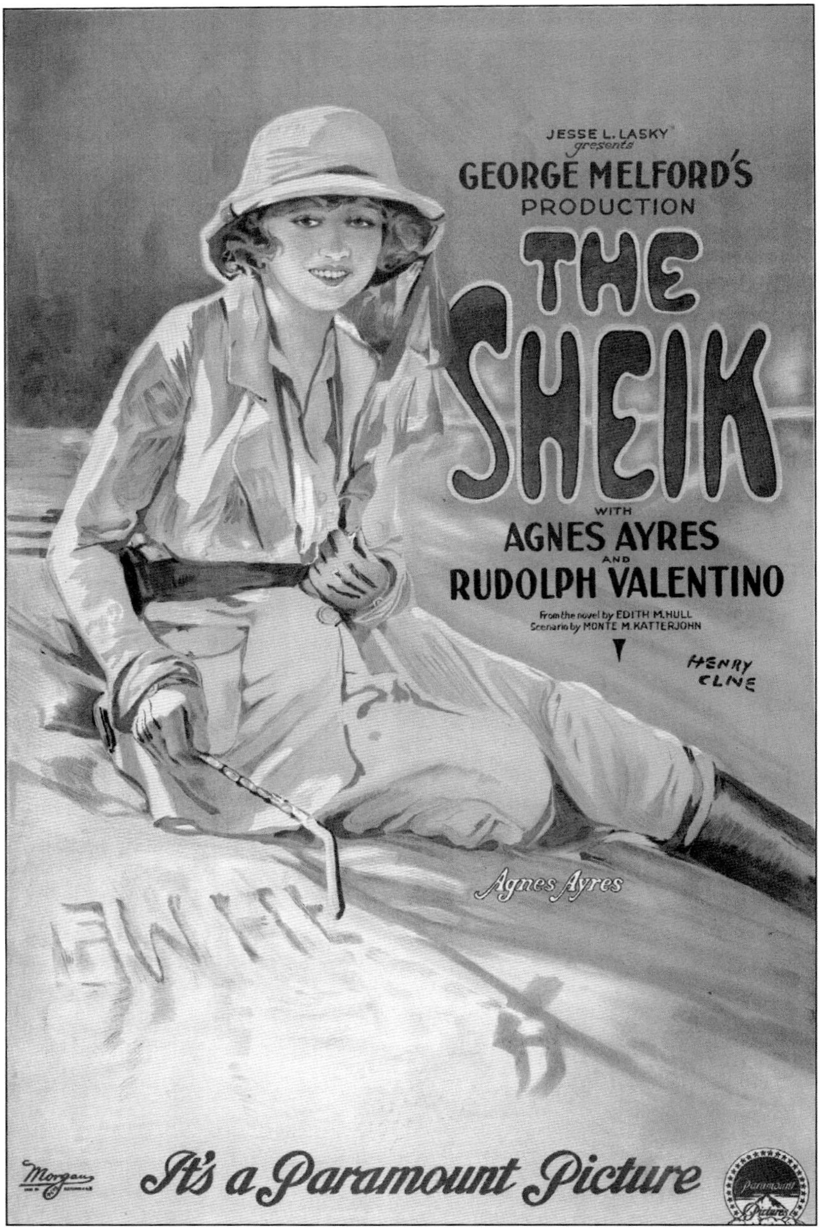

AGNES AYRES (1898–1940). Born Agnes Eyre Henkel in Illinois, Agnes Ayres saw her career in Hollywood blossom after she caught the eye of movie mogul, and H4E neighbor, Jesse L. Lasky. The two, both married at the time, began a long-term affair. Ayres became an international star with her portrayal of Lady Diana Mayo in *The Sheik* (1921) opposite Rudolph Valentino. She also appeared in Valentino's final film, the sequel, *Son of the Sheik*, in 1926. She landed major roles in several other films during the 1920s, including Cecil B. DeMille's epic *The Ten Commandments* (1923). Ayres's career waned after her affair with Lasky ended. Afterwards, she lost her fortune in the Wall Street crash of 1929. Despondent, she was committed to a sanitarium. In 1939, she lost custody of her only daughter due to her fragile mental state. A year later, Ayres died from a cerebral hemorrhage. She was only 42. (Chapel Columbarium, Floor 1, Lower South Wall, Tier 3, Niche 3D.) (Courtesy of the Library of Congress.)

Reginald Leslie "Snowy" Baker (1884–1953). Olympian Snowy Baker was one of the greatest athletes in Australian history and was the leading matinee idol Down Under. A boxing scandal prompted Baker's move to Hollywood, where he continued to make the occasional screen appearance and taught Elizabeth Taylor, Shirley Temple, Greta Garbo, and Rudolph Valentino how to swim. (Chapel Colonnade, North Wall, Tier 3, Niche 11.) (Courtesy of the State Library of Victoria.)

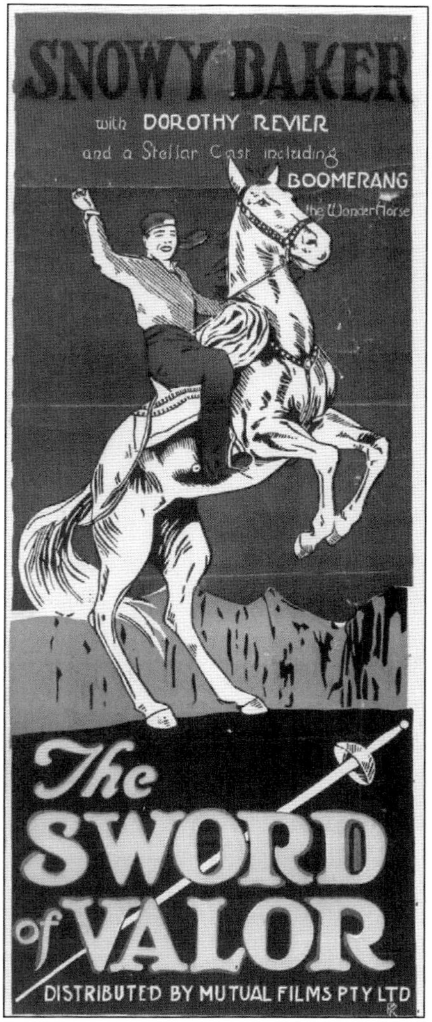

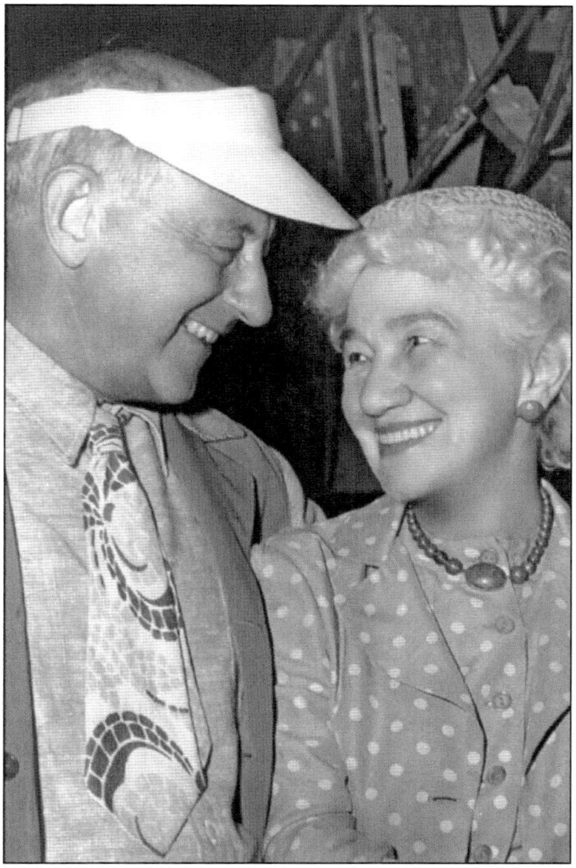

Anne Bauchens (1882–1967). Once upon a time, during Hollywood's pioneer days, women garnered a much larger share of filmdom's power than they do today. A case in point is Anne Bauchens, who for 40 years was Cecile B. DeMille's editor. Starting in the early silent era, Bauchens continued her partnership with DeMille up through his final film, *The Ten Commandments* (1956). Along the way, she was nominated for three Oscars. Bauchens is pictured here beside DeMille. (Chapel Columbarium, Floor 1, Northwest Wall, Tier 2, Niche 3.)

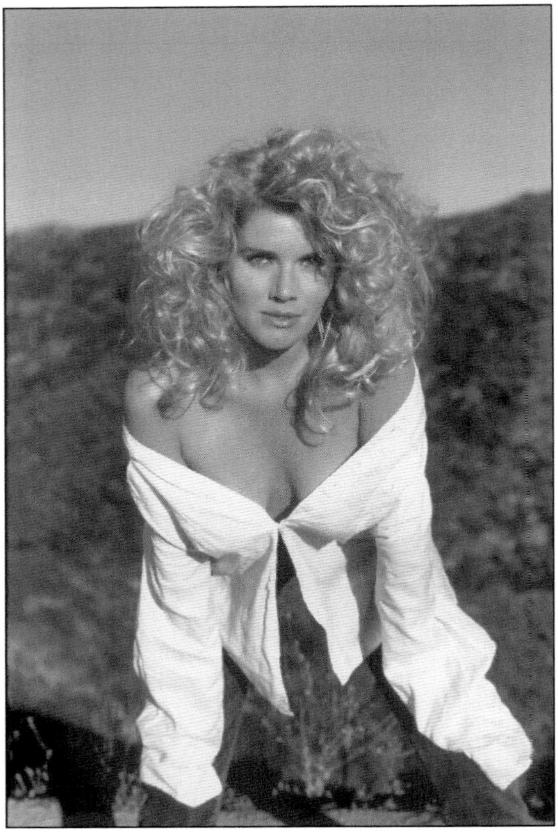

Lana Clarkson (1962–2003). B-movie queen and cult-film figure Lana Clarkson only achieved A-list fame in death. In 2003, she met music producer Phil Spector and accompanied him back to his mansion. An hour later, she was shot and killed in what Spector claimed was an "accidental suicide." Spector was convicted of her murder in 2009 and is currently serving 19 years to life in prison. (Chapel Columbarium, Floor 2, Upper South Wall, Tier 2-3, Niche 16-17.)

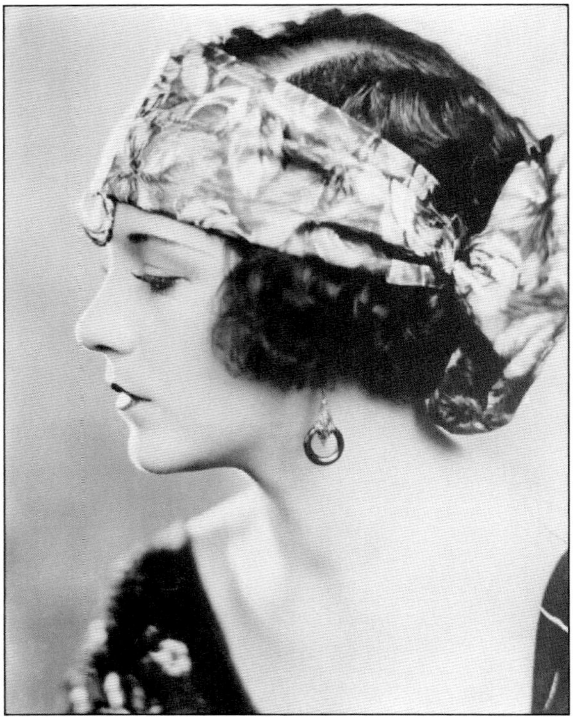

Viola Dana (1897–1987). Viola Dana was one of dozens of silent stars who saw their film careers disappear with the advent of talkies. Born Virginia Flugrath, she was a sister of actresses Edna Flugrath and Shirley Mason. She began appearing in films in 1910 and made over 100 screen appearances during her career. (Chapel Colonnade, North East Wall, Tier 4, Niche 6-7.) (Courtesy of the Library of Congress.)

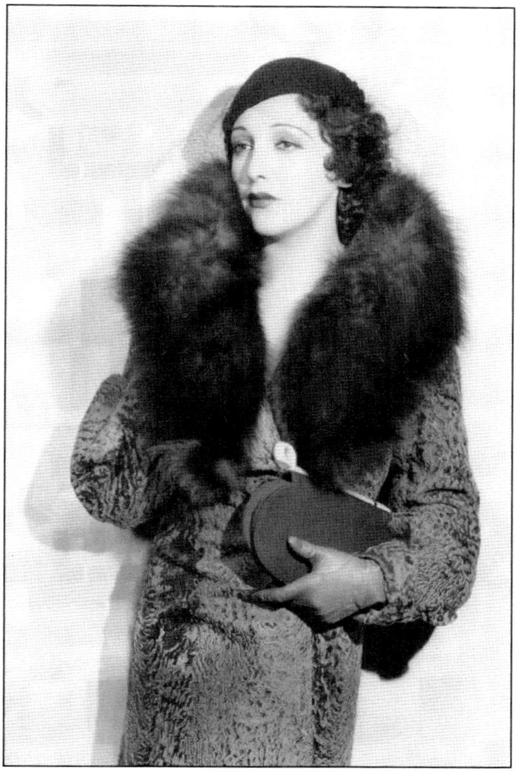

Bebe Daniels (1901–1971) and Ben Lyon (1901–1979). Actress, singer, dancer, writer, and producer Bebe Daniels made her stage debut at the tender age of four and was starring opposite silent comic Harold Lloyd by 14. Making the successful transition from child to adult star, she appeared with Valentino in *Monsieur Beaucaire* (1924). She continued to act until she retired from the screen in the mid-1930s, soon after singing in *42nd Street* (1933). She lived in London for many years with her longtime husband, Ben Lyon, who is interred at her side. Lyon was a Hollywood leading man during the silent era and, later, a 20th Century Fox executive who famously signed and even named Marilyn Monroe. Lyon and Daniels were married for over 40 years. They starred on radio and television in one of the United Kingdom's first reality shows during the 1950s and 1960s called *Life with the Lyons*, which featured Lyon, Daniels, and their two children. Lyon joined Daniels in death eight years after her passing. (Chapel Columbarium, Floor 2, Upper North Wall, Tier 3, Niche 7-8.) (Courtesy of the Library of Congress.)

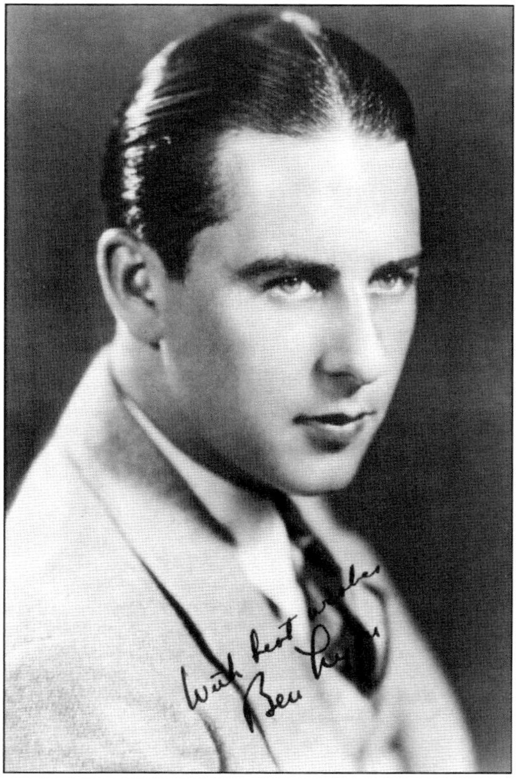

TOMATA DU PLENTY (1948–2000). Counter-culture figure Tomata du Plenty (born David Xavier Harrigan) was the singer for the punk rock group the Screamers and was later an artist. In the 1980s, he made several short films featuring H4E's own Vampira (Maila Nurmi). Du Plenty died of cancer at the age of 52. (Chapel Columbarium, Floor 1, Upper North Wall, Niche 2-3.)

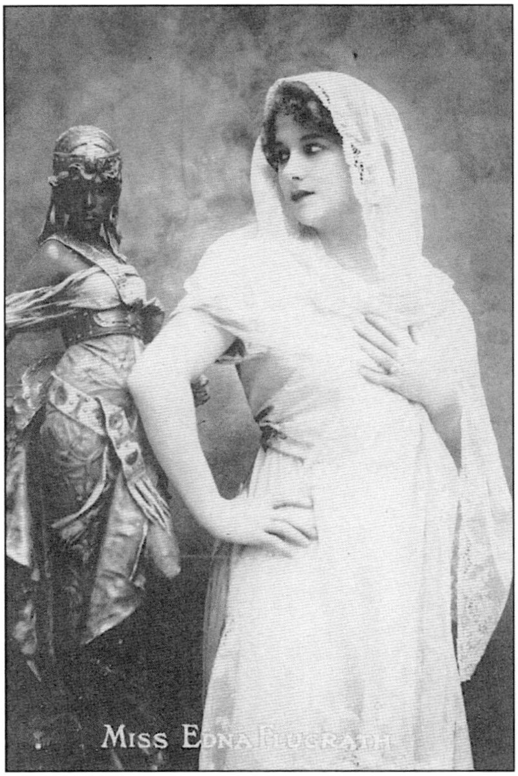

EDNA FLUGRATH (1893–1966). Edna Flugrath, along with sisters Viola Dana and Shirley Mason, left their mark on Hollywood during the silent era. Not a particularly close family, Edna's sisters were estranged for many years and only learned of her passing from a reporter. (Chapel Colonnade, North Wall, Tier 3.)

JEAN HAVEZ (1869–1925). Every Buster Keaton fan owes a debt of gratitude to Jean Havez, who wrote many of Keaton's most famous silent films. Havez also worked with silent comedians Roscoe "Fatty" Arbuckle and Harold Lloyd. He began his career in vaudeville writing novelty songs. Havez died of a heart attack at the age of 55 in 1925, at the height of the silent era. He is pictured here at far right with, from left to right, Joe Mitchell, Clyde Bruckman, and Buster Keaton. (Chapel Mausoleum, Building A, Crypt 218.)

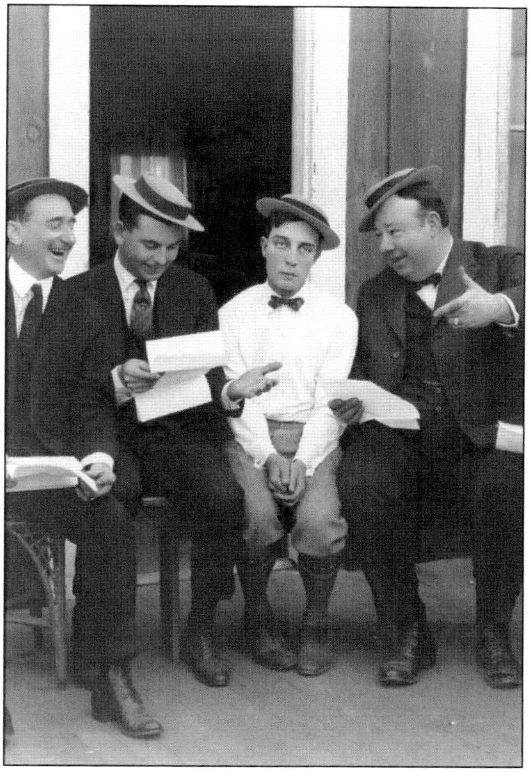

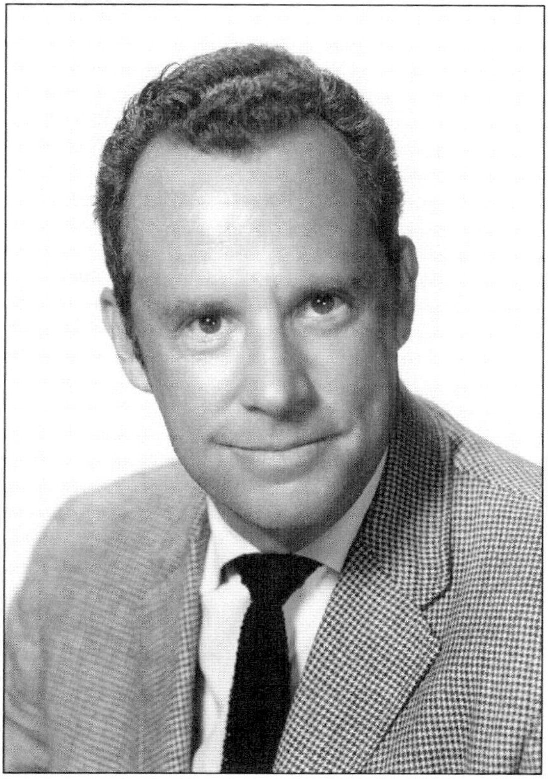

JESSE L. LASKY JR. (1910–1988). The son of Paramount cofounder Jesse L. Lasky Sr. (who is interred in a mausoleum nearby), Lasky Jr. was a screenwriter. He is best known for having penned eight screenplays for his father's one-time partner, Cecile B. DeMille, including *The Ten Commandments* (1956). (Chapel Columbarium, Floor 2, Upper East Wall, Tier 3, Niche 3.) (Courtesy of Pat Silver-Lasky.)

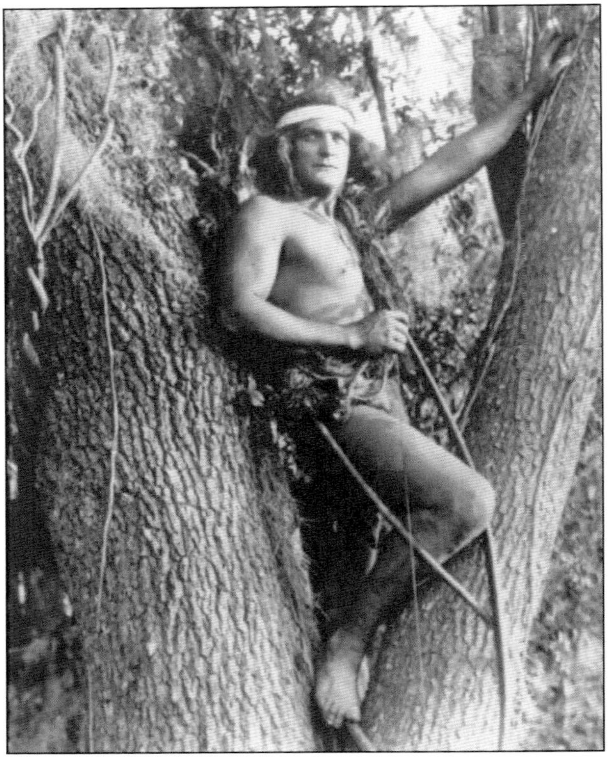

Elmo Lincoln (1889–1952). Elmo Lincoln is remembered by film historians as the "first Tarzan," having played the jungle-born character on-screen as early as 1918. He would appear in other Tarzan films over the next few decades, even as an uncredited extra in the 1940s. Lincoln died of a heart attack at the age of 63. (Chapel Colonnade, North Wall, Niche 20-J.) (Courtesy of Fine Art America.)

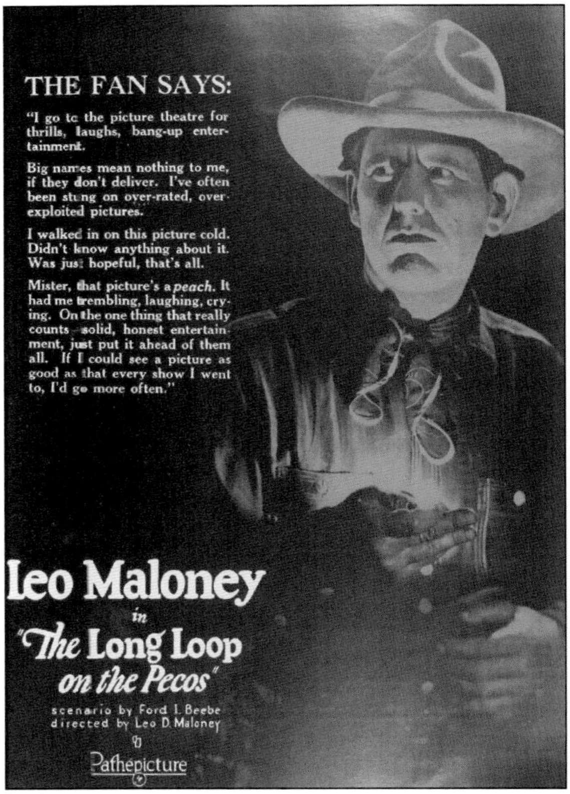

Leo D. Maloney (1888–1929). Maloney was an actor and director who built his own Western studio in the San Bernardino Mountains. He was at a party celebrating the completion of the film *Overland Bound* when he suffered a fatal stroke. (Chapel Columbarium, Floor 1, Southwest Wall, Tier 5, Niche 2.)

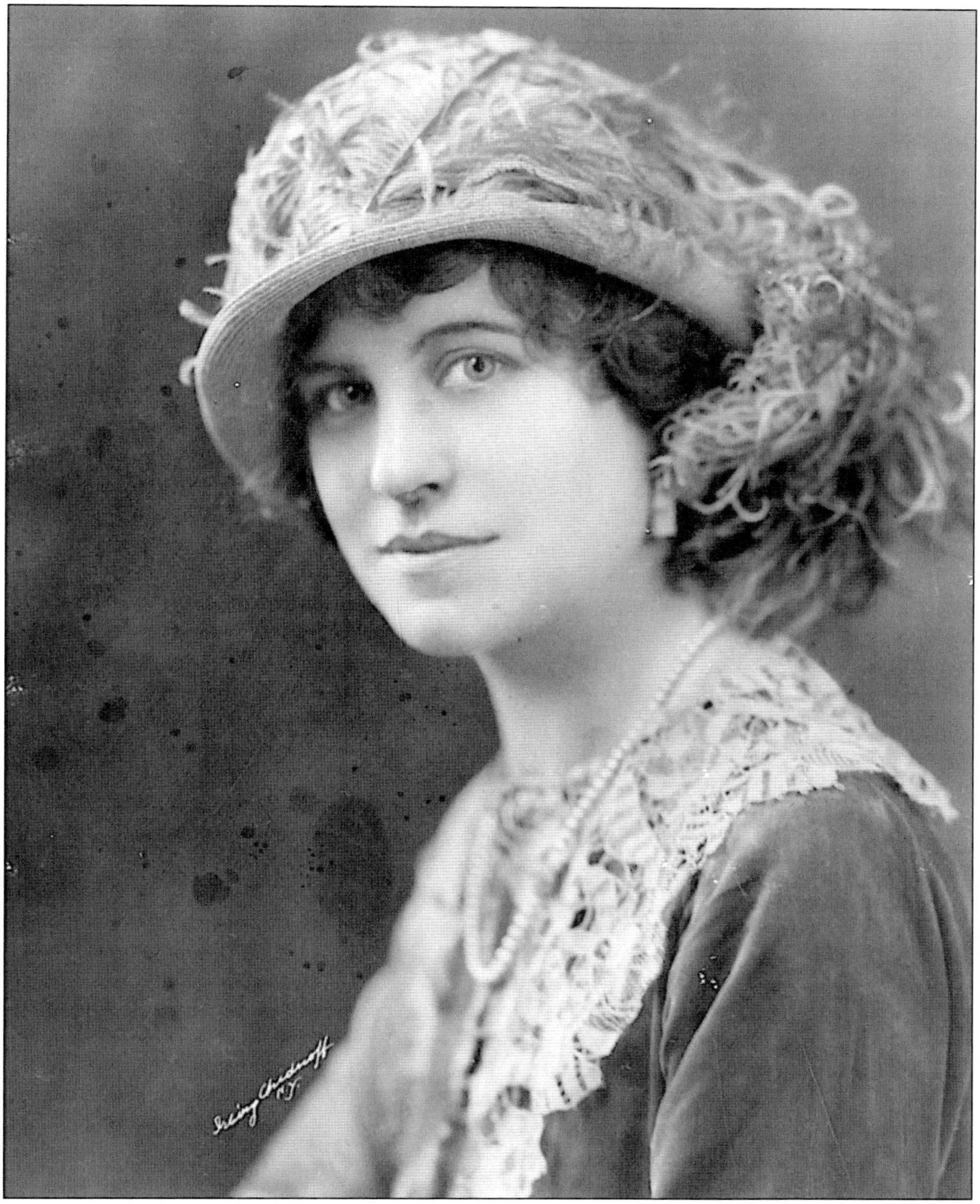

JEANIE MACPHERSON (1887–1946). MacPherson was a pioneering actress, writer, and director from 1908 through the 1940s. She was born into a wealthy Boston family and was schooled in Paris for a time before having to drop out when her family's fortune faded. Back in America, she studied in Chicago where she began her career as a dancer and actress. She began making movies in 1908 for D.W. Griffith and appeared on screen more than 100 times over the next nine years. In 1917, after directing a couple of films, MacPherson decided to concentrate on screenwriting and was hired in this role by Cecil B. DeMille. She formed one of the longest-lasting Hollywood partnerships with director (and supposedly lover) DeMille. MacPherson is credited as his screenwriter in over 30 films. She was one of the founders of the Academy of Motion Picture Arts and Sciences in 1927. (Chapel Colonnade, West Corridor, Southwest Wall, Tier 2.) (Courtesy of Detroit Public Library.)

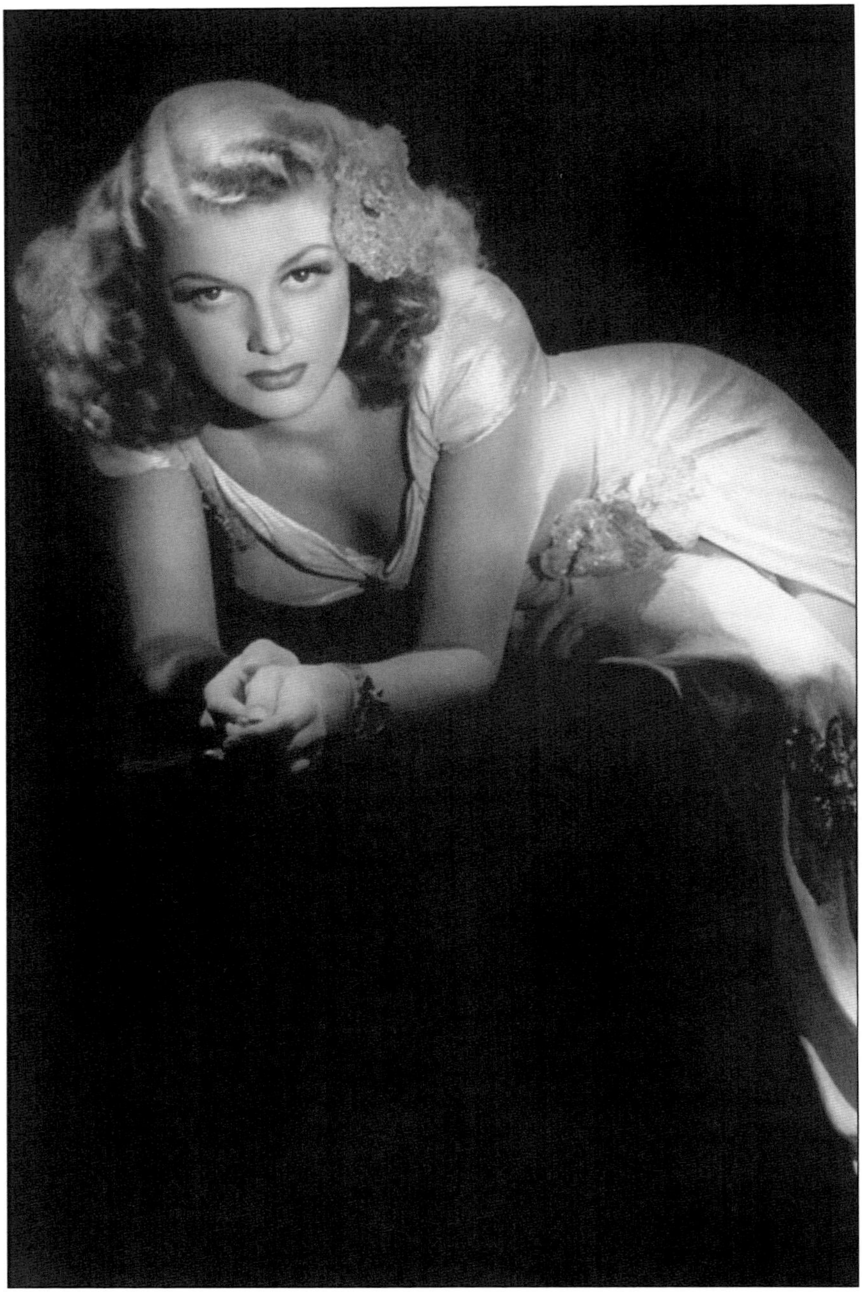

Ann Sheridan (1915–1967). Ann Sheridan was in college in her native Texas when she secured a bit part in a Hollywood movie as the prize for winning a beauty contest. Known as the "Oomph Girl," her beauty made her a pin-up model in the early part of the 1940s. She starred opposite a litany of Hollywood's leading men for much of her career, including James Cagney and Humphrey Bogart in *Angels with Dirty Faces* (1938), Errol Flynn in *Dodge City* (1939), Ronald Reagan in *Kings Row* (1942), and Cary Grant in *I Was a Male War Bride* (1949). She became a regular on television during the 1950s after her film career cooled. Sheridan died of cancer at age 52. Her ashes were originally housed at another LA cemetery for nearly 40 years before they were moved here in 2005. (Chapel Columbarium, Floor 2, Upper East Wall, Tier 3, Niche 24.)

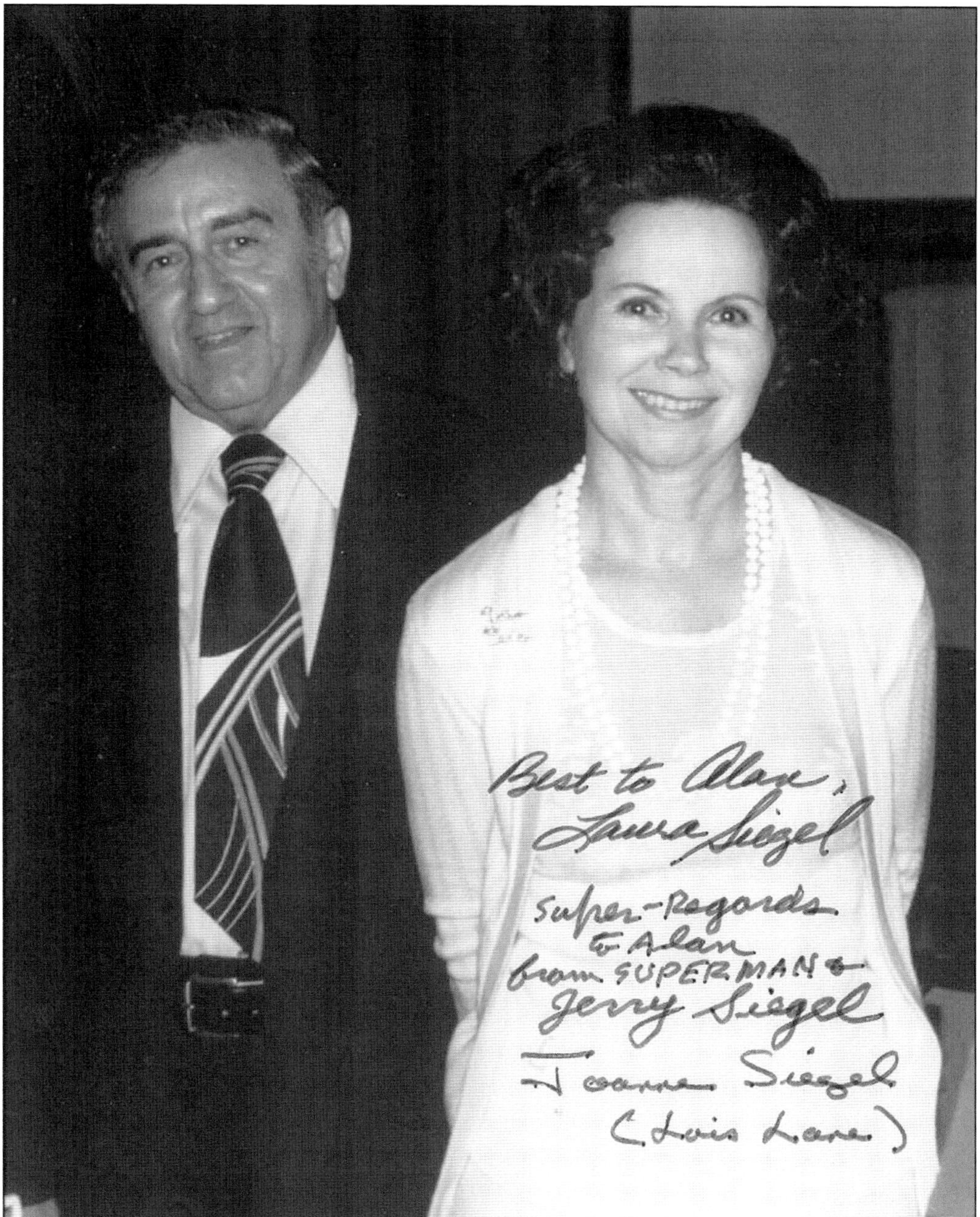

JERRY SIEGEL (1914–1996) AND JOANNE SIEGEL (1917–2011). Cleveland native Jerry Siegel met his comic book collaborator Joe Shuster in high school. Together, the duo created Superman, the iconic alien superhero good guy, and many other characters. Siegel's urn displays the names of many of his creations, including Slam Bradley, Dr. Occult, Superboy, the Spectre, and of course, Superman. He is interred beside his wife, Joanne, who was the original model for Joel Shuster's drawings of Lois Lane. Joanne married Siegel in 1948 and remained at his side until his death. She worked tirelessly at the end of her life to recover her husband's and partner Shuster's copyrights to the character Superman, which they sold in 1939 for $130. (Chapel Columbarium, Floor 2, East Wall.) (Courtesy of Alan Light.)

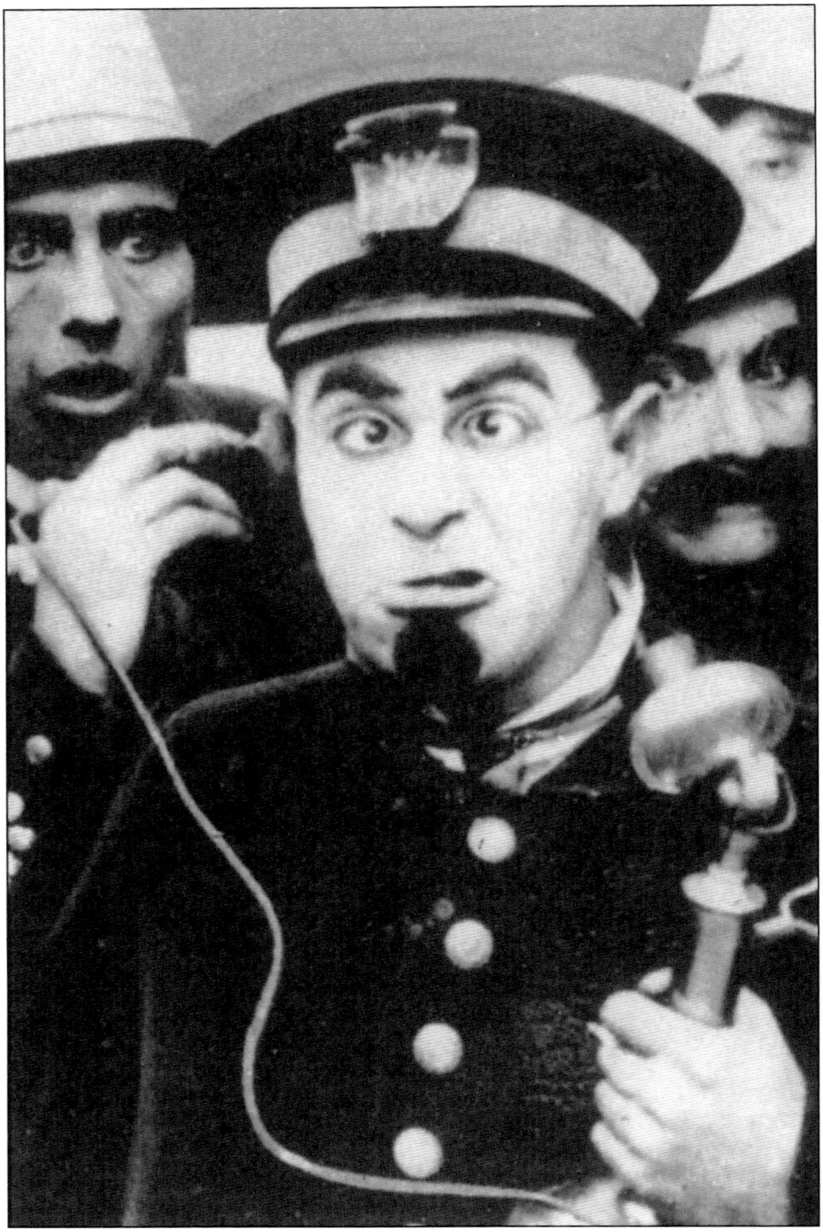

FORD STERLING (1883–1939). Ford Sterling began his show business career when he literally ran away from home to join the circus. He would go on to make 270 screen appearances during a film career that lasted 25 years, bridging both the silent and talkie eras. His greatest success came in the role of Chief Teeheezal, the leader of Mack Sennett's madcap Keystone Cops. Sterling died penniless in 1939 at age 55 after a heart attack. His ashes were placed in a cardboard box and interred here in an unmarked crypt. As one of the authors' proudest achievements, they, along with friend Steve Goldstein, convinced H4E to place a plaque on Sterling's crypt in 2013 for his 130th birthday. The unfurling was attended by about a dozen fans of Sterling's work. On his plaque, they chose to spell "Cop" with a "C" instead of a "K." It was discovered that "Kop" did not come into vogue until years after the Keystone Cop films were made, so they went with the original spelling to appease the purists. (Chapel Colonnade, South Wall, Dawn Niche.)

Gregg Toland (1904–1948). Innovative cinematographer Gregg Toland packed in a legendary career during his brief lifetime. Most famous for his work on Orson Welles's classic *Citizen Kane* (1941), during one seven-year span, Toland was nominated for the Academy Award for Best Cinematography five times. He died in his sleep from coronary thrombosis. He is pictured here on the left with an unidentified student. (Chapel Columbarium, Floor 1, Lower Column H, Tier 4, Niche 2.)

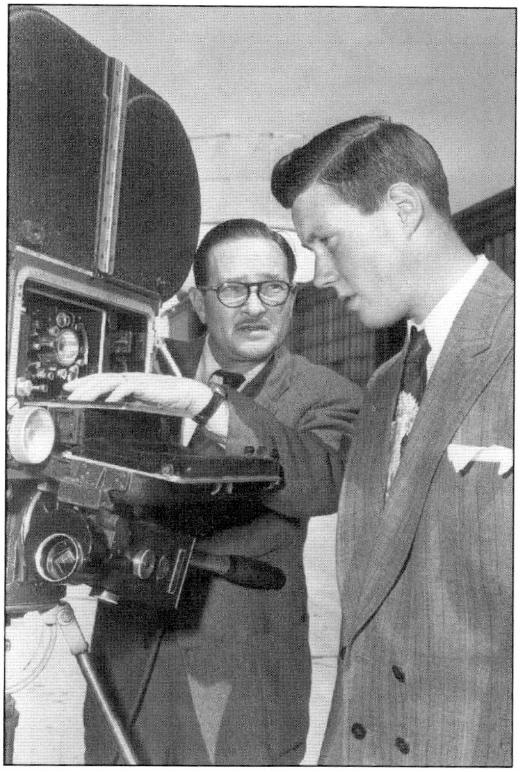

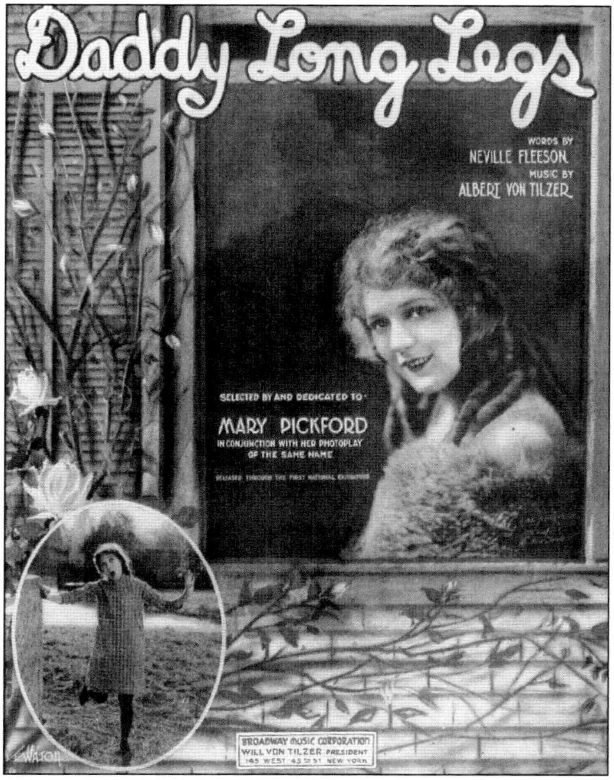

Carrie Clark Ward (1862–1926). Born in Nevada during the Civil War, Carrie Clark Ward acted in over 60 films during the silent era. Ward worked with the biggest stars in Hollywood, appearing in *The Bank* (1915) with Charlie Chaplin, *Daddy-Long-Legs* (1919) with Mary Pickford, and *The Eagle* (1925) with Rudolph Valentino. (Chapel Mausoleum, Corridor C, Crypt 121.)

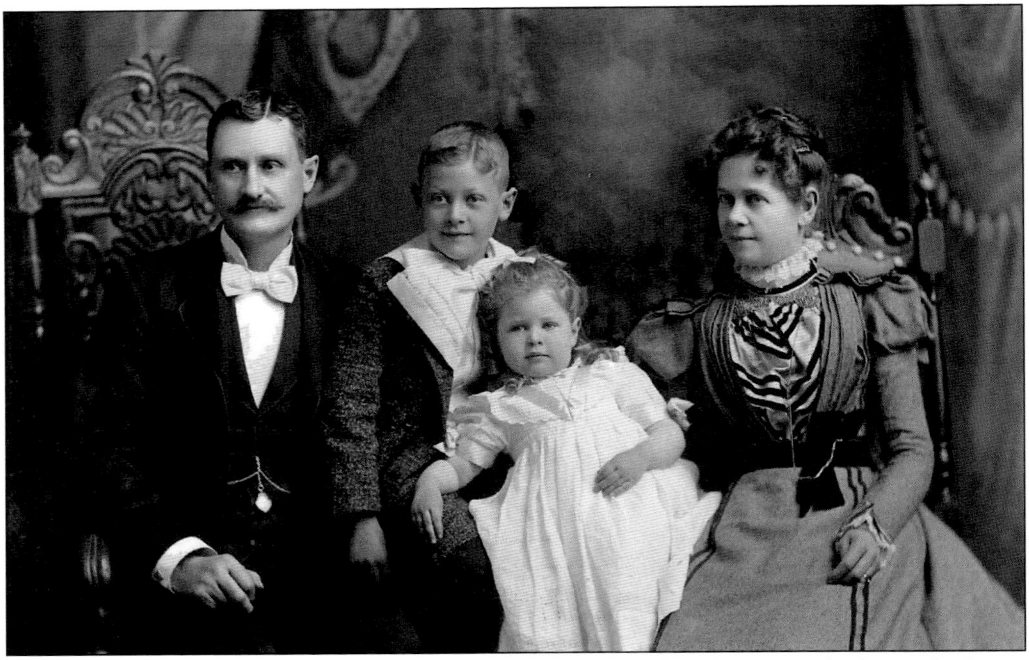

HOBART JOHNSTONE WHITLEY (1847–1931). Canadian railroader H.J. Whitley rushed into Oklahoma Territory in 1889 and helped establish several towns. After moving west, Whitley built the Hollywood Hotel and developed Hollywood's Whitley Heights. He claimed to have given Hollywood its name (as did H4E resident Daeida Wilcox Beveridge). Whitley is pictured here with his family. (Chapel Colonnade, South Wall, Column 2, Tier 1, Niche O.)

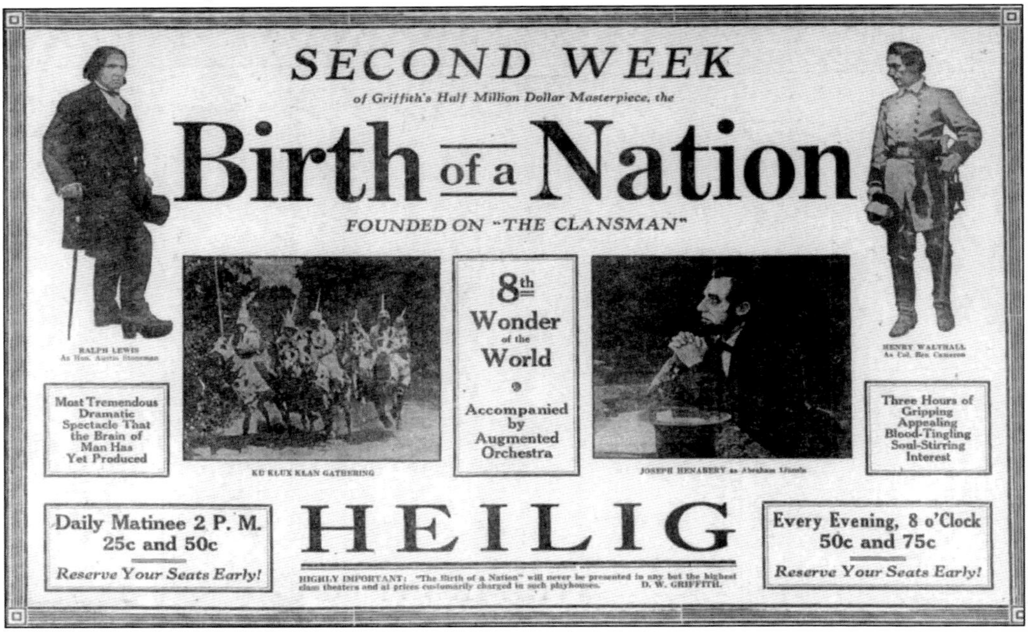

FRANK WOODS (1860–1939). A founder of the Academy of Motion Picture Arts and Sciences, Woods began his career as a screenwriter and is credited with co-writing the script for *The Birth of a Nation* (1915). He later became a pioneering film critic. (Chapel Columbarium, Floor 1, Lower North Wall, Tier 4, Niche 9A.)

Two

Abbey of the Psalms

The Abbey of the Psalms, which parallels Hollywood Forever's western boundary, is today the final resting place of some of the most interesting people in Hollywood's history (which is saying a mouthful).

Found along its long corridors are the crypts of many of the colorful characters from the early days of film. Jesse L. Lasky, who partnered with Adolph Zukor to found Paramount Pictures, is here. As is legendary director Victor Fleming, who, in 1939, had a year like no other.

There are also several character actors represented, like Louis Calhern, Gertrude Astor, Tom Kennedy, and Almira Sessions, whose faces, if not their names, were once familiar to all.

Many accomplished women can be found here. Near the main entrance is the crypt of Renee Adoree, a talented beauty of the silent screen who died at a young age from tuberculosis, far from her native France. Nearby is the room containing the Talmadge sisters, once among the most famous women in the world. Darla Hood from *Our Gang* is here, as is Peruvian songstress Yma Sumac and the former crypt of author Gene Stratton-Porter. Along one wall is the popular crypt of Joan Hackett, whose message reads, "Go Away—I'm Asleep."

Perhaps the most famous woman in the cemetery is multi-talented Judy Garland, whose body was recently moved here after being housed for decades in a New York mausoleum.

Musicians and artists are represented prominently in Abbey of the Psalms. Here, one can find Carl Stalling, whose peppy, staccato rhythms and orchestrated industrial sounds will entertain *Looney Tunes* fans for the rest of time. The crypt of Bob Mitchell, who was the first organist at Dodger Stadium, is also in here, as is that of artist Harry Lachman, who painted in Paris with Picasso, Matisse, and Renoir before becoming a director in Hollywood.

Charlie Chaplin has a strong connection to Abbey of the Psalms, as his son and one of his wives are interred here.

Even a restless spirit or two is said to wander the halls, like in the case of Clifton Webb, who has reportedly been seen strolling along the corridor outside his crypt.

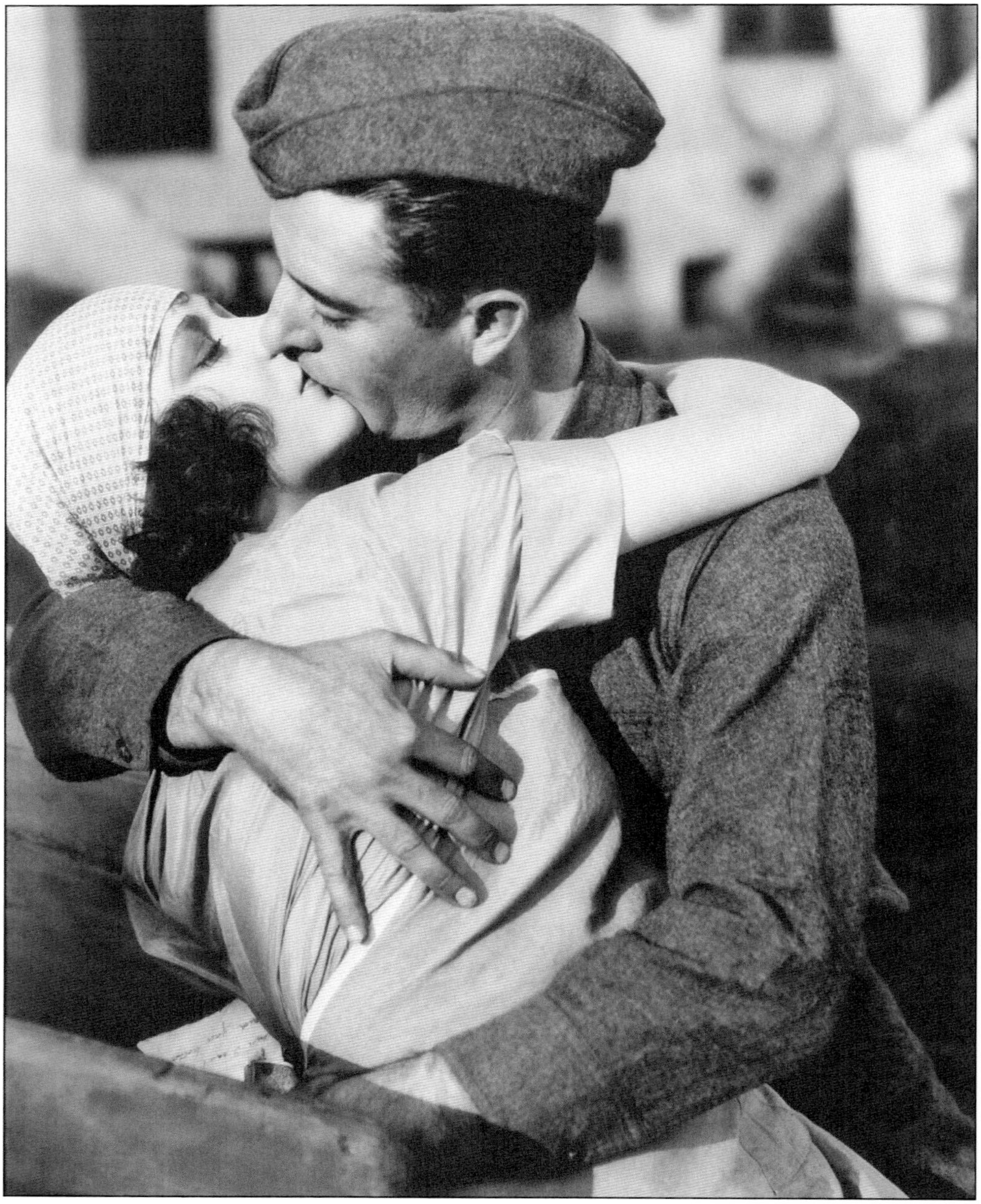

Renee Adoree (1898–1933). Young Jeanne de la Fonte was born into a family of circus performers and was entertaining the masses under the big top when she was five. She was touring with an acting troupe in Russia when World War I broke out, forcing her to flee to London. After the war ended, Adoree went to America, where she toured the east coast dancing on the vaudeville circuit before heading to Hollywood. Fans of silent movies remember Adoree today for her starring role opposite John Gilbert in *The Big Parade* (1925), one of the silent era's finest films. Adoree's French accent was pleasing to audiences, and she seemed primed to continue her film career well into the talkie era until she was diagnosed with tuberculosis in 1930. She died at the age of 35 in a sanitarium in Sunland, California. She is pictured here with costar Gilbert in a scene from *The Big Parade*. (Abbey of the Psalms, Foyer F, Crypt 219.)

Gertrude Astor (1887–1977). Gertrude Astor was a character actress who made her mark in over 250 films, primarily during the silent era. Astor began her entertainment career as a trombonist on a riverboat. Her last screen appearance was in *The Man Who Shot Liberty Valance* (1962). She died in Woodland Hills, California, on her 90th birthday. (Abbey of the Psalms, Haven of Worship, North Wall, Tier 13, Niche 5.)

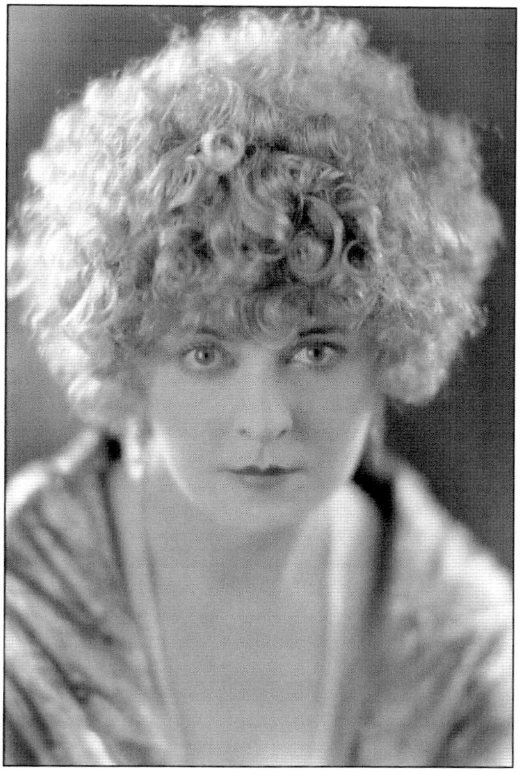

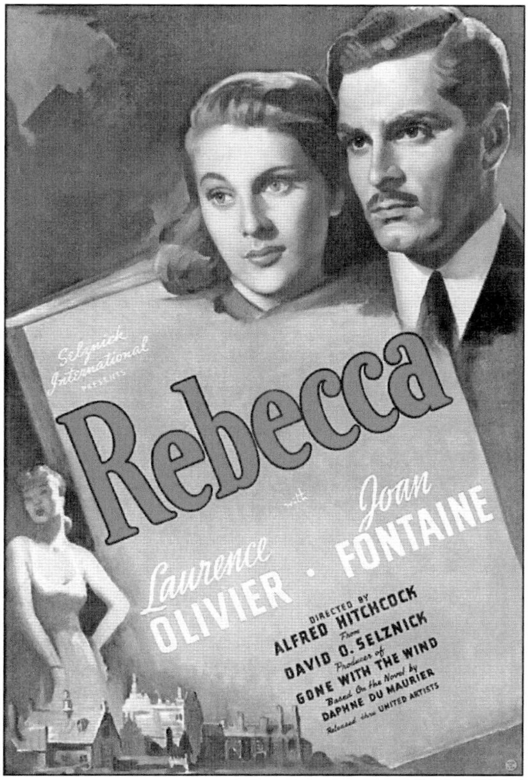

George S. Barnes (1892–1953). Early cinematographer George S. Barnes began working in film during the silent era and continued working in the field until his death. Nominated for eight Academy Awards, he won once for *Rebecca* (1940). (Abbey of the Psalms, Sanctuary of Refuge, Corridor G-2, Crypt 2087.)

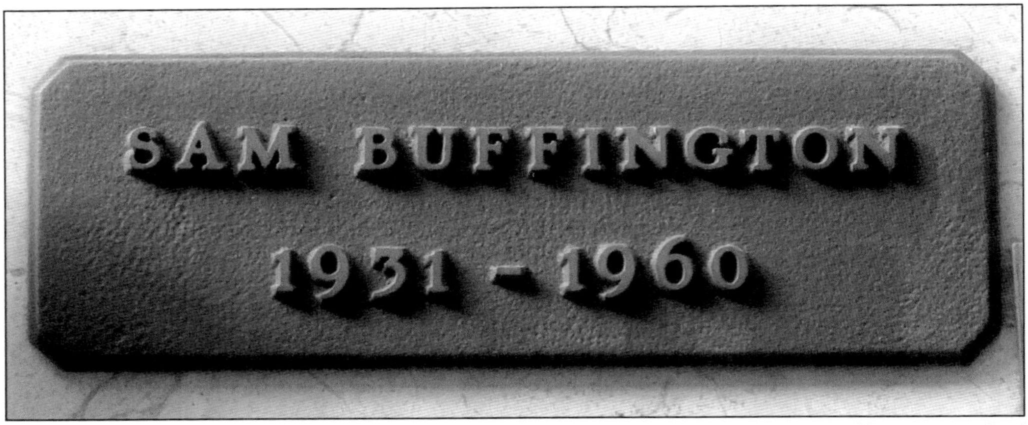

SAM BUFFINGTON (1931–1960). A busy character actor in the late 1950s, Buffington packed dozens of radio, television, and movie appearances into a career that lasted only a few years. Often cast in mature roles, most often in Westerns, Buffington was a young man who looked much older. He committed suicide in 1960 when he was only 28 years old. (Abbey of the Psalms, Haven of Repose.)

LOUIS CALHERN (1895–1956). A star of both stage and screen, Louis Calhern had a 35-year Hollywood career that ended when he suffered a fatal heart attack in Japan on the set of *The Teahouse of the August Moon*. Calhern regularly worked with some of the leading actors and directors in Hollywood. He was married and divorced four times, including a nine-year pairing with Natalie Schafer, who played Lovey Howell on television's *Gilligan's Island*. He is pictured here with Cary Grant in a publicity still from Alfred Hitchcock's *Notorious* (1946). (Abbey of the Psalms, Foyer F, South Wall, Tier 3, Niche 308.)

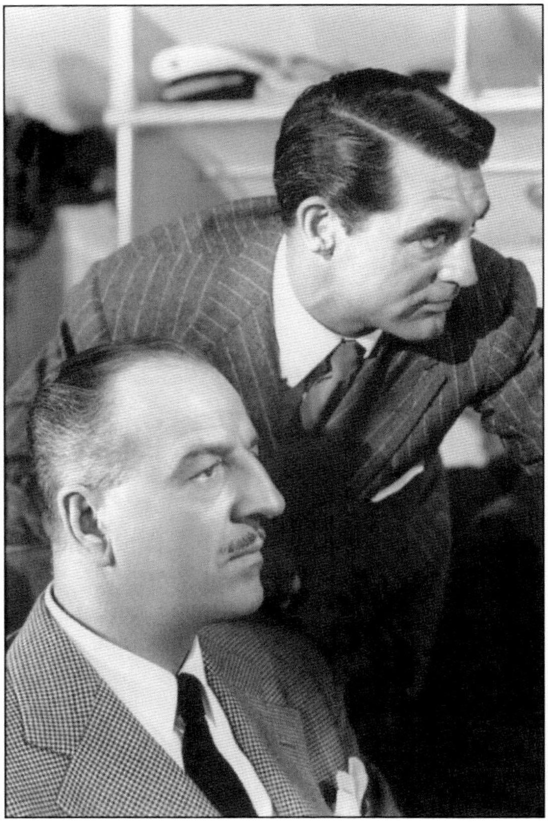

Charles Chaplin Jr. (1925–1968). The eldest son of silent superstar Charlie Chaplin, the younger Chaplin had a movie career of his own, appearing in 13 films, including alongside his father in *Limelight* (1952). Chaplin died from a pulmonary embolism at age 42, and is interred in the same crypt as his maternal grandmother. His mother, Lita Grey, is entombed in a nearby building. The Chaplins, with the son playing a cop and the father as the clown, are pictured here in a scene from *Limelight*. (Abbey of the Psalms, Sanctuary of Trust, E-2, Crypt 1065.) (Courtesy of Roy Export SAS.)

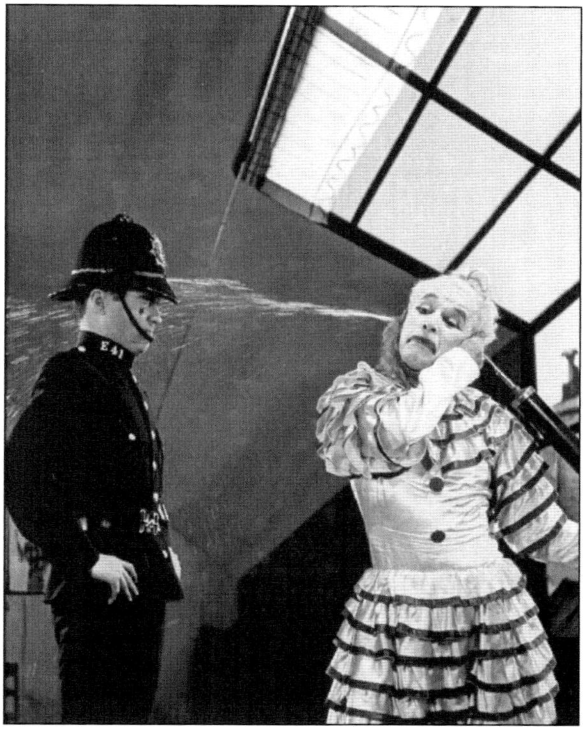

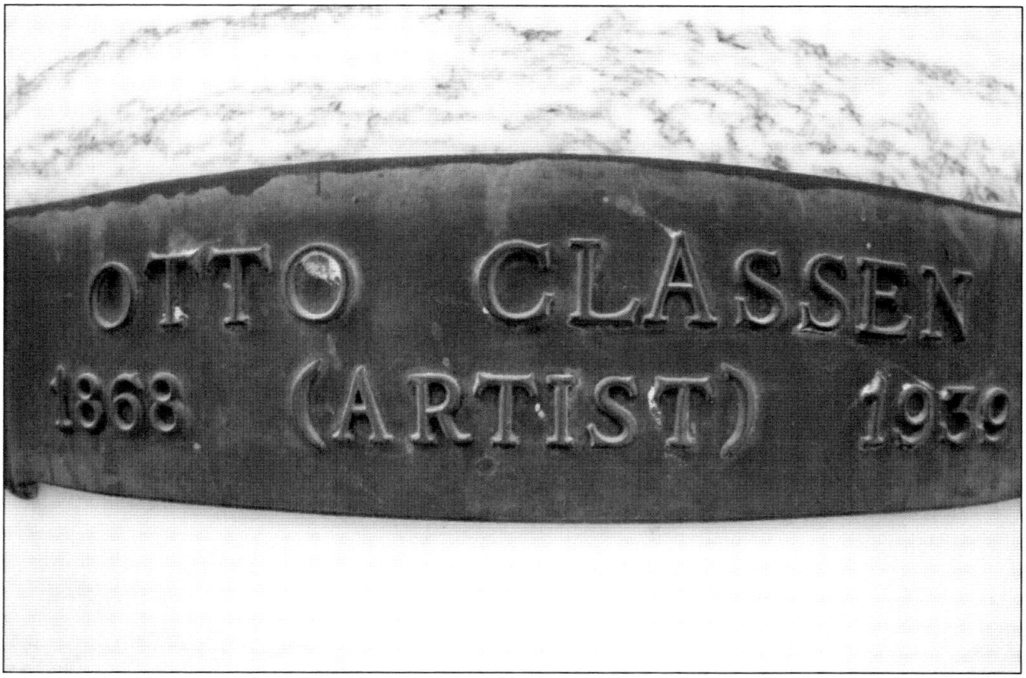

Otto Classen (1868–1939). German artist Otto Classen was a well-known impressionistic portrait and landscape painter during the early 20th century. Born in Dresden, Classen came to Los Angeles around his 30th birthday. He created several works of "Californiana," often of the California deserts. (Abbey of the Psalms, Sanctuary of Hope, Crypt 137.) (Courtesy of Pentax Forums.)

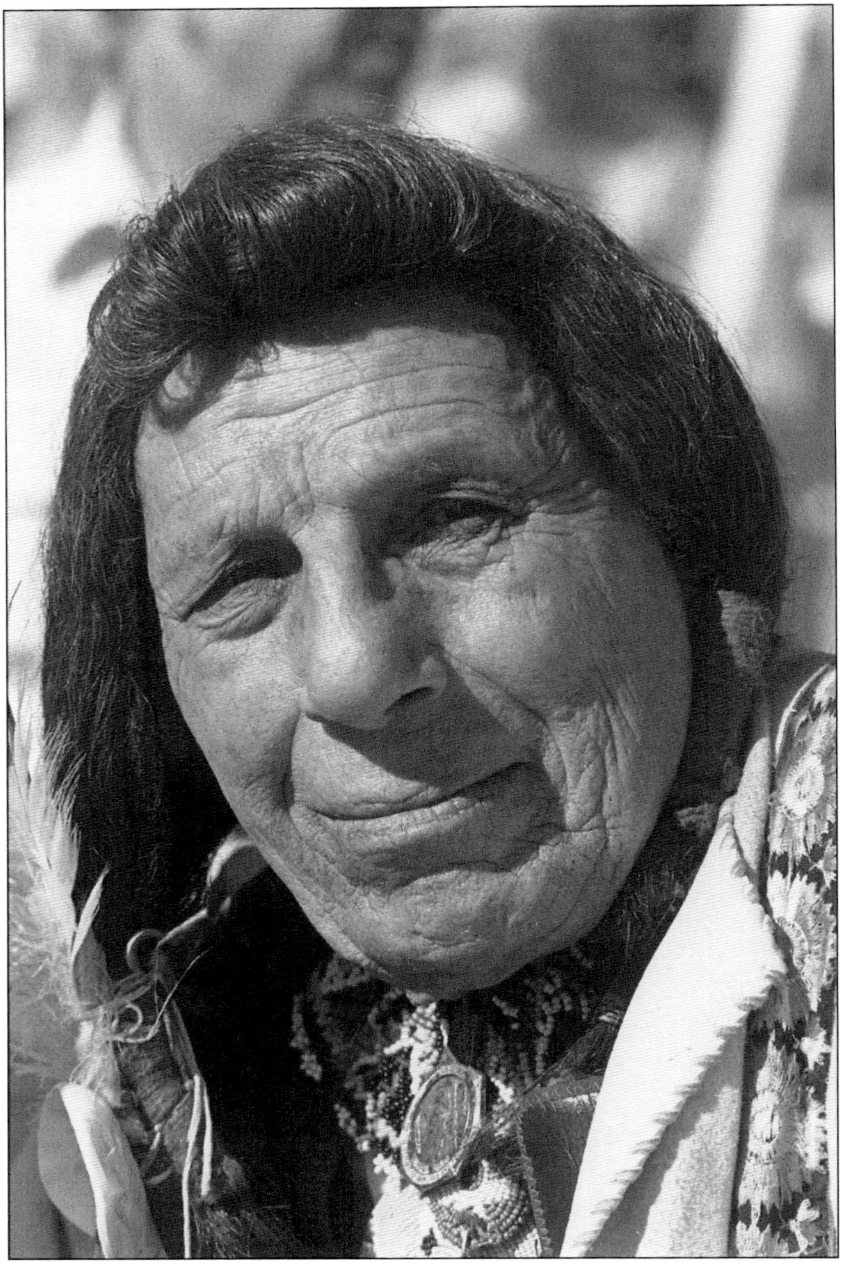

IRON EYES CODY (1904–1999). Iron Eyes Cody was at one time the country's most famous Native American. Cody claimed to be a member of the Cherokee tribe, but in one of Hollywood's endless ironies, he may not have been an Indian at all. Cody began acting in the early 1930s, with his dark complexion making him a regular on screen playing Native Americans. He appeared in Westerns for his entire career, both on screen and on television, and acted alongside some of the biggest cowboy stars of the day, including John Wayne in *The Big Trail* (1930). Cody appeared in over 200 films, but it was his appearance as an Indian with a lone tear in "Keep America Beautiful," a 1970s environmental commercial, that gave him lasting fame. Near the end of his life, it was suggested that he was in fact born in Louisiana to Sicilian immigrants, a claim he vehemently denied. (Abbey of the Psalms, Sanctuary of Memories, Corridor H-4-1, Crypt 3301.)

James Cruze (1884–1942). Born Jens Vera Cruz Bosen, James Cruze acted in, directed, or produced over 100 films in his career, mostly during the silent era. He was busy directing a Roscoe "Fatty" Arbuckle film in 1921 when a scandal involving Arbuckle and starlet Virginia Rappe torpedoed Fatty's career. Cruze directed his wife, Betty Compson, in *The Great Gabbo* (1929). They divorced the following year. (Abbey of the Psalms, Foyer F, Tier 2, Niche 211.)

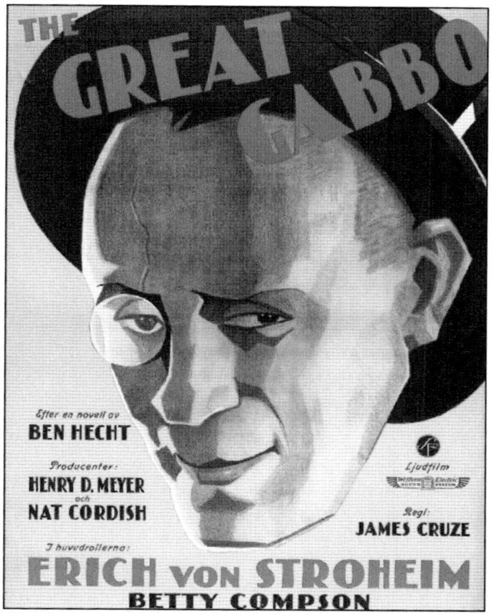

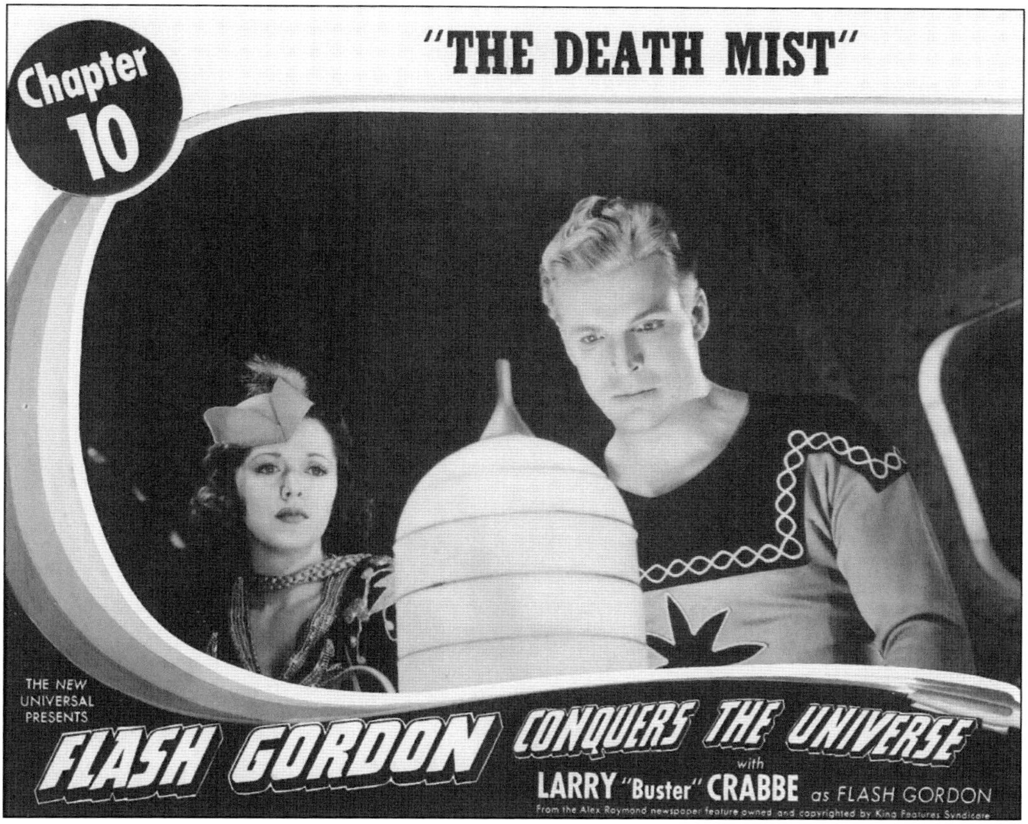

Basil Dickey (1880–1958). Screenwriter Basil Dickey penned over 140 scripts during his career. He collaborated on *The Perils of Pauline* (1914), a popular serial that starred Pearl White, and *Flash Gordon Conquers the Universe* (1940). Dickey's brother Paul was also a screenwriter and playwright. (Abbey of the Psalms, Foyer.)

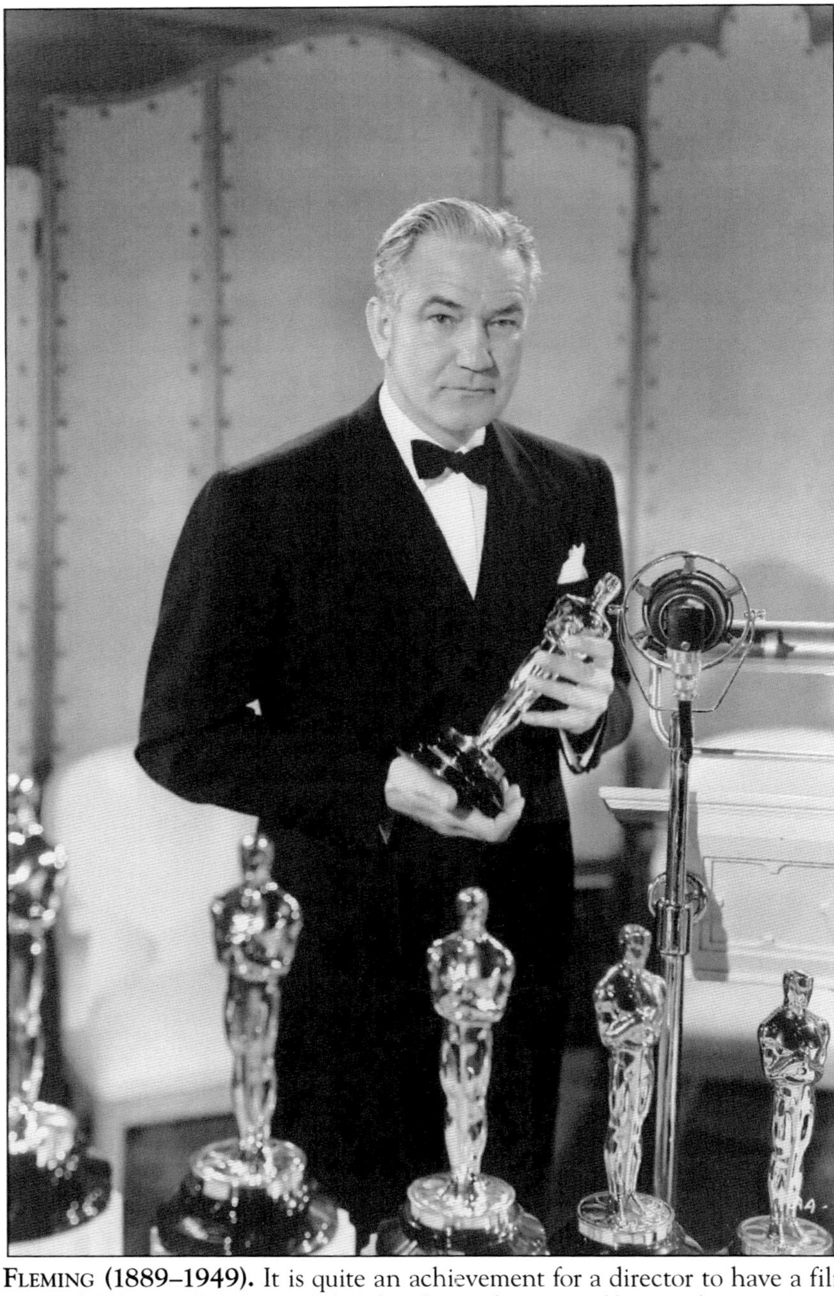

Victor Fleming (1889–1949). It is quite an achievement for a director to have a film appear in the top 10 of AFI's 100 Years, 100 Films list, but to have two films in the top 10 and to have filmed both during the same year is truly astounding. In 1939, director Victor Fleming directed both *The Wizard of Oz* and *Gone with the Wind*, for which he won the Academy Award for Best Director. Fleming worked in silent films with Allan Dwan and D.W. Griffith before serving as Pres. Woodrow Wilson's photographer at the Versailles Peace Conference in France at the end of World War I. Back in the states, Fleming cranked out an enviable string of hits for decades in both the silent and talkie eras, but today he is remembered mostly for his 1939 achievements. Fleming died suddenly in 1949 from a heart attack. (Abbey of the Psalms, Sanctuary of Refuge, Crypt 2081.)

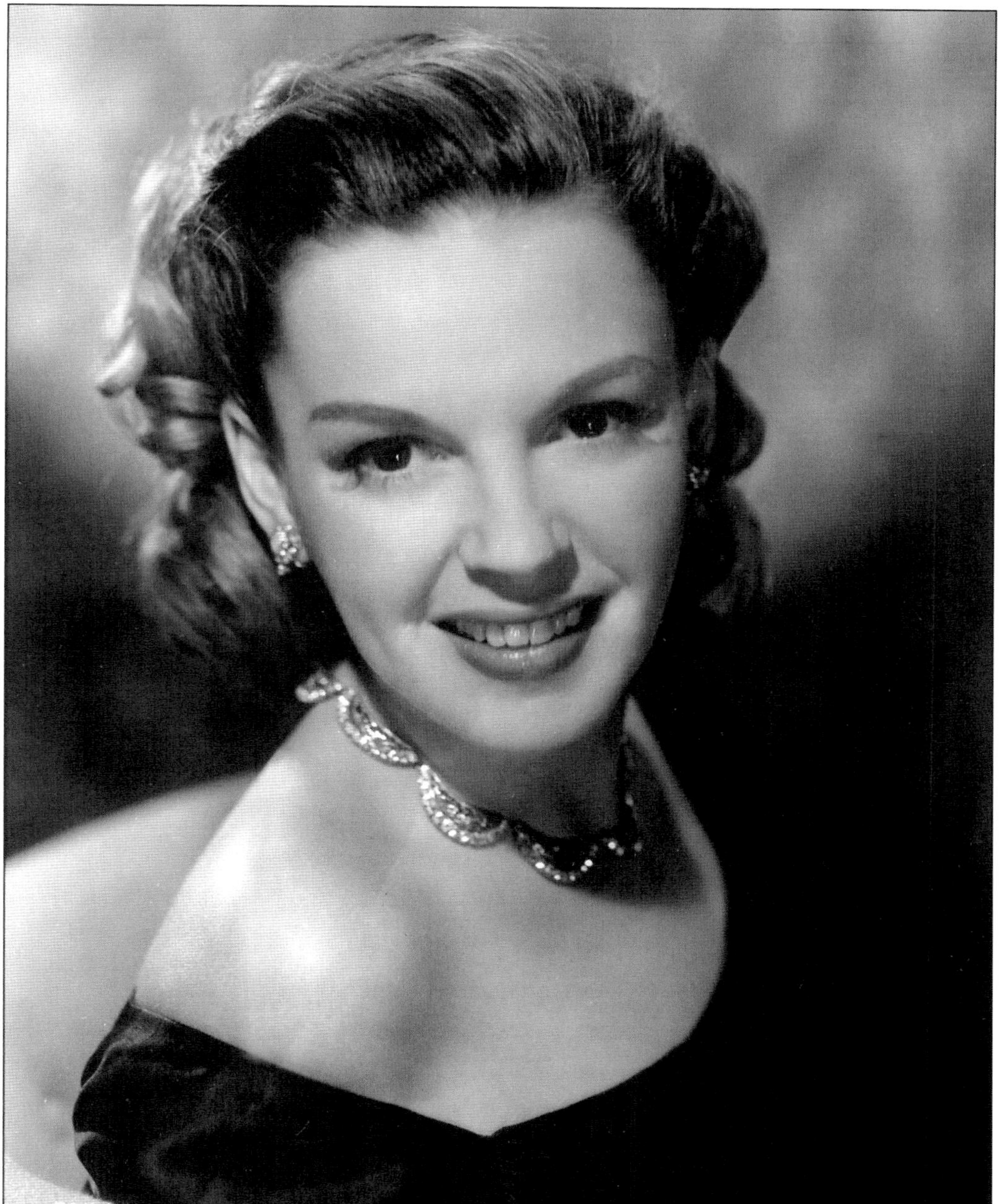

Judy Garland (1922–1969). One of the world's most beloved entertainers, Judy Garland was recently moved to H4E after nearly 50 years in a New York mausoleum. Born Frances Ethel Gumm, Garland was singing on stage at the age of two with her older sisters. The group performed together until 1935, when Garland signed a contract with MGM. What followed was a string of some of MGM's best musicals, including *The Wizard of Oz* (1939), *Meet Me in St. Louis* (1944), *The Harvey Girls* (1946), and *Easter Parade* (1948). Garland also appeared in several Andy Hardy movies with H4E neighbor Mickey Rooney. As an adult, she returned to her first love, live performances. Garland struggled with addiction for most of her life and died from an accidental overdose of sleeping pills. (Abbey of the Psalms, Garden of Israel, Private Room.)

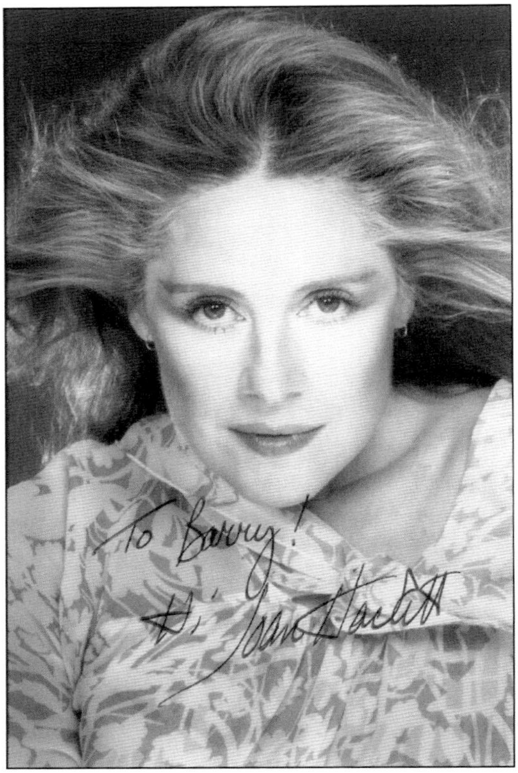

Joan Hackett (1934–1983). One of the most visited tombs in H4E is that of Joan Hackett in the Sanctuary of Faith, where guests are instructed to "Go Away—I'm Asleep." A talented actress on film, stage, and television, Hackett died of ovarian cancer when she was 49. (Abbey of the Psalms, Sanctuary of Faith, D-3, Crypt 2314.)

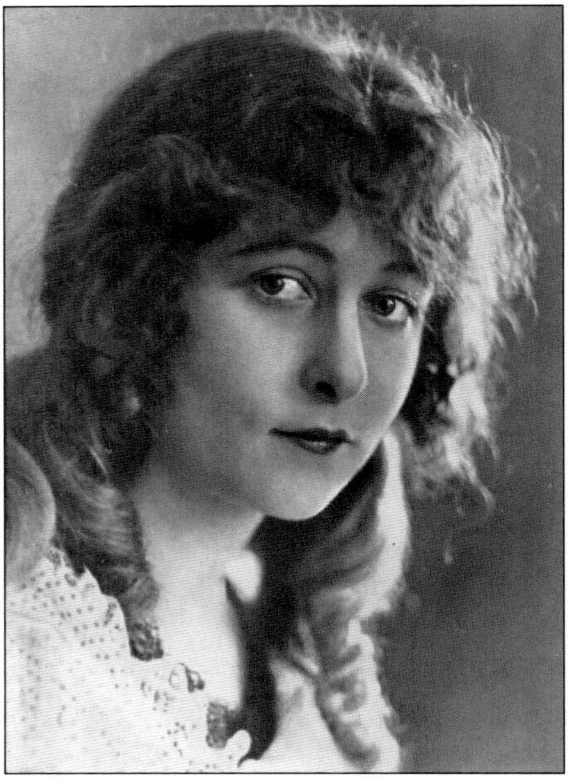

Mildred Harris (1901–1944). A child star at 11, Harris became the first of four wives of Charlie Chaplin only five years later, after she became pregnant. The marriage was essentially over following the death of their newborn child. They were divorced after only one year together. Harris became a leading lady in film throughout the 1920s, but saw her career decline with the arrival of sound. She died from pneumonia at 42. (Abbey of the Psalms, Corridor G-1, Crypt 740.)

WANDA HAWLEY (1893–1963). Wanda Hawley is another of the legions of silent film stars whose careers ended when talking pictures became the rage. Pretty, Pennsylvania-born Hawley costarred with H4E neighbors Douglas Fairbanks in *Mr. Fix-It* (1918) and Rudolph Valentino in *The Young Rajah* (1922). She was often seen in the films of director Cecil B. DeMille. Out of work and broke in the 1930s, Hawley was said to have spent time as a call girl. She is pictured here on the left with Edythe Chapman in a scene from *Secret Service* (1919). (Abbey of the Psalms, Haven of Peace, Tier 2, Niche 3.)

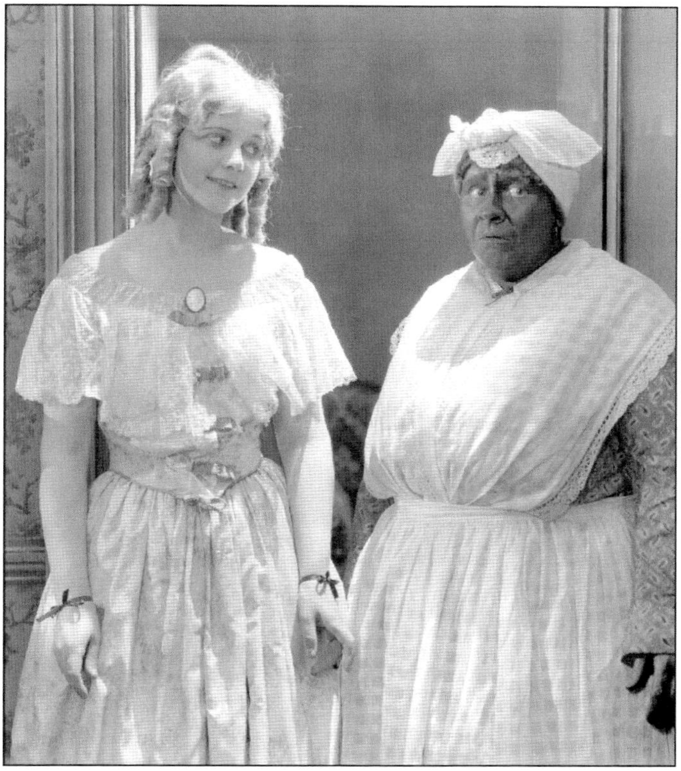

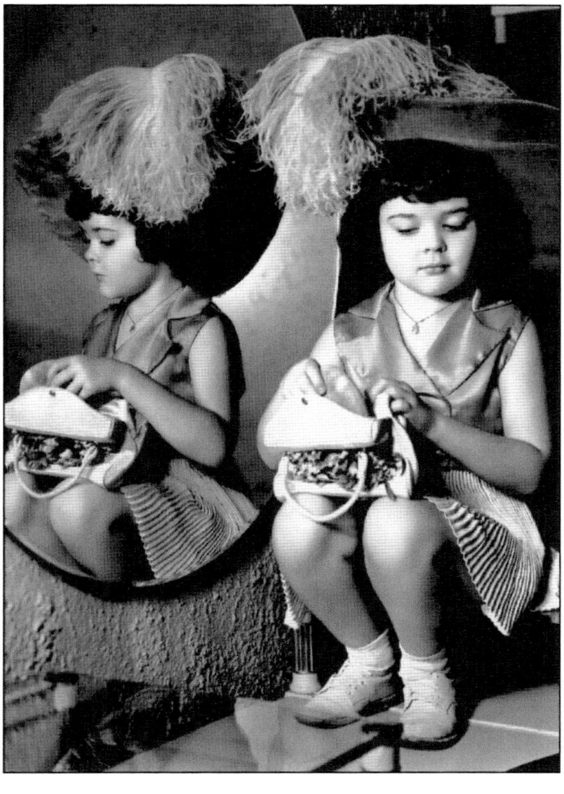

DARLA HOOD (1931–1979). Cute Oklahoma-native Darla Hood made her debut as Darla in Hal Roach's *Our Gang* comedies at the age of four and continued in the role until 1941. Hood became a professional singer as an adult and appeared regularly on television shows. Her singing voice was familiar to millions of television viewers during the 1960s due to her work in commercials for Campbell's Soup and Chicken of the Sea tuna. She died at the age of 47 from acute hepatitis contracted from a blood transfusion. (Abbey of the Psalms, Sanctuary of Light, Corridor G-4, Crypt 7213.)

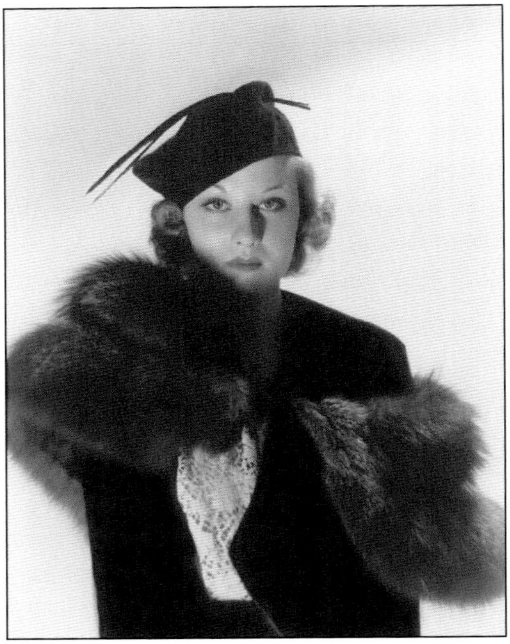

JEAN HOWARD (1910–2000). Jean Howard was born in Texas as Ernestine Mahoney. After being a Ziegfeld girl, she turned her attention to photography, becoming the chronicler of Hollywood's Golden Age. Despite divorcing her husband in 1948, the couple continued to live together for the next 20 years. Howard inherited a fortune from her friend Cole Porter, which allowed her to live in Italy for several years. (Abbey of the Psalms, Haven of Meditation, Tier 8, Niche 1.)

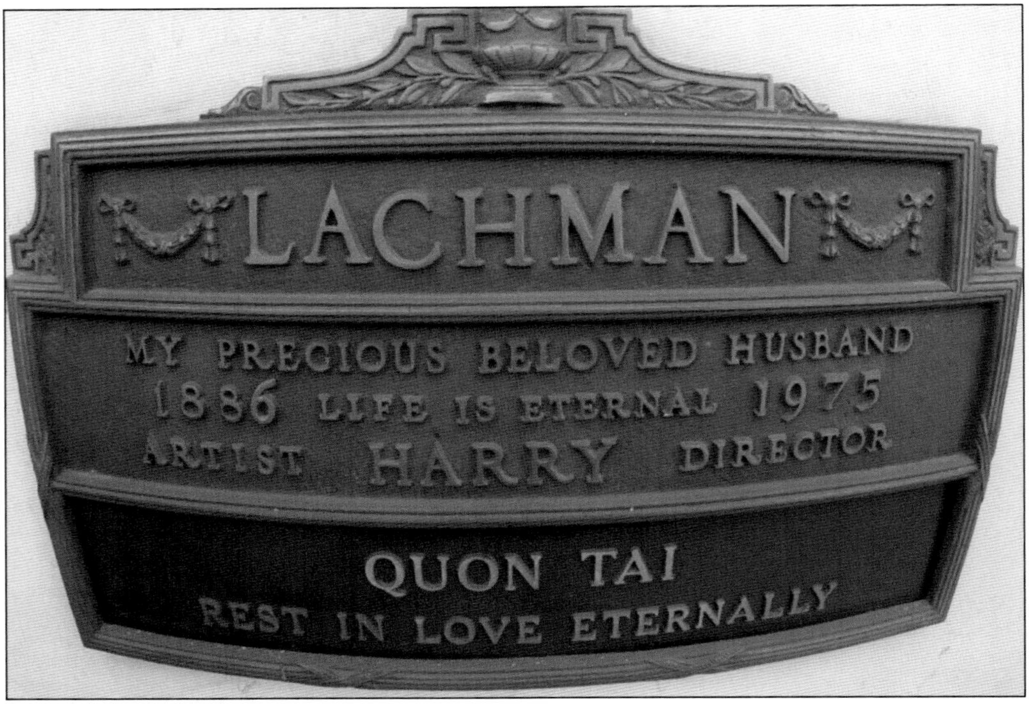

HARRY LACHMAN (1886–1975). American artist Harry Lachman was a Légion d'Honneur–winning Post-Impressionist painter in Paris in the 1910s and 1920s. He was friends with Pablo Picasso, Henri Matisse, and Pierre-Auguste Renoir. Lachman made his first films in Europe before coming to Hollywood, where he directed the likes of Spencer Tracy, Rita Hayworth, Cary Grant, Janet Gaynor, and Laurel and Hardy. After retiring from pictures, Lachman again picked up the paint brush. His creations are still exhibited in some of the finest art museums in the world. (Abbey of the Psalms, Shrine of Adoration, Crypt 1388.) (Courtesy of Pentax Forums.)

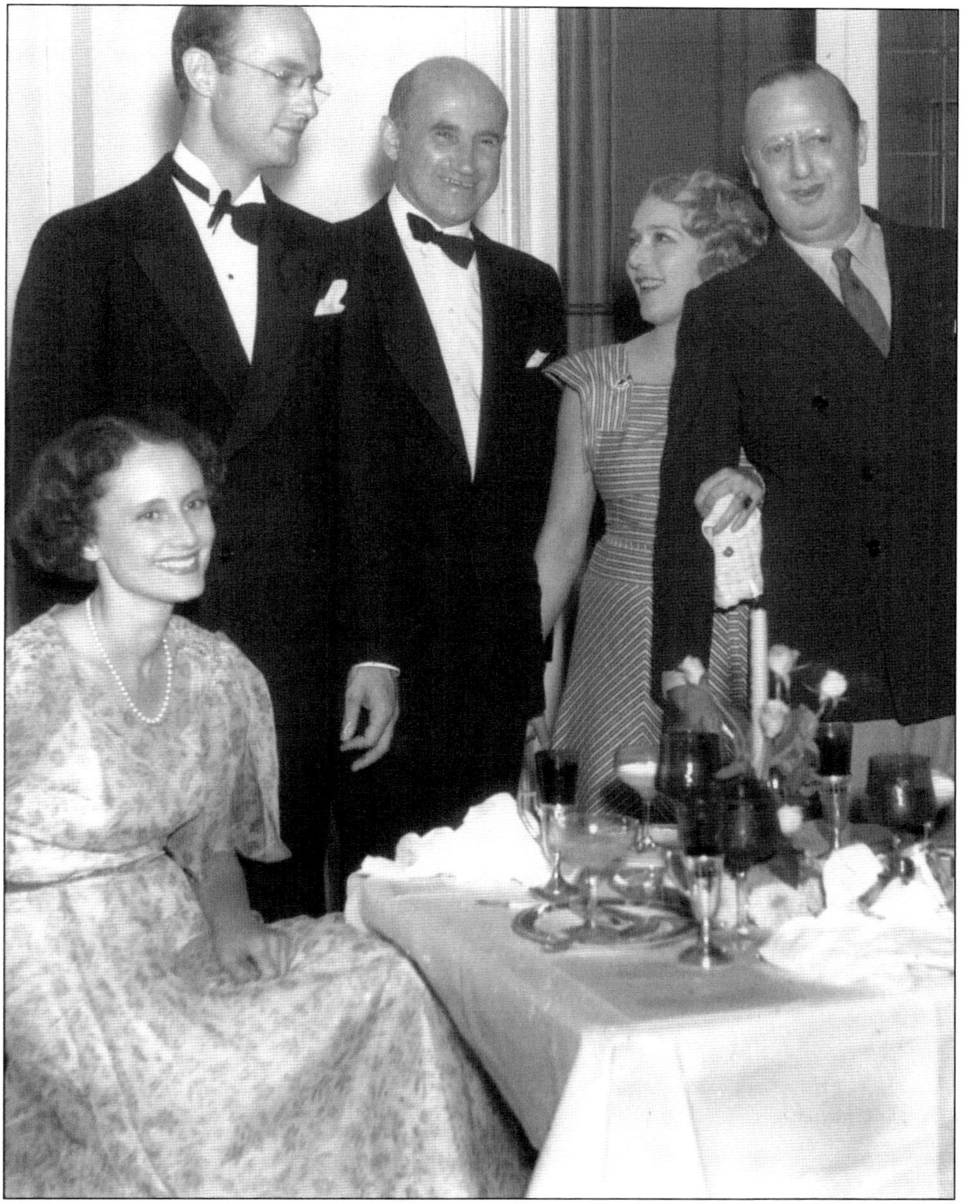

Jesse L. Lasky (1880–1958). One of the true pioneers of American cinema, Jesse L. Lasky permanently placed Hollywood on the movie-making map when he sent his friend and partner Cecile B. DeMille west to film *The Squaw Man* (1914). Part of the film was shot in a rented barn in the tiny borough of Hollywood, six miles north of downtown Los Angeles. The film was so successful that other crews flooded to Hollywood, quickly making it the filmmaking capital of the world. In 1916, Lasky helped create what became Paramount Pictures when his studio, the Jesse L. Lasky Feature Play Company, merged with Adolph Zukor's Famous Players Film Company. A plaque on his tomb reads, "Beloved son of California who in 1913 headed the company that made the first feature length motion picture made in Hollywood." Today, the barn DeMille used for *The Squaw Man* still exists as the Lasky-DeMille Barn and serves as the home of the Hollywood Heritage Museum. Both Lasky and DeMille are interred in H4E just steps away from their creation, Paramount Studios. (Abbey of the Psalms, Corridor G-3, Crypt 2196.)

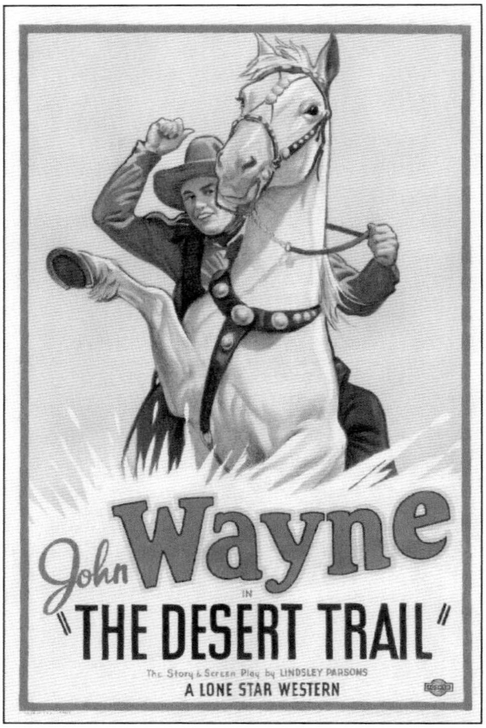

Paul Malvern (1902–1993) and Jean Huntley (1893–1979). Paul Malvern began his career in show business as a member of his family's acrobatic troupe before becoming a stunt man in Hollywood. A severe injury on set sent him behind the camera, where he produced more than 100 films. Nearly 40 of them starred a young Western actor named John Wayne. His wife was actress Jean Huntley, who appeared in Charlie Chaplin's *The Gold Rush*. (Abbey of the Psalms, Sanctuary of Memories, Crypt 1301.)

Robert "Bob" Mitchell (1912–2009). Pianist Bob Mitchell first accompanied silent films in theaters when he was 12. He later became a choir director, a position he held in one fashion or another for the next 80 years. Along the way, he founded the Robert Mitchell Choir Boys troupe, which appeared in 100 films and was the subject of an Academy Award–nominated short. Mitchell was the first organist at Dodger Stadium when it opened in 1962. (Sanctuary of Memories, Elevation 8, Crypt C-49.)

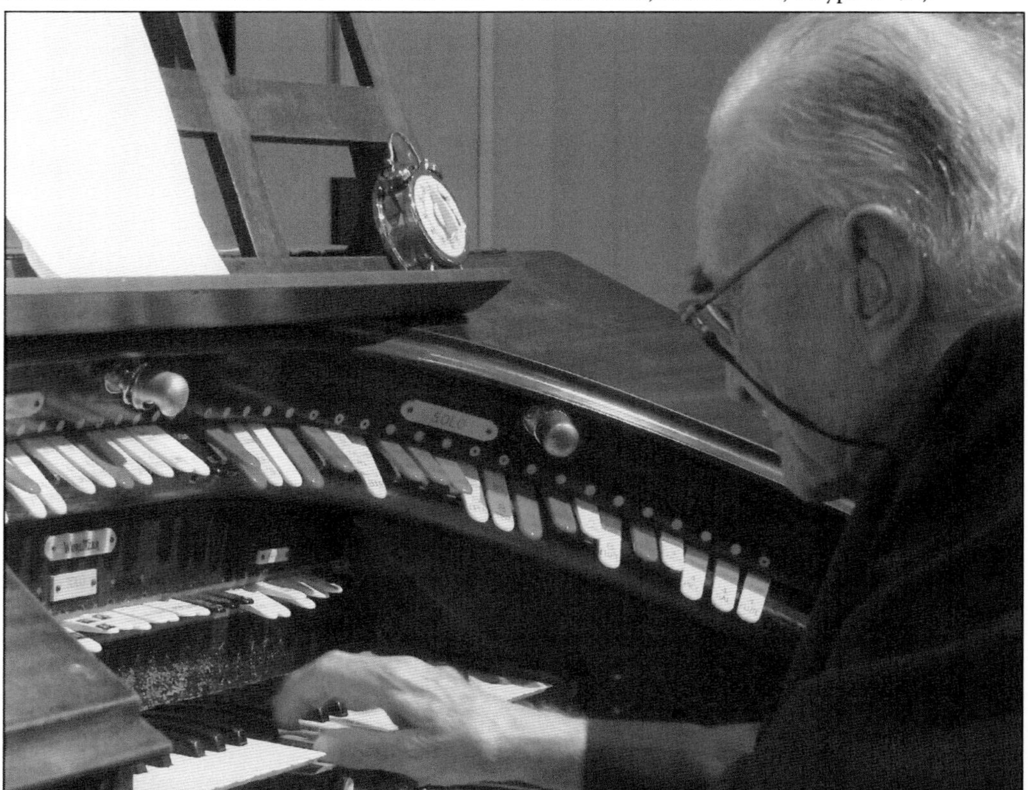

Bernice Petkere (1901–2000). Petkere was a successful pianist and songwriter during the Great Depression, earning the title "Queen of Tin Pan Alley." She penned such standards as "Close Your Eyes" and "Starlight," which was recorded by Bing Crosby. (Abbey of the Psalms, Sanctuary of Faith, Crypt 1273.)

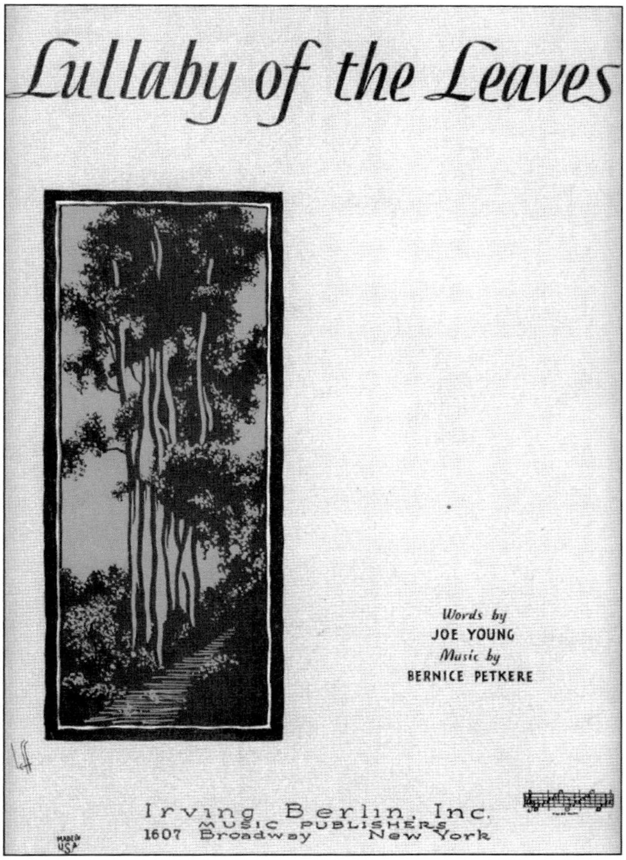

Almira Sessions (1888–1974). Character actress Almira Sessions racked up over 500 film and television appearances during her 60-plus year career. She was featured in such well known hits as *It's a Wonderful Life* (1947), *The Bishop's Wife* (1948), *Harvey* (1950), and *Rebel Without a Cause* (1955). One of her last roles was in Roman Polanski's chiller *Rosemary's Baby* (1968). Sessions is seen here at far left, with Una O'Connor (center) and Dorothy Vaughan in a scene from 1941's *Three Girls About Town*. (Abbey of the Psalms, Haven of Worship, H-1-1, Niches.)

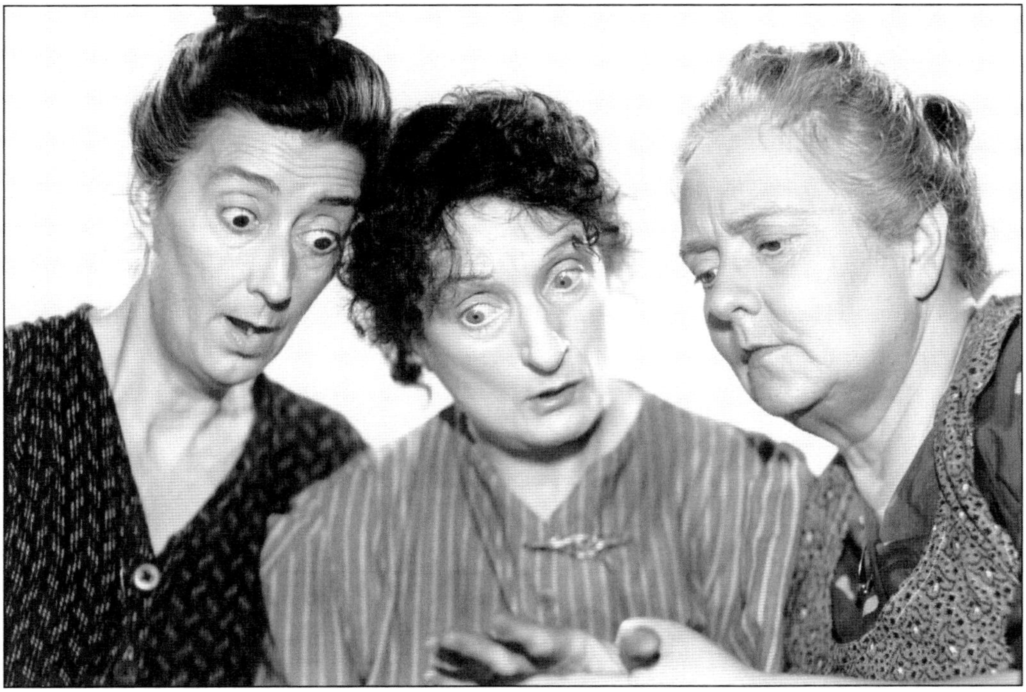

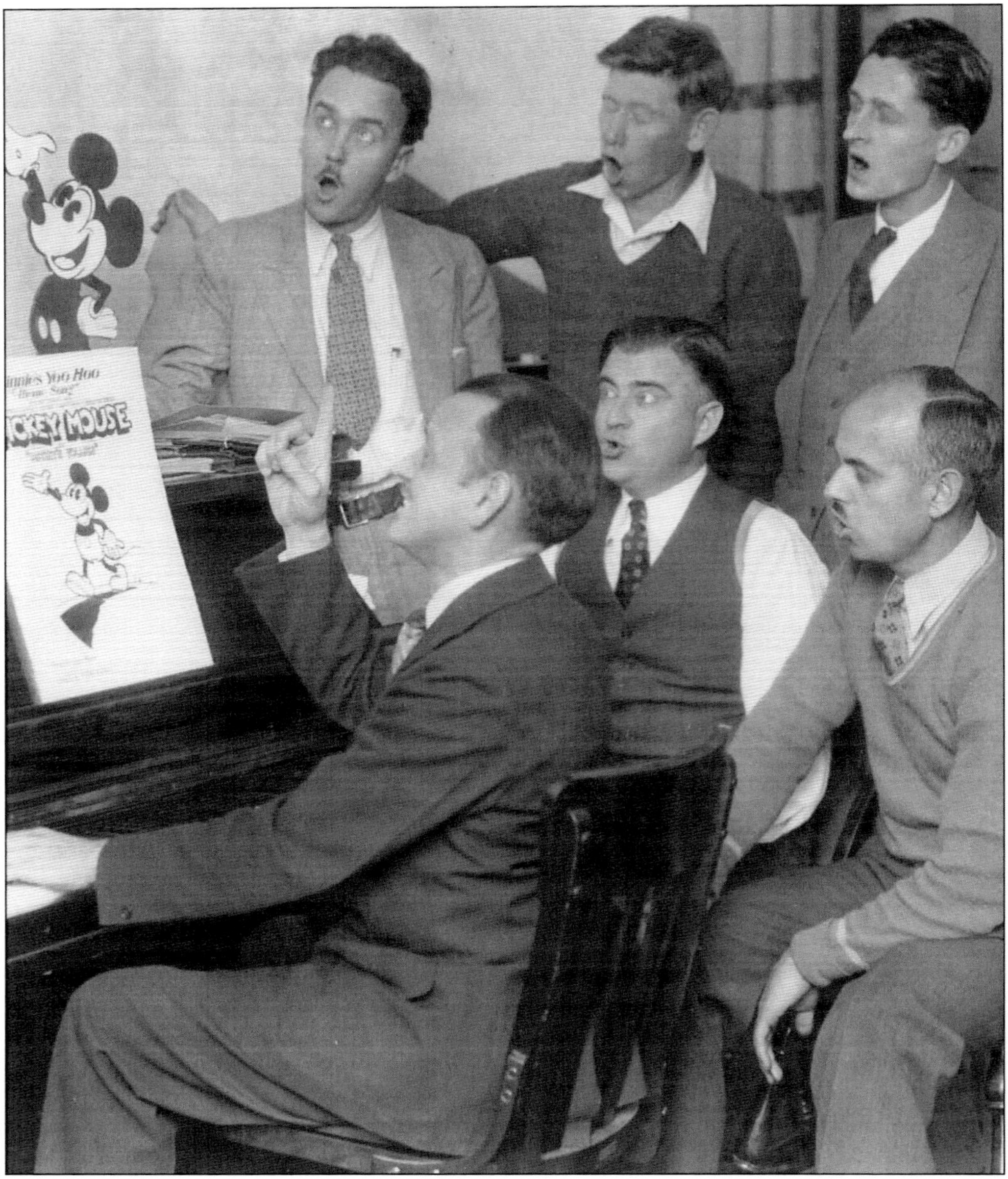

Carl Stalling (1891–1972). An otherwise hilarious *Looney Tunes* or *Merrie Melodies* cartoon is only half as funny with the sound turned off. That's because the scores created by composer Carl Stalling perfectly capture the pace and energy of the motion on screen, lifting the humor to an even higher plateau. Stalling was famous for adding "musical puns"—references to other popular songs—into his seven-minute masterpieces. He began his career playing piano for silent films in Missouri, where he befriended a young animator named Walt Disney. With the end of silent films in sight, Stalling accepted an offer from Disney to come west to be his music director. He worked there for two years before leaving to join the studio of Disney's former partner Ub Iwerks. Stalling later joined Leon Schlesinger's animation team at Warner Bros., where he remained until his retirement in 1958. In the 22 years Stalling was at Warner Bros., he composed over 600 scores. Stalling is seen here at the piano in 1929 along with the Disney animation staff. (Abbey of the Psalms, Corridor D-2, Crypt 7149.)

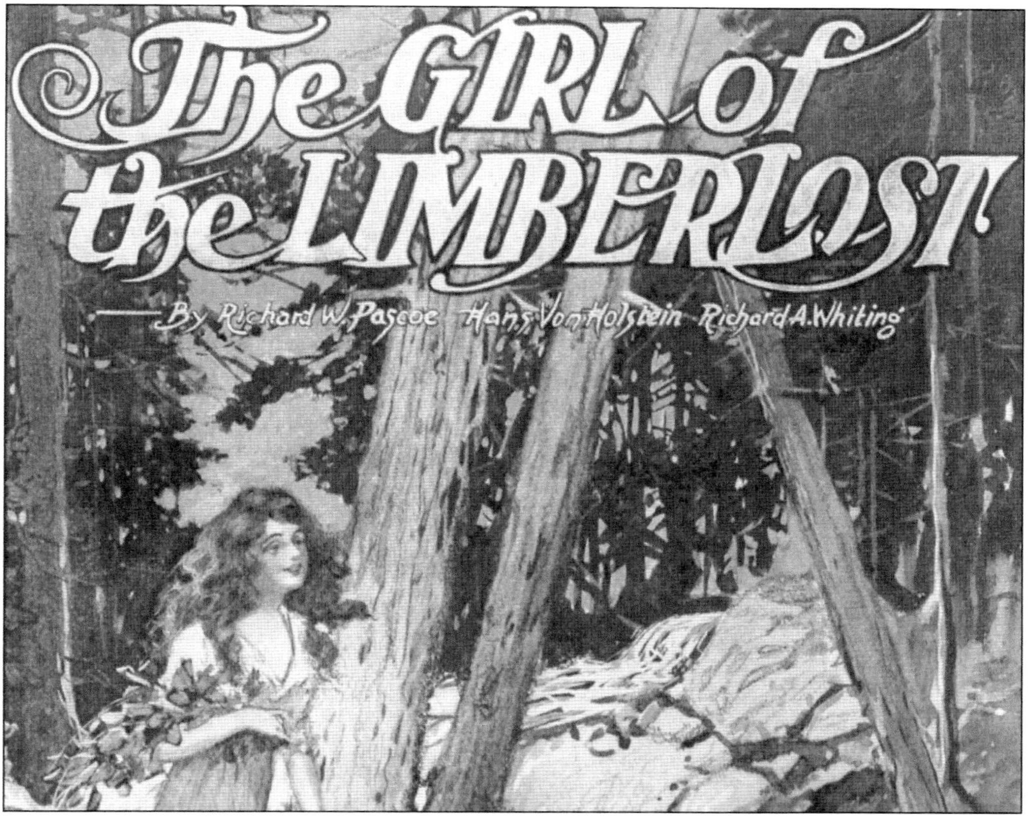

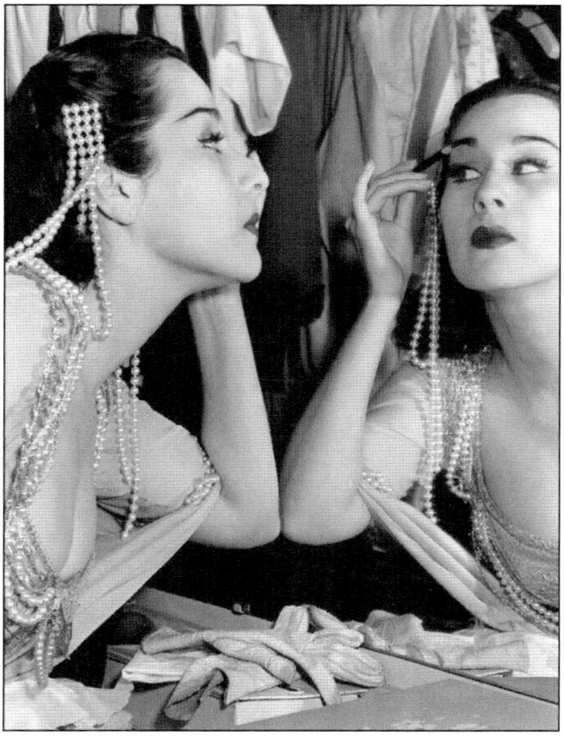

GENE STRATTON-PORTER (1863–1924). American author Gene Stratton-Porter wrote several best-selling novels, including *A Girl of the Limberlost*. An early environmentalist and nature photographer, she was killed in a streetcar accident when she was 61. Her original crypt is here, but her body is not, having been reburied near Limberlost swamp in Indiana, a wetland she worked to preserve. (Abbey of the Psalms, Foyer F, Crypt 217.)

YMA SUMAC (1922–2008). Peruvian American soprano Sumac possessed a five-octave vocal range that was captured on million-selling albums for Capitol Records. Known as the "Peruvian Songbird," Sumac claimed to be a direct descendant of the last Incan emperor. (Abbey of the Psalms, Sanctuary of Memories, Elevation 19, Crypt C-116.)

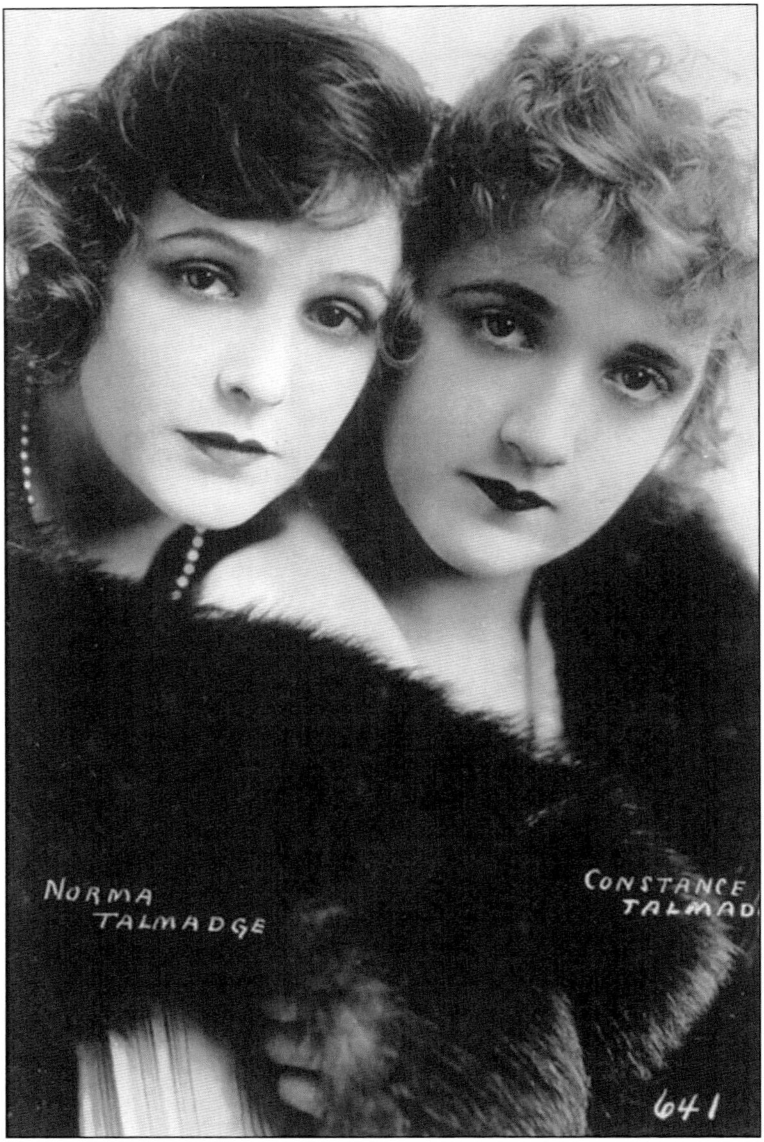

Constance (1898–1973), Norma (1894–1957), and Natalie Talmadge (1896–1969). Norma and Constance Talmadge (pictured) were two of the biggest stars of the silent era. Beautiful brunette Norma excelled at emotional dramas, whereas tall, mischievous Constance preferred light romantic comedy roles. They began their film careers as teenagers in New York before heading west with sister Natalie, who also acted for a time and became Buster Keaton's first wife. Constance's career got a major boost after she appeared in D.W. Griffith's *Intolerance* (1916). Norma's skyrocketed after she married Joseph Schenck, one of the most powerful producers in Hollywood. By the early 1920s, the Talmadges were ranked the No. 1 (Norma) and No. 2 (Constance) most popular screen actresses. Their careers stalled at the end of the silent era, and all three sisters battled addiction and alcoholism. Norma was the first to die in 1957, followed by Natalie in 1969, and Constance four years later. One story—most likely apocryphal—about the origin of the footprints in front of Hollywood's Grauman's Theater suggests that Norma inadvertently began the tradition when she stepped in wet cement on her way to a screening. (Abbey of the Psalms, Corridor G-7, Family Room B.)

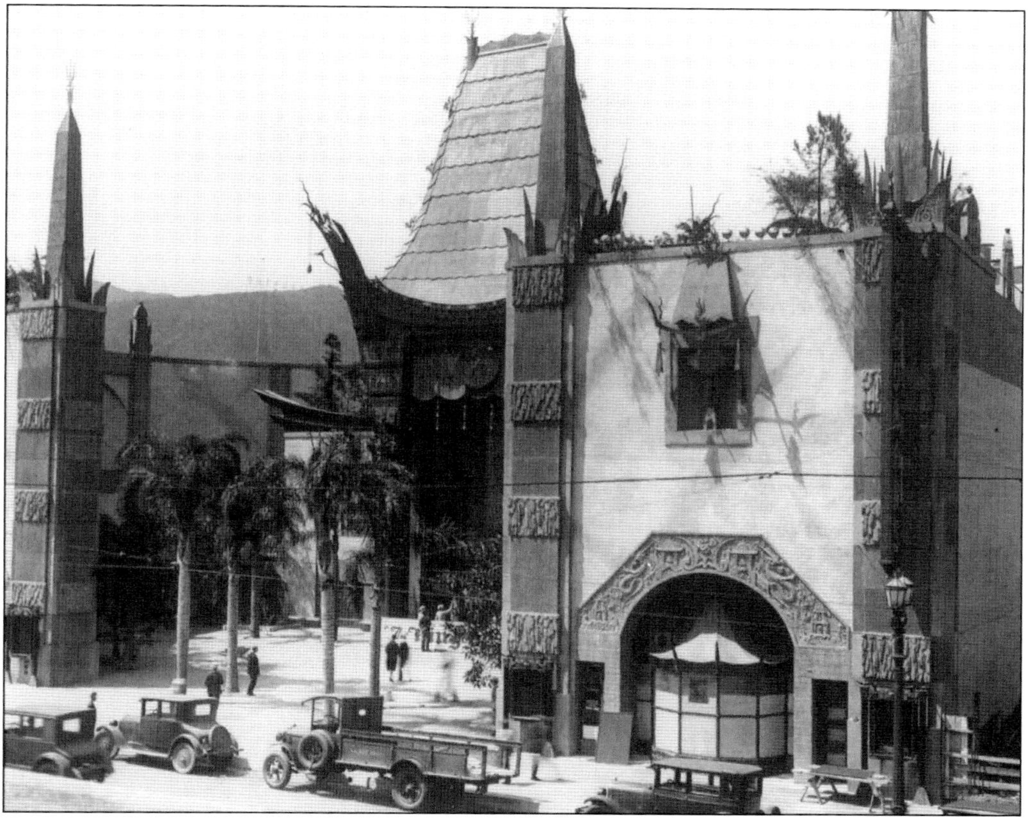

Charles E. Toberman (1880–1981). Real Estate developer Charles Toberman created many of the more notable Hollywood structures, including Grauman's Chinese Theater (pictured). He lived to be 101. (Abbey of the Psalms, Building G-9, Room E, Crypt 4.)

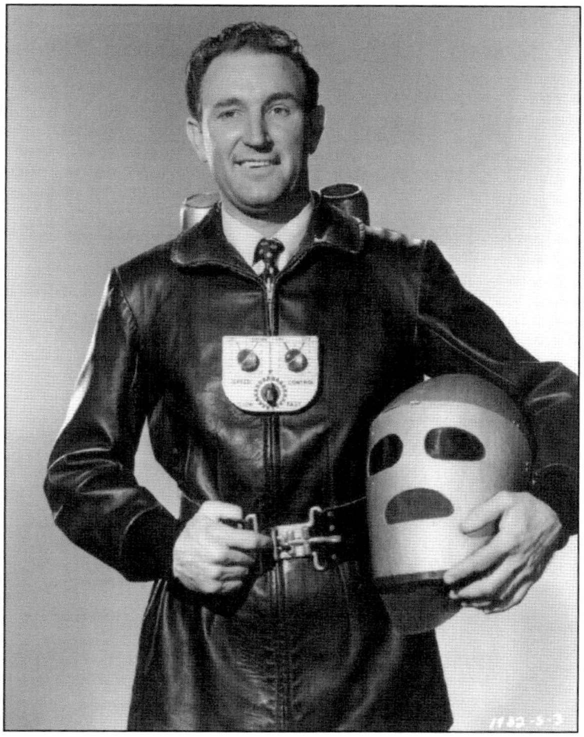

George D. Wallace (1917–2005). Actor George D. Wallace's most recognizable role was as Commando Cody in the serial *Radar Men from the Moon* (1952). Wallace's leather jacket, rocket pack, and silver bullet-shaped helmet later inspired Billy Campbell's costume in *The Rocketeer* (1991). Transitioning from the screen to the stage, Wallace enjoyed a long career on Broadway. (Abbey of the Psalms, Foyer Columbarium.)

HENRY B. WALTHALL (1878–1936). One of the most enduring images from the silent era is of Henry B. Walthall jamming a flag into a cannon in *The Birth of a Nation* (1915). A son of the South, he was born on a cotton plantation in Alabama, and his father had been a captain in the Confederacy. Walthall appeared in hundreds of films, many for director D.W. Griffith, and died soon after collapsing on the set of his final film. (Abbey of the Psalms, Corridor D-1, Crypt 370.)

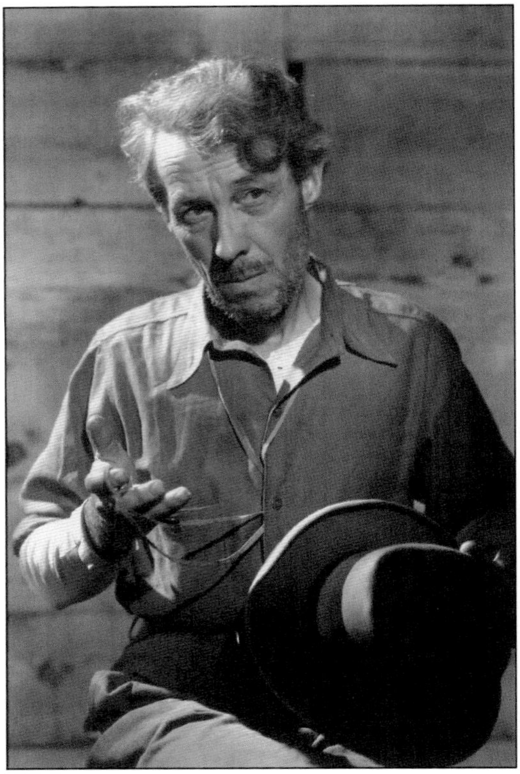

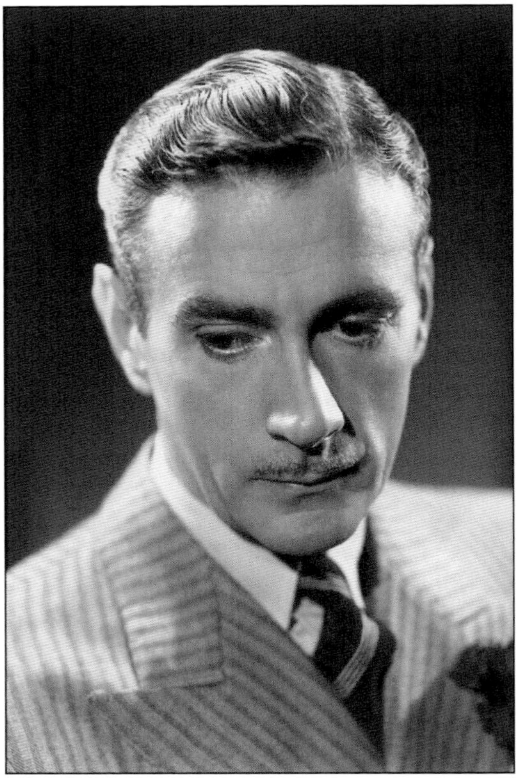

CLIFTON WEBB (1889–1966). Actor Clifton Webb enjoyed a 50-year Hollywood career playing snobby characters in well-known films like *Laura* (1944), *The Razor's Edge* (1946), and *Cheaper By The Dozen* (1950). Unusually close to his mother, who lived with him until her death at the age of 91, she is now interred beside him. (Visitors to his crypt may want to take along their autograph book, as Webb's ghost is said to haunt the corridor.) (Abbey of the Psalms, Corridor G-6, Crypt 2350.)

Three

Beth Olam Cemetery

Many years ago, a portion of Hollywood Forever on the south side of the property was named Beth Olam and set aside for Jewish burials. Today, Beth Olam is again a part of Hollywood Forever, and consists of two mausoleums: the Hall of David and the Hall of Solomon. (Beth Olam also has outdoor burials. The names included in this book from these gardens are listed in the fourth chapter.)

People belonging to the Jewish faith have made a huge impact on Hollywood from its earliest days. Many of these individuals are now housed in either the Hall of David or the Hall of Solomon.

Along these corridors are the crypts of such luminaries as bandleader Nelson Riddle, one of America's most famous musicians, as well as Leon Schlesinger, who wrangled a team of legendary artists during animation's golden age to produce some of the funniest cartoons ever made. The Ritz Brothers are all here, as are actors Rudolph Schildkraut and his son Joseph.

Hank Mann, whose hangdog face brought laughter to millions, is in Beth Olam, as is Edgar G. Ulmer, one of Hollywood's most underrated directors. Ann Savage, who Ulmer directed to a stunning performance in 1945's *Detour*, is interred nearby. Sound engineer Nathan Levinson is entombed here; he worked closely with Sam Warner at Warner Bros. to create talking pictures.

A real "rocket scientist," Theodore Von Karman, can be found here, as can mobster Benjamin Siegel, who was called "Bugsy," but never to his face.

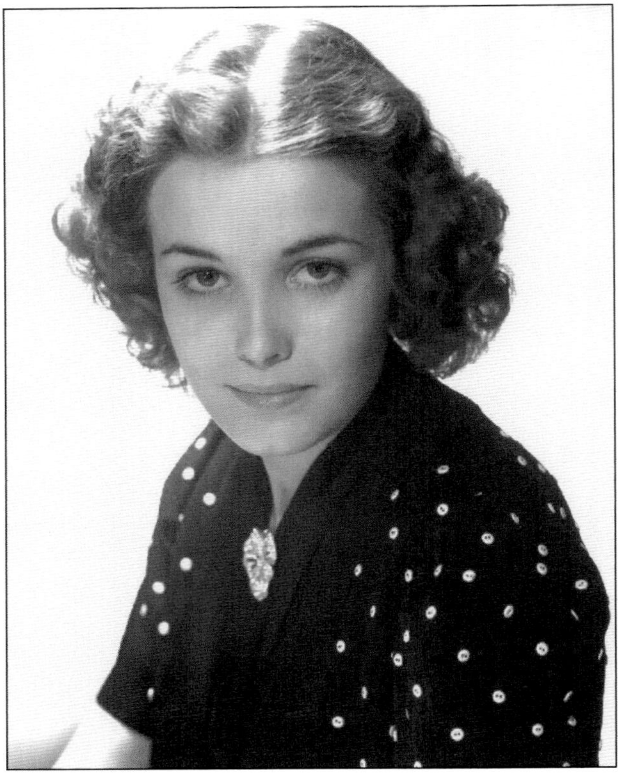

Lois Collier (1919–1999). Diminutive South Carolinian Collier was bitten by the acting bug on a tour of Hollywood at the age of 15. She began her acting career in 1938 and appeared in several B-Westerns with cowboy stars Bob Steele and Tom Tyler. She was the female lead in seven *Three Mesquiteers* films for Republic during the 1940s. Collier retired after appearing in all 58 episodes of the *Boston Blackie* television show in the 1950s. (Hall of David, Corridor T-6-2, Crypt 6386.)

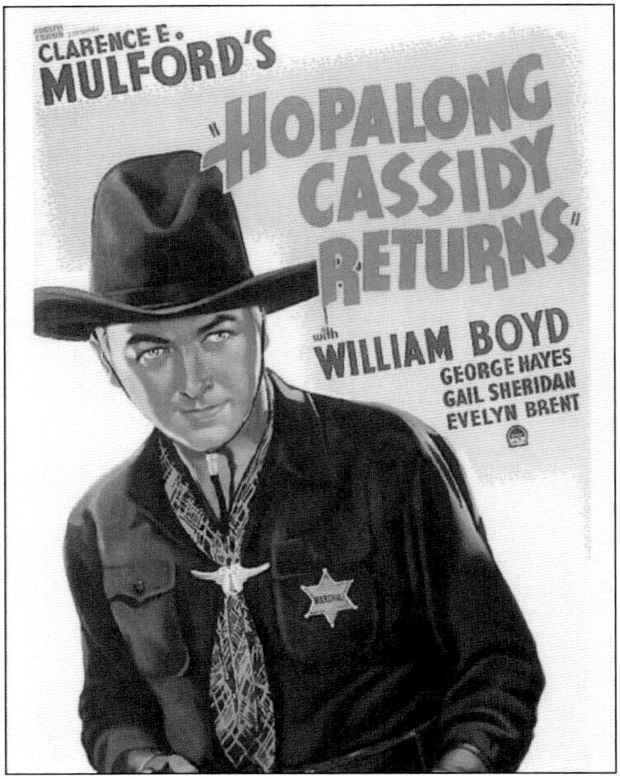

Harrison Jacobs (1892–1968). Harrison Jacobs was a prolific screenwriter, mostly in the Western genre. He is credited with writing over a dozen of the Hopalong Cassidy films that starred William Boyd. (Hall of David, Corridor T-7-2, Crypt 6477.)

Bronislaw Kaper (1902–1983). Polish composer Bronislaw Kaper scored over 150 films and won an Oscar for *Lili* in 1953. He began his career playing the piano in Berlin cabarets, where he met fellow H4E resident Walter Jurmann. The two teamed up and headed to Hollywood after fleeing the Nazis. One of their original collaborations was for the Marx Brothers comedy classic *A Night at the Opera* (1935). (Hall of David, Corridor T-1, Tier 15, Niche 1513.)

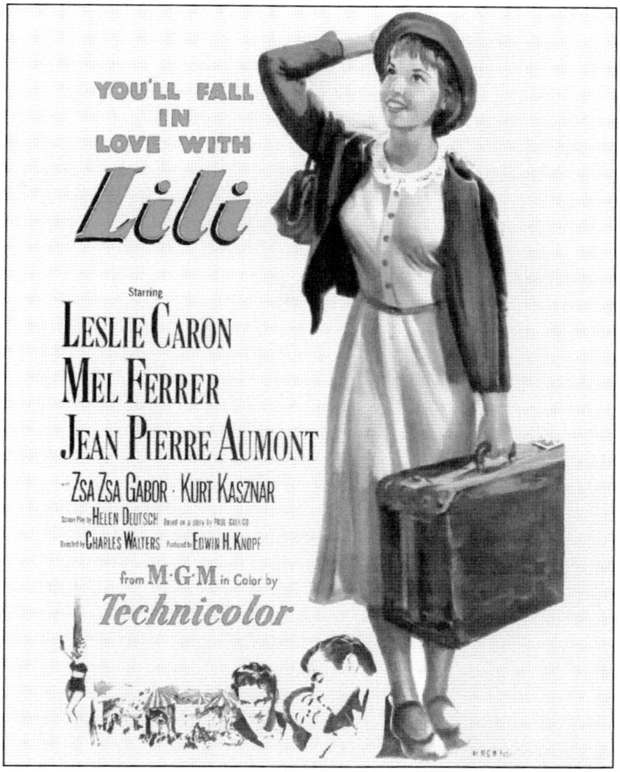

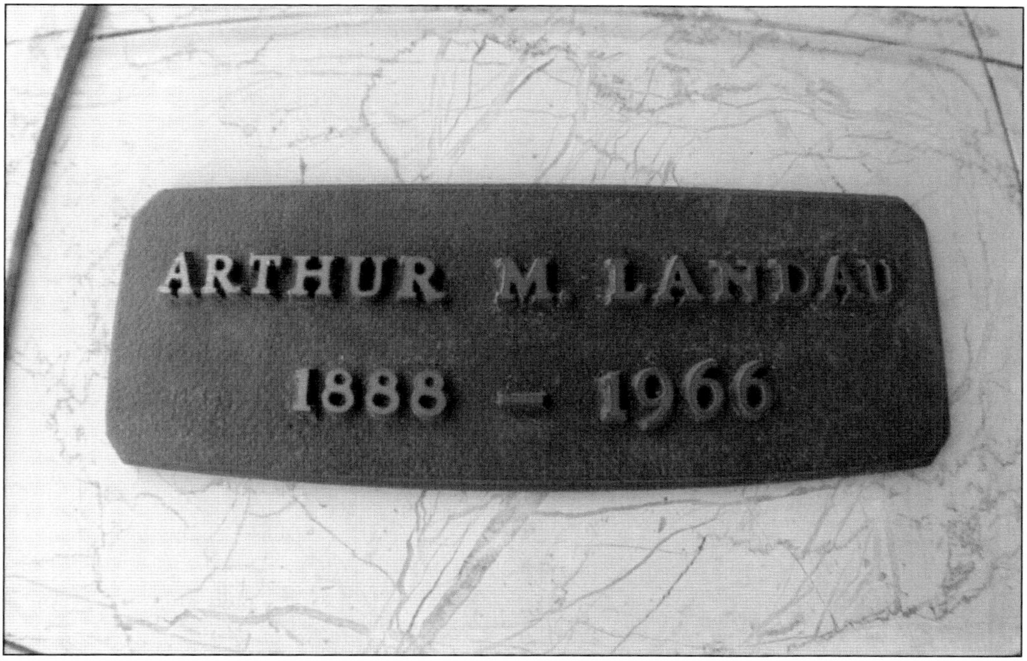

Arthur Landau (1888–1966). Agent Arthur Landau launched and guided the career of blonde bombshell Jean Harlow. He was portrayed by Red Buttons in the Paramount production of *Harlow* shortly before his death. (Hall of David, Corridor T-1, Tier 13, Niche 130S.) (Courtesy of Pentax Forums.)

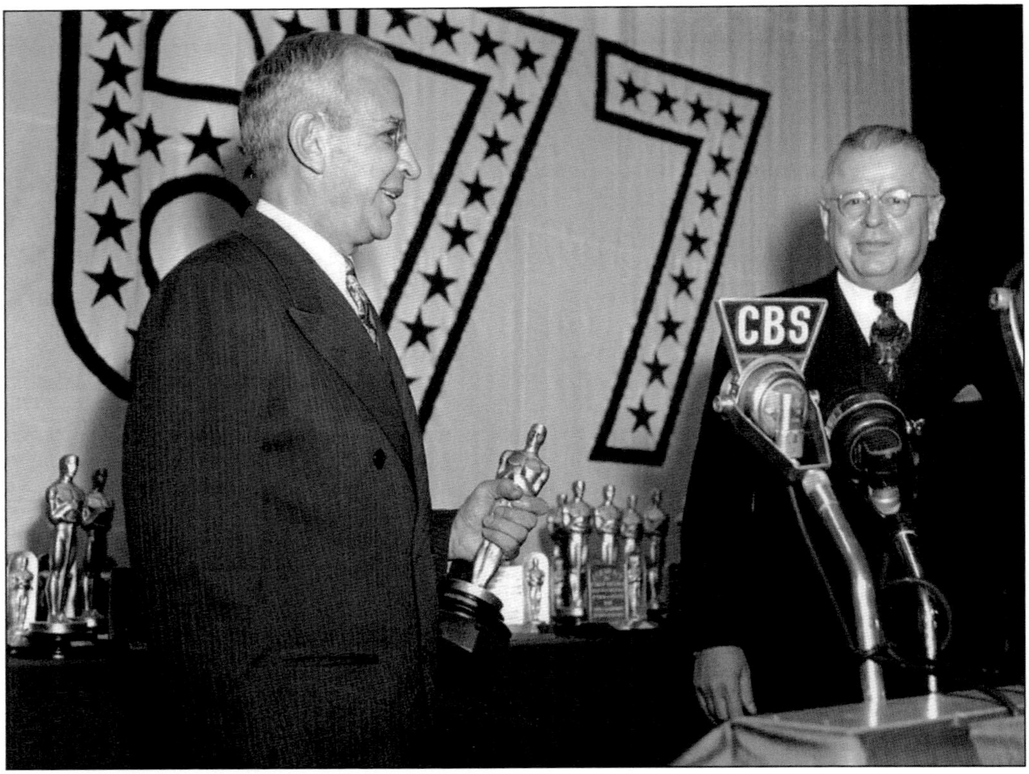

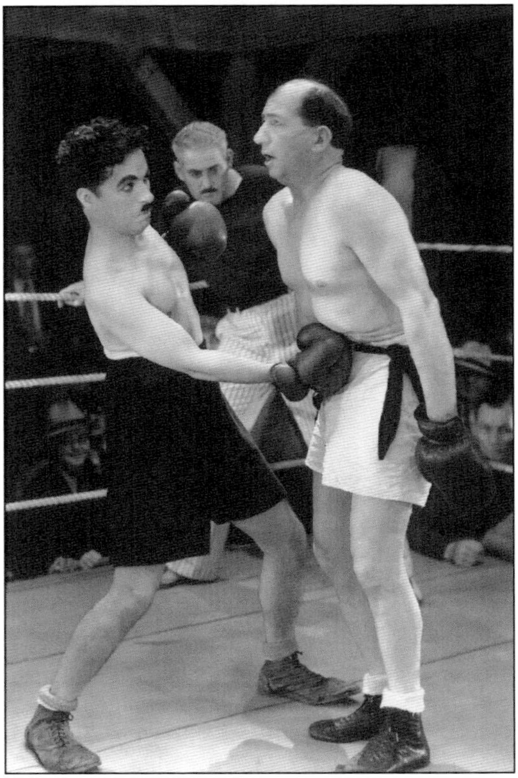

NATHAN LEVINSON (1888–1952). Sound engineer Nathan Levinson had a significant role in bringing voices to movies, thereby ending the silent era. Levinson convinced producer Sam Warner to try Western Electric's sound-on-disc process to bring sound effects to the film *Don Juan* (1926) and actual voices to *The Jazz Singer* the following year. Levinson won an Academy Award for Best Sound for *Yankee Doodle Dandy* in 1942. He is pictured here accepting his Oscar. (Hall of David, Foyer O, Tier 8, Niche 7.)

HANK MANN (1888–1971). One of the funniest scenes of the silent era is the boxing match between Charlie Chaplin and Hank Mann in *City Lights* (1931), pictured here. Mann was born in Russia as David William Lieberman. He made his way to Hollywood, where he landed a job working for Mack Sennett at Keystone Studios. It was here that he first met Chaplin, who he would work with for the next 25 years. He was one of the original Keystone Cops and appeared in *Abbott and Costello Meet the Keystone Kops* in 1955. (Hall of David, Corridor T-J-1-1, Crypt 7672.)

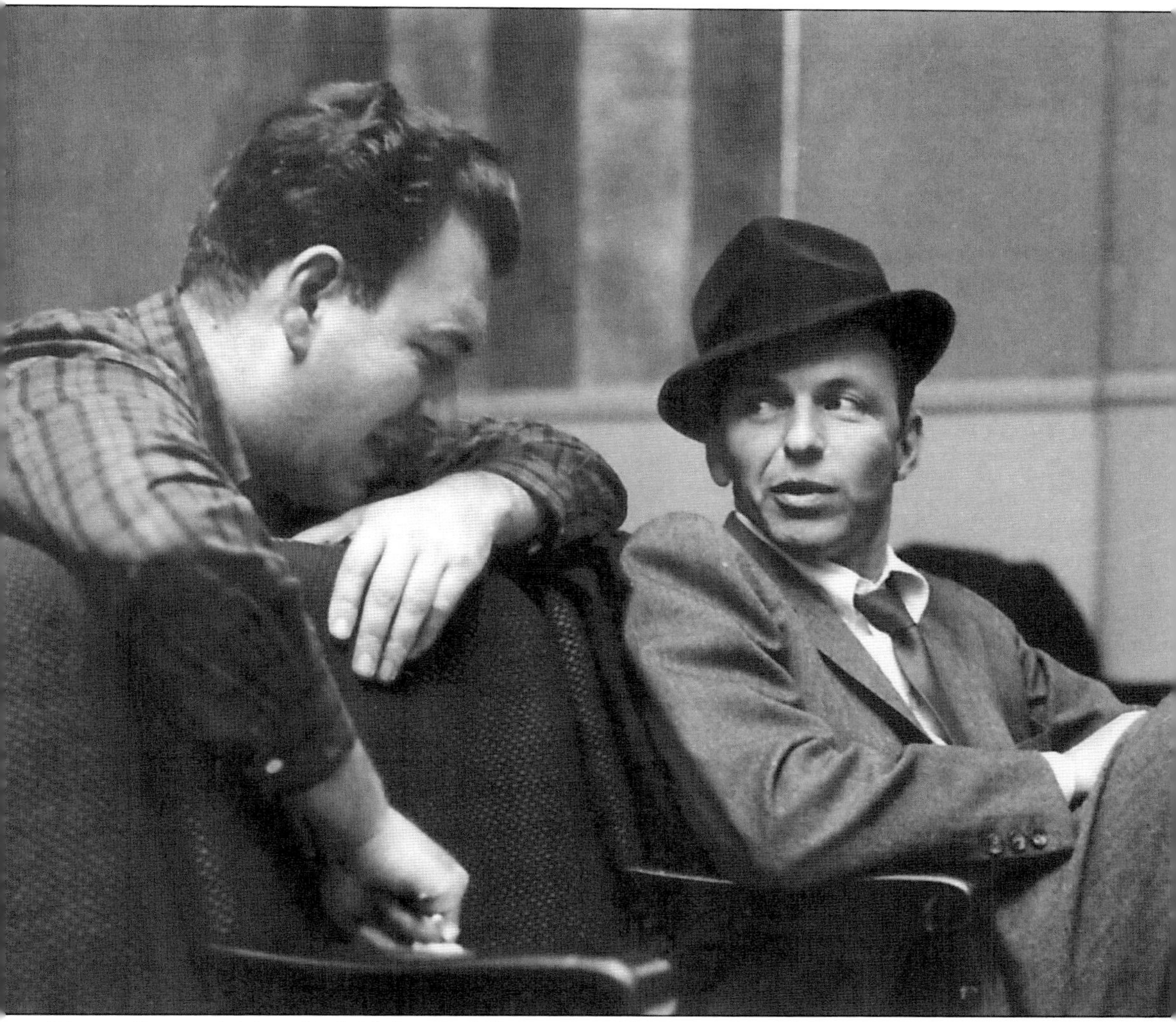

Nelson Riddle (1921–1985). Nelson Riddle was one of the most successful American bandleaders, composers, and arrangers. He was born in New Jersey, where he began studying the piano when he was eight years old and the trombone at 14. Riddle played trombone for Tommy Dorsey's orchestra for a few months before being drafted into the Army during World War II. He began his career in Hollywood as an arranger after the war ended and contributed to the films *High Society* (1956), *Pal Joey* (1957), *Ocean's 11* (1960), and *Paint Your Wagon* (1969). Over the course of Riddle's career, he worked with nearly every big-named singer of the era, including Frank Sinatra, Nat King Cole, Judy Garland, Johnny Mathis, and Rosemary Clooney. His career revived near the end of his life when he worked with Linda Ronstadt on three platinum-selling albums of jazz standards. He is pictured above with Frank Sinatra. (Hall of David, Corridor T-1, East Wall, Niche 702.)

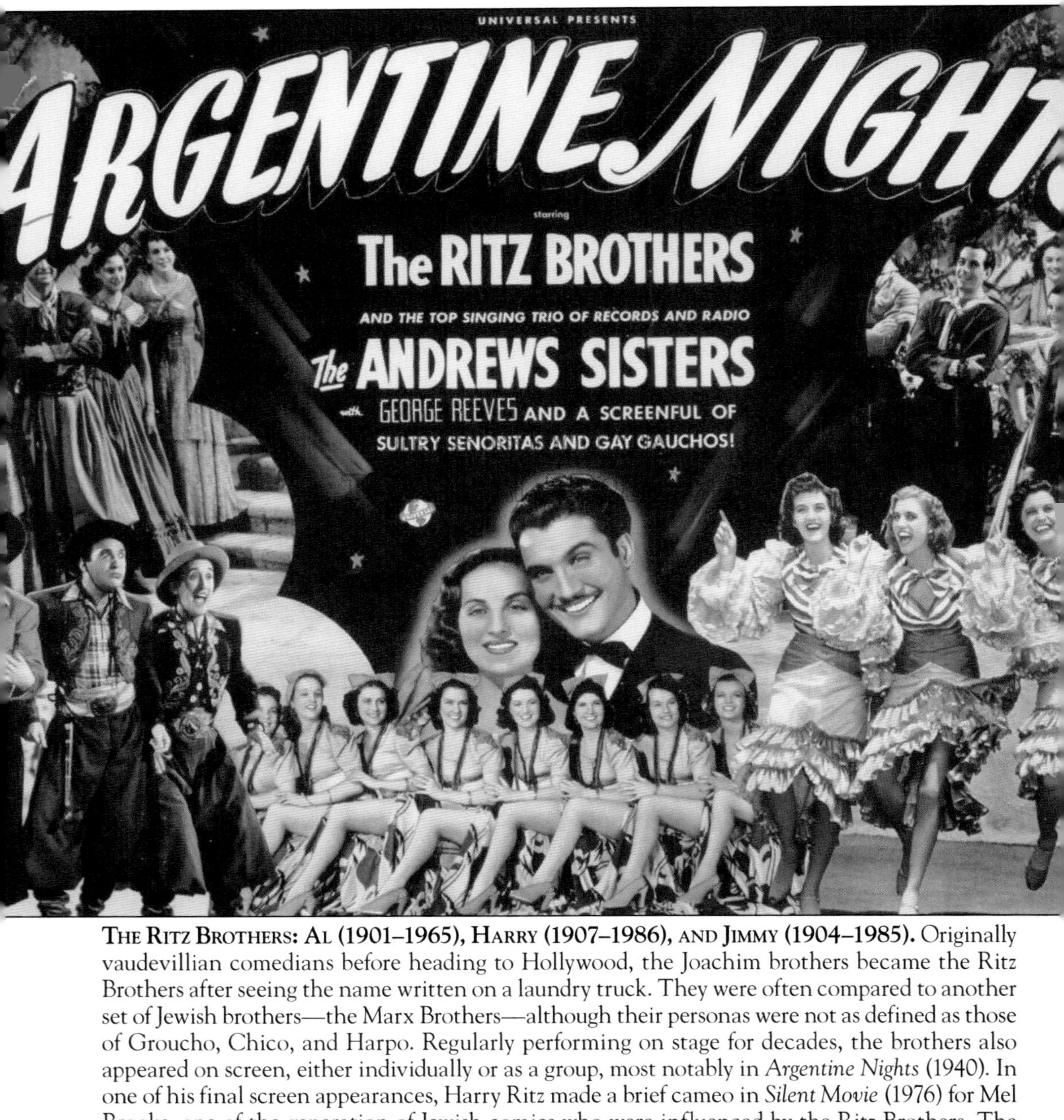

The Ritz Brothers: Al (1901–1965), Harry (1907–1986), and Jimmy (1904–1985). Originally vaudevillian comedians before heading to Hollywood, the Joachim brothers became the Ritz Brothers after seeing the name written on a laundry truck. They were often compared to another set of Jewish brothers—the Marx Brothers—although their personas were not as defined as those of Groucho, Chico, and Harpo. Regularly performing on stage for decades, the brothers also appeared on screen, either individually or as a group, most notably in *Argentine Nights* (1940). In one of his final screen appearances, Harry Ritz made a brief cameo in *Silent Movie* (1976) for Mel Brooks, one of the generation of Jewish comics who were influenced by the Ritz Brothers. The brothers remained close throughout their lives and are now interred close to one another. (Al: Hall of David, Corridor T-J-1-4; Harry: Hall of David, Corridor T-J-1-3, Crypt 7776; and Jimmy: Hall of David, T-J-1-1, Crypt 5659.)

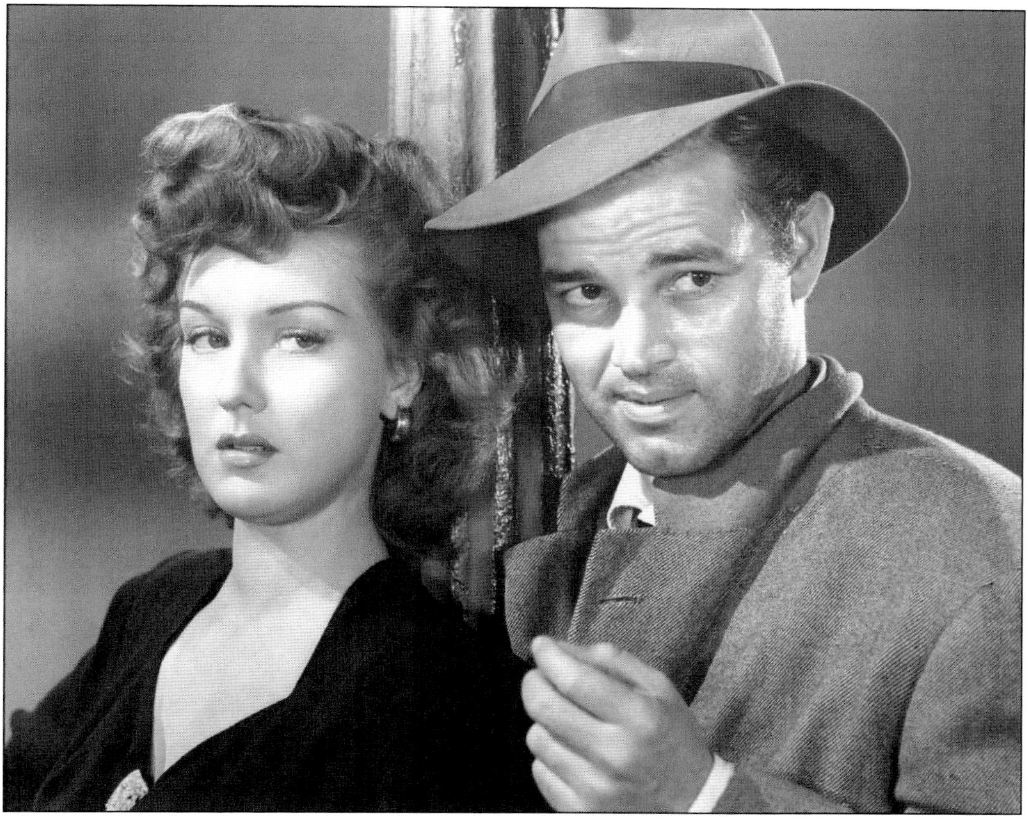

Ann Savage (1921–2008). Anyone who has seen the low-budget film noir classic *Detour* (1945) will never forget the performance of actress Ann Savage as the hard-edged blackmailer Vera. This role was later voted one of the Top Ten Movie Villains by the Academy of Motion Picture Arts and Sciences. She is pictured here with the film's costar, Tom Neal. In her later years, Savage worked closely with the organization Hollywood Heritage to preserve Hollywood landmarks. (Hall of Solomon, Hall M-3, Tier 5, Niche 2.)

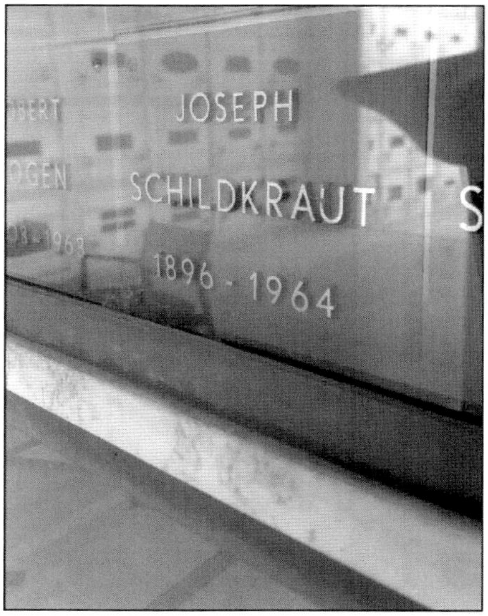

Joseph Schildkraut (1896–1964) and Rudolph Schildkraut (1862–1930). Austrian-born actor Joseph Schildkraut starred alongside Lillian and Dorothy Gish in D.W. Griffith's *Orphans of the Storm* (1921) and Cecil B. DeMille's 1927 epic *The King of Kings*. He won an Oscar for *The Life of Emile Zola* (1937). His father, Rudolph, acted in German silent films before he came to Hollywood. He also appeared in *The King of Kings*. Both Schildkraut men died at the age of 67 from heart attacks. Joseph's urn is pictured; Rudolph's crypt, across the hall, is visible in the reflection directly above the chair. (Joseph: Hall of Solomon, Foyer R Niches, Tier 6, Niche 43; Rudolph: Hall of Solomon, Foyer R, Crypt 214.)

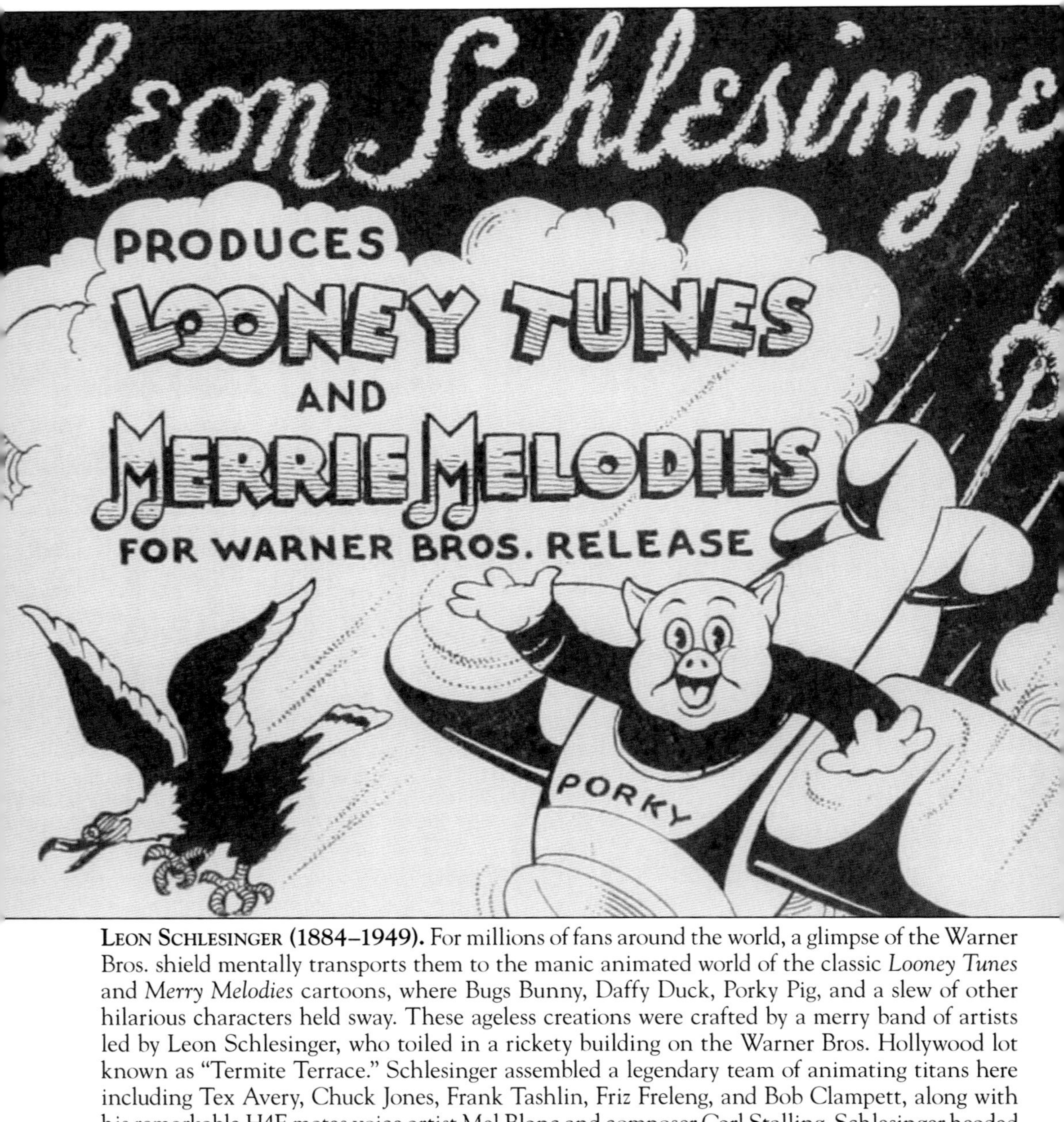

Leon Schlesinger (1884–1949). For millions of fans around the world, a glimpse of the Warner Bros. shield mentally transports them to the manic animated world of the classic *Looney Tunes* and *Merry Melodies* cartoons, where Bugs Bunny, Daffy Duck, Porky Pig, and a slew of other hilarious characters held sway. These ageless creations were crafted by a merry band of artists led by Leon Schlesinger, who toiled in a rickety building on the Warner Bros. Hollywood lot known as "Termite Terrace." Schlesinger assembled a legendary team of animating titans here including Tex Avery, Chuck Jones, Frank Tashlin, Friz Freleng, and Bob Clampett, along with his remarkable H4E mates voice artist Mel Blanc and composer Carl Stalling. Schlesinger headed Warner Bros.'s cartoon studio from 1930 to 1944. He also produced B-Westerns during the 1930s. (Hall of David, T-5-2, Crypt 1275.)

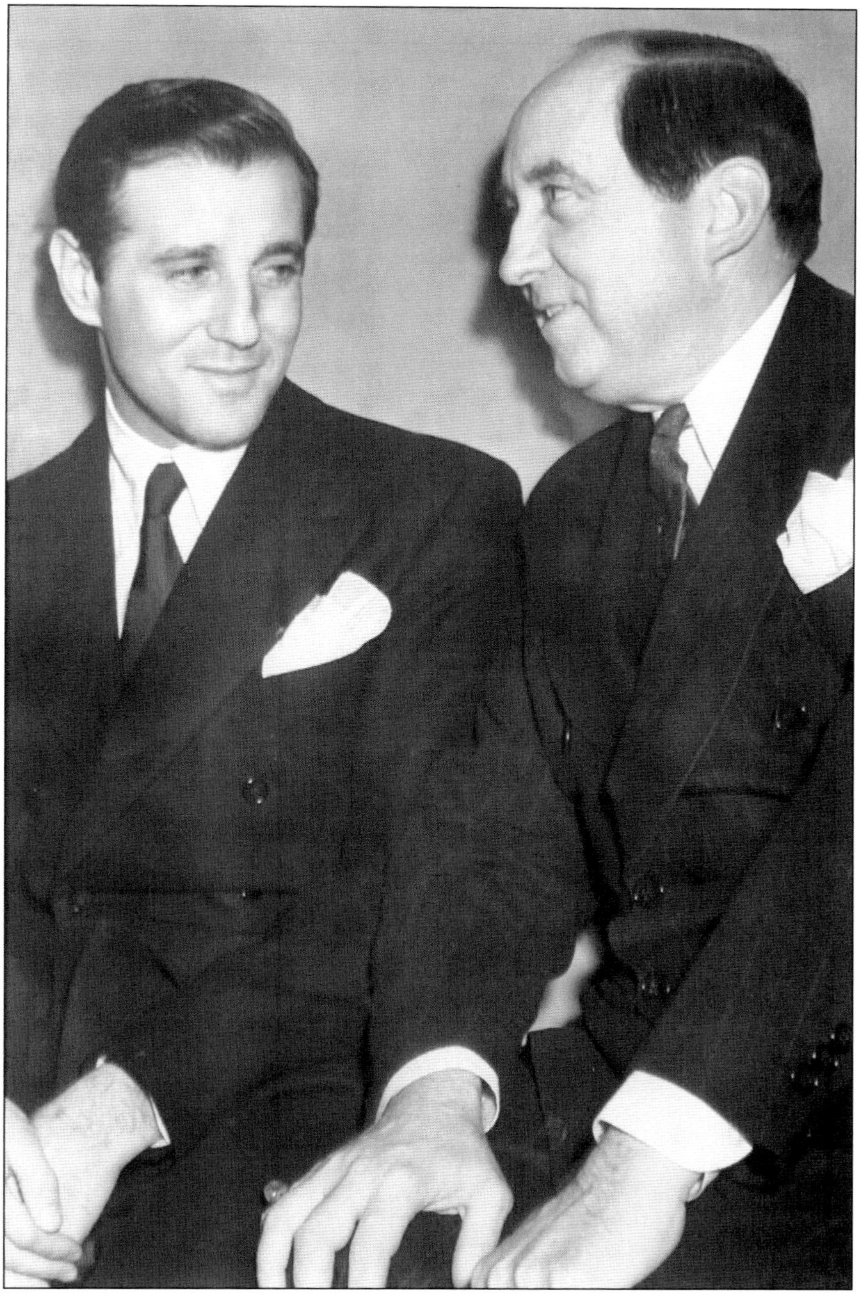

Benjamin "Bugsy" Siegel (1906–1947). Handsome, charismatic Benjamin Siegel, known as "Bugsy"—a nickname he detested—was one of the most feared gangsters of his day. He committed his first murder as a teenager and became one of the founders of Murder Inc., a hitman-for-hire organization. Moving to Southern California, Siegel mingled regularly with many of Hollywood's biggest stars. He created the Las Vegas that is known today when he took over the construction of the Flamingo Hotel with borrowed mob money. Cost overruns angered his partners, who had him gunned down in the Beverly Hills home of his girlfriend. Warren Beatty played Siegel in the 1991 film *Bugsy*. Siegel (left) is pictured here with his lawyer, Jerry Geisler. (Hall of Solomon, M-2, Crypt 1087.)

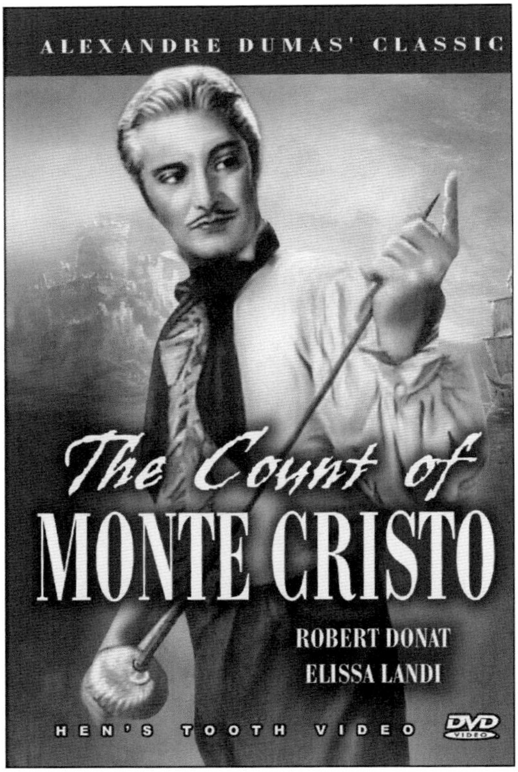

EDWARD SMALL (1891–1977). Edward Small produced hundreds of films across all genres over a 50-year career. Among Small's credits are *The Count of Monte Cristo* (1934), *The Man in the Iron Mask* (1939), and *Brewster's Millions* (1945). He produced both *Solomon and Sheba* and *Witness for the Prosecution* in 1959. (Hall of David, Corridor T-1, Crypt 1046A.)

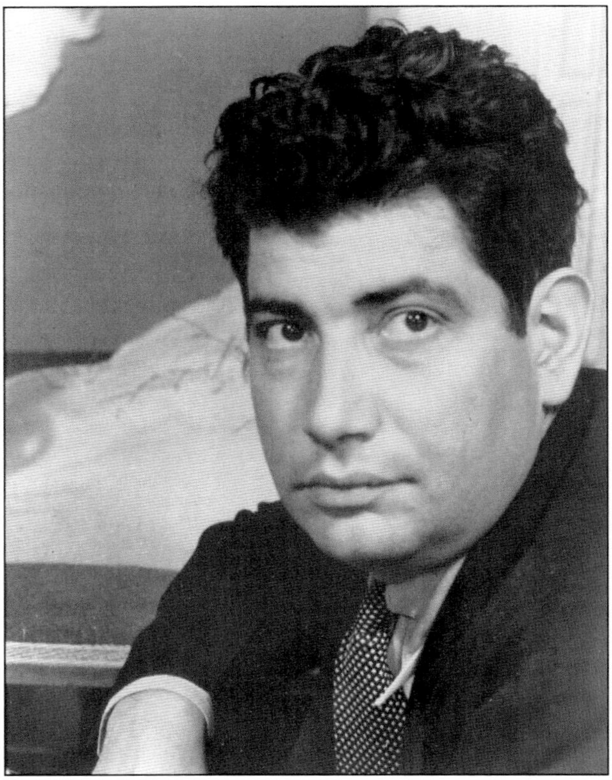

EDGAR G. ULMER (1904–1972) AND SHIRLEY ULMER (1914–2000). Director Edgar Ulmer learned filmmaking at the feet of director F.W. Murnau in Europe and followed him to Hollywood in 1926. Ulmer directed the hit horror film *The Black Cat* (1934) for Universal but was later barred from working at the studio after he began an affair with Shirley Kassler, the wife of the nephew of Carl Laemmle, the head of Universal. Ulmer was forced to work for Poverty Row producers with miniscule budgets. Even with these hurdles, he made both the highly-acclaimed *Club Havana* and the film noir classic *Detour* in 1945. Kassler became Ulmer's wife in 1946 and is interred with him. The phrase "Talent Obliges" is inscribed on Edgar's crypt. (Hall of David, T-9-2, Crypt 1587.)

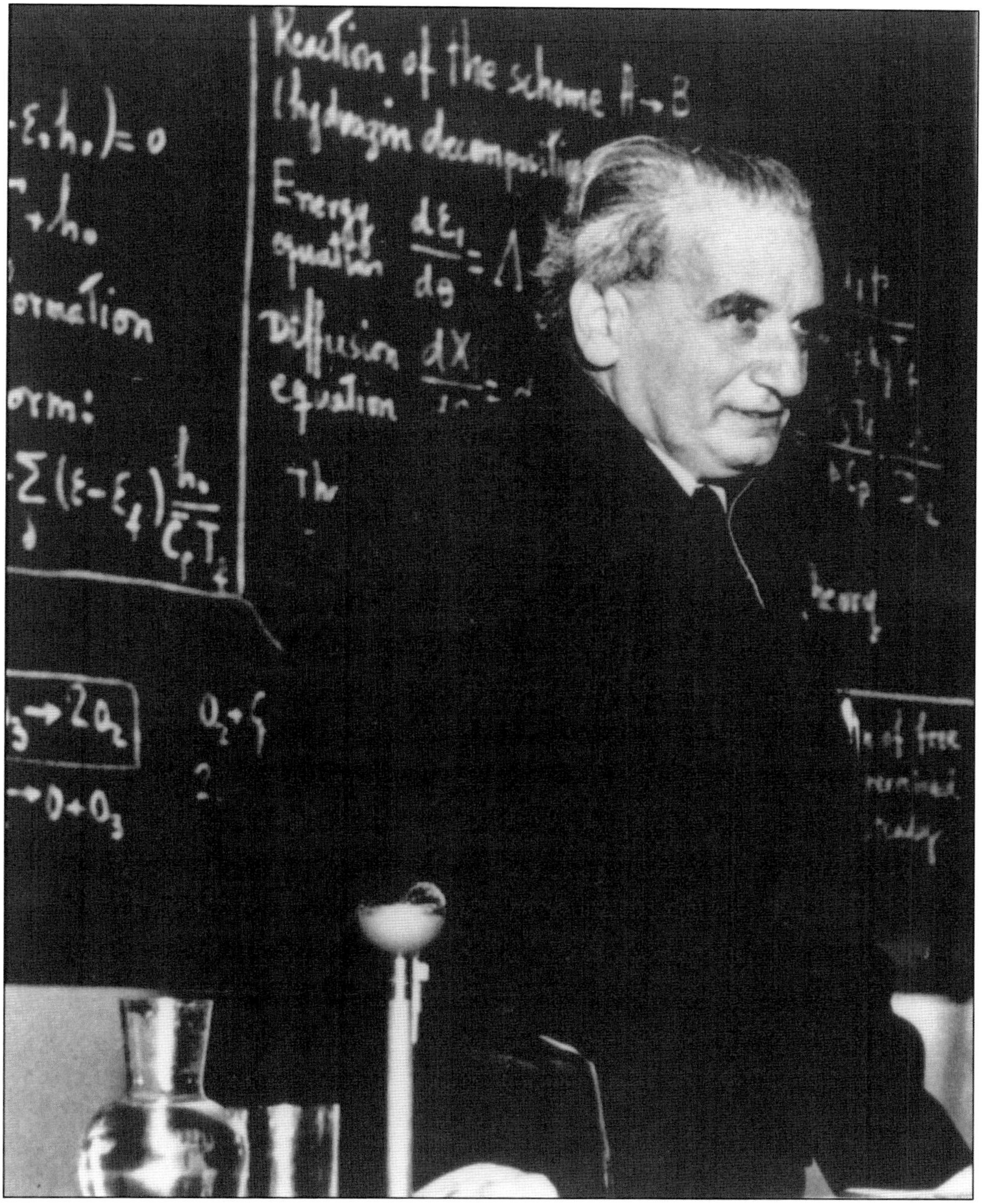

THEODORE VON KARMAN (1881–1963). Hungarian Theodore Von Karman is one of the giants of the tiny segment of the population who actually hold the job title of "rocket scientist." An expert in aeronautics and aerospace engineering, Von Karman designed one of the first helicopters in Europe. He moved to America to accept a position at Caltech in Pasadena, California. While there, he helped found the Aerojet Corporation with Jack Parsons, one of America's most brilliant and controversial scientists. He was later one of the cofounders of the Jet Propulsion Laboratory (JPL), which today is responsible for America's unmanned space probes. Von Karman was the very first recipient of the National Medal of Science, which was presented to him by Pres. John F. Kennedy. Von Karman died while on vacation in Germany in 1963. (Hall of David, Section N-1, Crypt 142.)

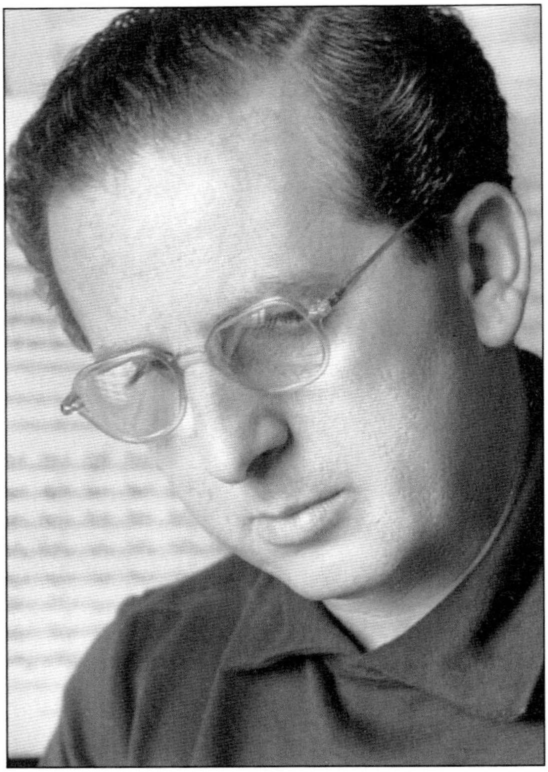

Franz Waxman (1906–1967). Waxman was a German Jewish composer who came to Hollywood in 1934 after getting a fierce beating in Berlin from a group of Nazis. While in Hollywood, Waxman composed the scores for such classics as *The Bride of Frankenstein* (1935), *Rebecca* (1940), *Sorry, Wrong Number* (1948), *Stalag 17* (1953), and *Rear Window* (1954). Waxman won Oscars in consecutive years for his scores for *Sunset Boulevard* (1950) and *A Place in the Sun* (1951). (Hall of Solomon, Foyer O Niches, Tier 5, Niche 1.)

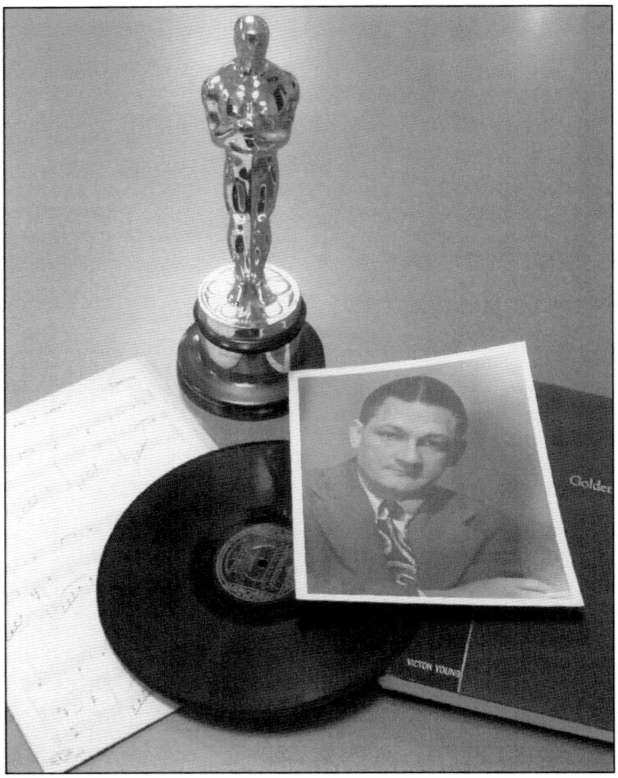

Victor Young (1900–1956). Composer, arranger, violinist, and conductor Victor Young was born in Chicago and had much of his musical training in Europe. In the mid-1930s, he came to Hollywood to score films. For the next 25 years, he would write several of the best-known scores in Hollywood history, earning 22 Academy Award nominations (often with multiple nominations during the same year), while winning one. (Hall of Solomon, Memorial Hall, Crypt 0046.) (Courtesy of Brandeis University.)

Four

Under Heaven

Death has been called the "great leveler." This concept has been carried to its extreme in most modern cemeteries, where only markers that are flat to the ground are allowed. While this is more democratic, and undoubtedly makes the property much easier to maintain, it loses the atmosphere of grandeur and permanence offered by above-ground monuments.

Hollywood Forever was founded before cemeteries were "Forest Lawn-ed" into flat, character-lacking fields. As a result, H4E often attracts those who choose to memorialize their loved ones with ornate monuments, while others choose simple markers. H4E is one of the dwindling number of cemeteries where a choice is still offered.

Maila Nurmi, television's Vampira, is here, with her grave shadowed by Derrin McGavin, who once played a vampire hunter on television. His grave in turn, is overlooked by that of Mr. Blackwell, who may well be critiquing the monuments of his neighbors in the afterlife.

The grounds of H4E contain their share of tough-luck tales, like that of Florence Lawrence, the world's first movie star. She was badly burned in a studio fire, which ended her career. Forgotten by the world, she took her own life. Karl Dane, who also committed suicide after losing his career to sound, is here as well. So is the grave of Carl "Alfalfa" Switzer, who had the double bad luck of being shot (which was bad enough) and then having his funeral on the same day as Cecil B. DeMille's, therefore being overlooked in the news.

Some of the world's great voice actors are in Hollywood Forever. Mel Blanc, animation's "Man of a Thousand Voices," is here. So is Don LaFontaine, the voice of 5,000 movie trailers, who made the phrase "In a world . . ." part of the American vocabulary.

Under one of the grandest monuments in Hollywood is the beautiful white marble crypt of the former "King of Hollywood," Douglas Fairbanks, and his heir. Fairbanks's grave used to read, "Goodnight sweet prince, and flights of angels sing thee to thy rest." With the internment of his son Douglas Fairbanks Jr. into the same crypt in 2000, the wording was changed to read, "Goodnight sweet *princes* . . ."

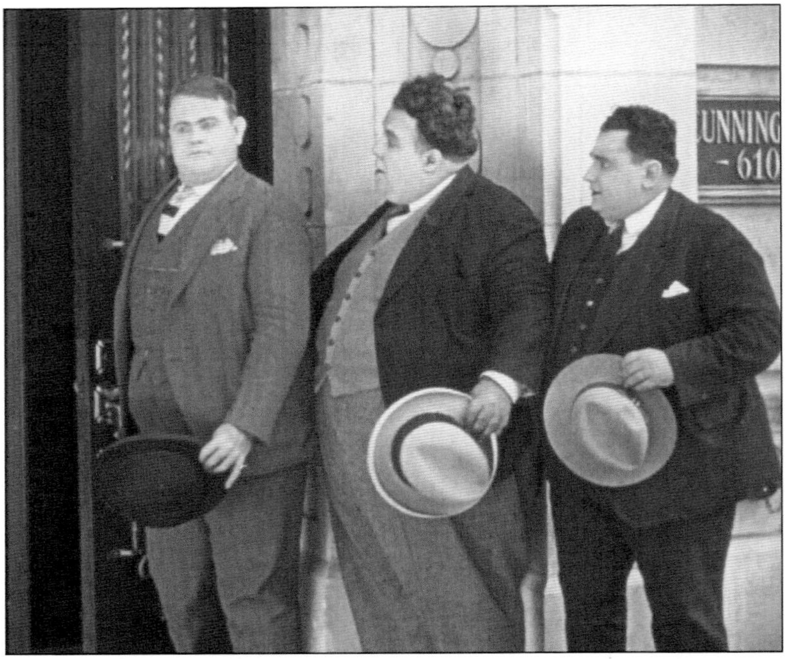

Frank Alexander (1879–1937). Rotund comic Frank Alexander was a silent film actor who appeared as a villain in many of the Larry Semon comedies of the 1910s. The 350-pound Alexander (center) was joined with portly comedians Kewpie Ross (left) and Hilliard Karr (right) to form a comedy trio known as A Ton of Fun. (Garden of Beginnings, Plot 10 [unmarked].)

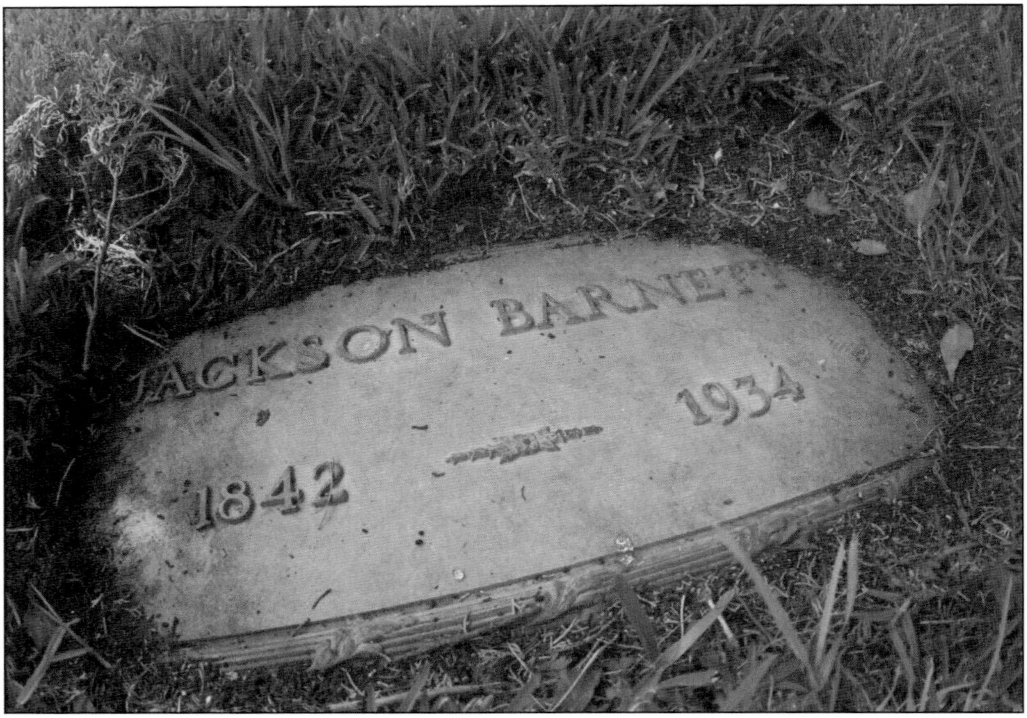

Jackson Barnett (1856–1934). Native American Jackson Barnett made millions after striking oil on his Oklahoma farm, earning the nickname "the World's Richest Indian." He married and moved to a mansion in Los Angeles. Barnett died in 1934 after having his marriage annulled. His former wife, now his caretaker, refused to leave the mansion for four years until she was finally evicted with tear gas. She spent the remainder of her life in an unsuccessful fight to regain control of Barnett's fortune. (Plains of Abraham Section.) (Courtesy of Pentax Forums.)

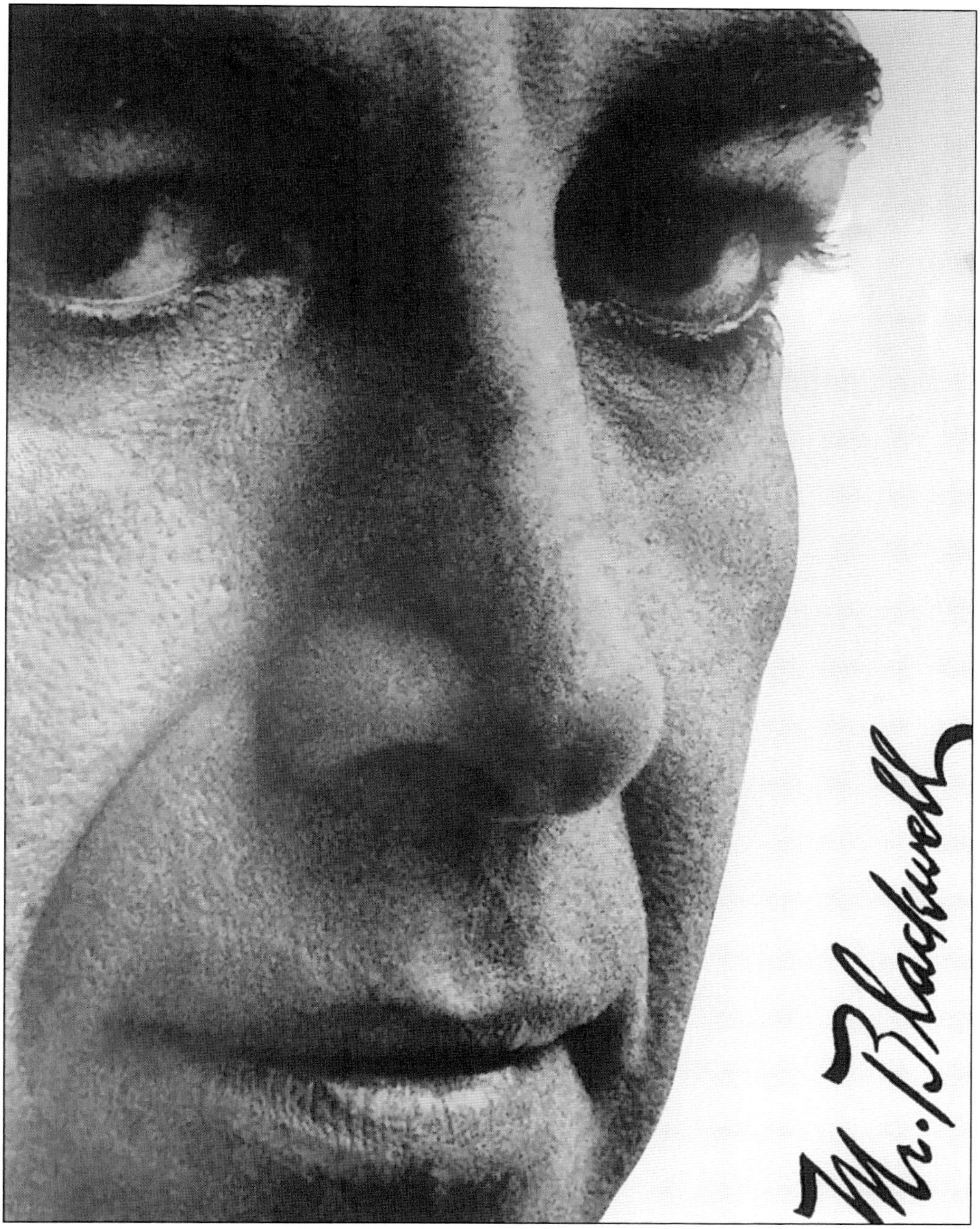

Richard "Mr. Blackwell" Blackwell (1922–2008). For decades, celebrities lived in fear of finding themselves included on one of Mr. Blackwell's worst-dressed lists. A screen actor as a teenager, Blackwell later became an agent before transitioning to fashion design and criticism. He launched his own fashion line called the House of Blackwell in the late 1950s. During its two-decade run, the House of Blackwell designed clothing for Jayne Mansfield, Yvonne De Carlo, Dorothy Lamour, Jane Russell, and Nancy Reagan. Blackwell began his worst-dressed list in 1960 and continued it for nearly 50 years, until his death in 2008. He lived in the Hancock Park district of Los Angeles with Richard Spencer, his partner of over 60 years. The couple are now buried together under a black obelisk. (Griffith Lawn Section.)

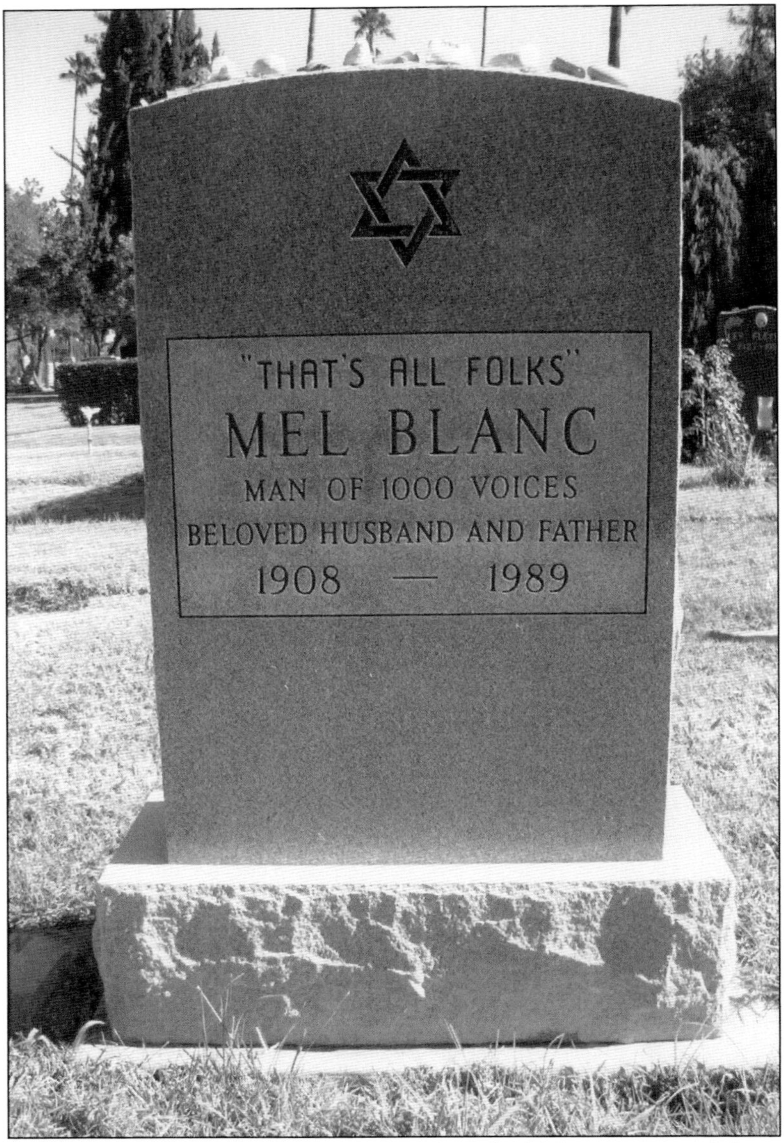

Mel Blanc (1908–1989). The voice of Mel Blanc breathed life into many of the most beloved animated characters of all time. A comedian during the Golden Age of Radio, Blanc, known as "the Man of a Thousand Voices," vocalized almost all the male Warner Bros. *Looney Tunes* and *Merry Melody* characters: Bugs Bunny, Daffy Duck, Porky Pig, Tweety Bird, Sylvester the Cat, Yosemite Sam, Foghorn Leghorn, Marvin the Martian, Pepe Le Pew, Speedy Gonzales, Wile E. Coyote, Road Runner, and the Tasmanian Devil. He also voiced *The Flintstones*' Barney Rubble, and Mr. Spacely on *The Jetsons* for Hanna-Barbera. Blanc was not the original voice of Elmer Fudd, but began voicing this character after his original voice actor passed away. Blanc was in a near-fatal automobile accident in 1961 that left him in a coma. Although he was unresponsive as himself, he would communicate with his doctors as Bugs Bunny. After Blanc died, a famous poster called "Speechless" was released, showing a spotlight on an empty microphone with Blanc's animated characters standing to the side with their heads bowed. Blanc's tombstone is one of the most popular in Hollywood Forever. It reads, "That's All Folks." (Garden of the Exodus, Lot 149, Space 102.) (Photograph by Kim Stephens.)

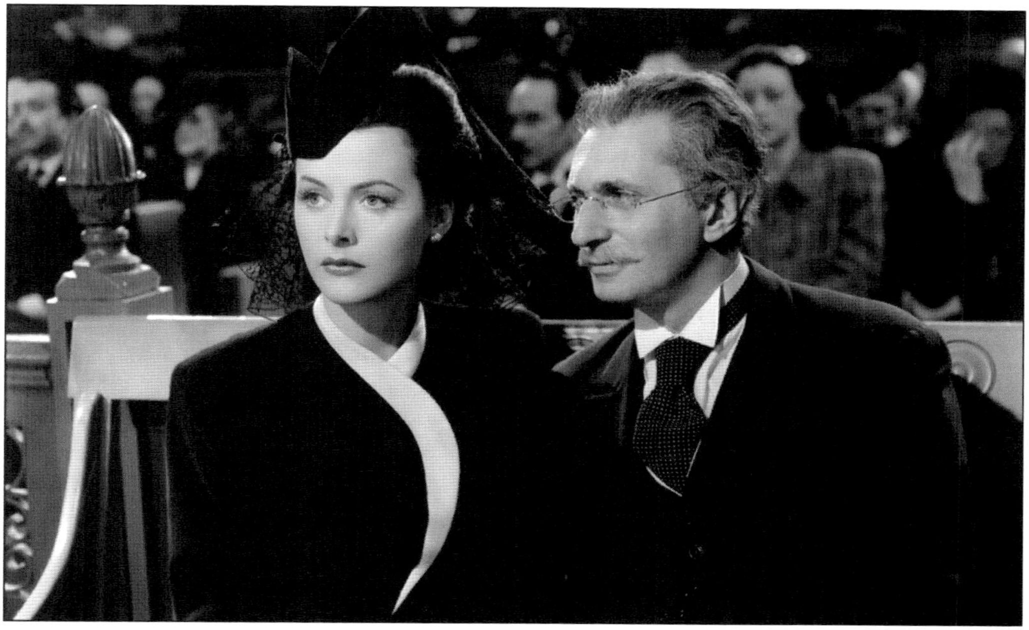

Felix Bressart (1892–1949). Bressart was a Jewish character actor who arrived in Hollywood after fleeing from the Nazis in Europe. He made memorable appearances in *Ninotchka* (1939), *The Shop Around the Corner* (1940), and *To Be or Not to Be* (1942). He continued acting until his death from leukemia. He is pictured here with Hedy Lamarr in MGM's *Crossroads* (1942). (Plains of Abraham, Row J, Grave 89.)

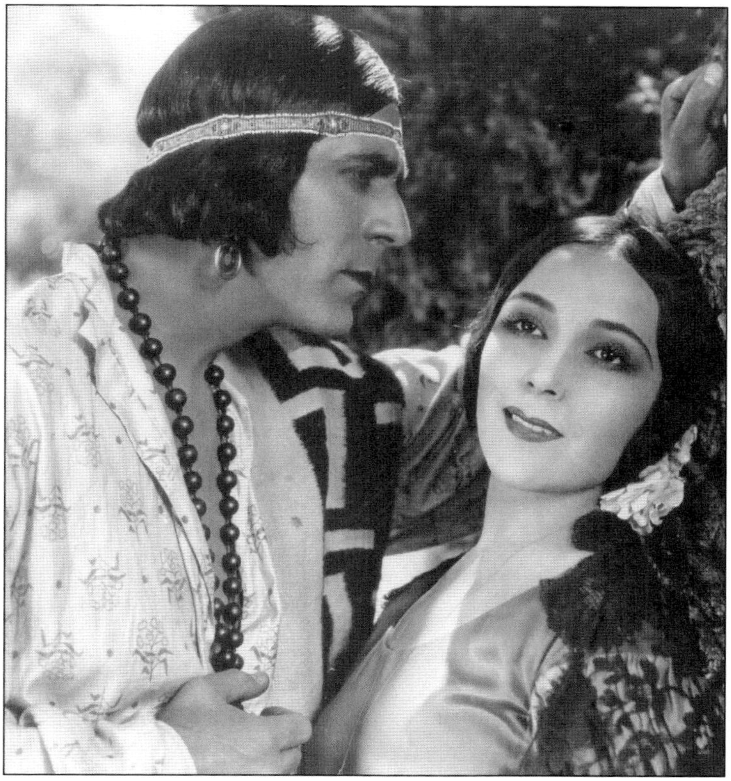

Edwin Carewe (1883–1940). Edwin Carewe was a Native American who broke through prejudicial barriers to become a successful Hollywood actor and director during the silent era. He directed nearly 60 films for most of the major studios and discovered many of that era's stars. Carewe was unable to make a successful switch to sound films. He died in 1940 from a heart ailment. He is pictured here in a scene from *Evangeline* (1929) with Dolores del Rio. (Garden of Ancestors, Plot 471.)

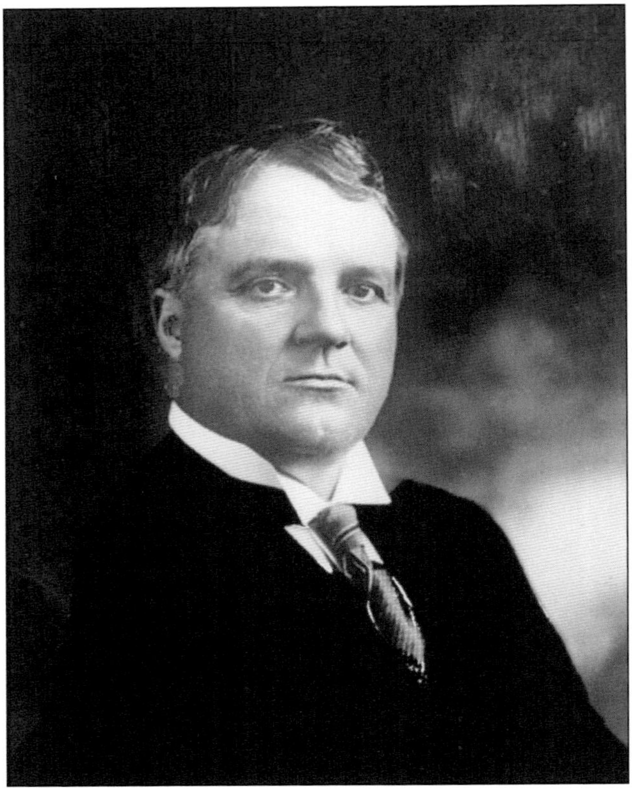

HARRY CHANDLER (1864–1944). Harry Chandler married *Los Angeles Times* publisher Harrison Gray Otis's daughter in 1894 and took over the paper's publishing duties when Otis died in 1917. Chandler spent the rest of his life transforming Los Angeles into a world-class city while investing in real estate, making him the largest property owner in the country. His holdings included the Hollywoodland housing development, which was advertised with 50-foot letters on the side of Mt. Lee. The "-land" was later removed, leaving the famous Hollywood Sign, which is visible from Chandler's grave. His son Norman assumed the paper's publishing duties after Chandler's death in 1944. (Chandler Gardens, Lot 39.)

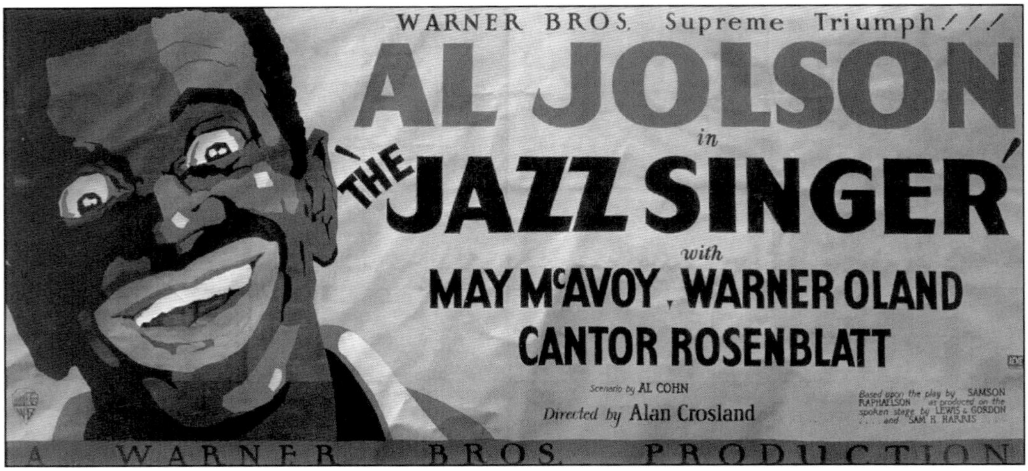

ALAN CROSLAND (1894–1936). Alan Crosland directed *Don Juan* (1926), Hollywood's first major film with a recorded soundtrack but no spoken dialogue. A year later, he helmed *The Jazz Singer* (1927), filmdom's first talkie, which pealed the death knell for silent films. Crosland was killed in 1936 in an automobile accident. His grave was unmarked for decades until a monument was donated in 2003 by the charitable organization Hollywood Underground. (Garden of the Exodus, Single Space 777.)

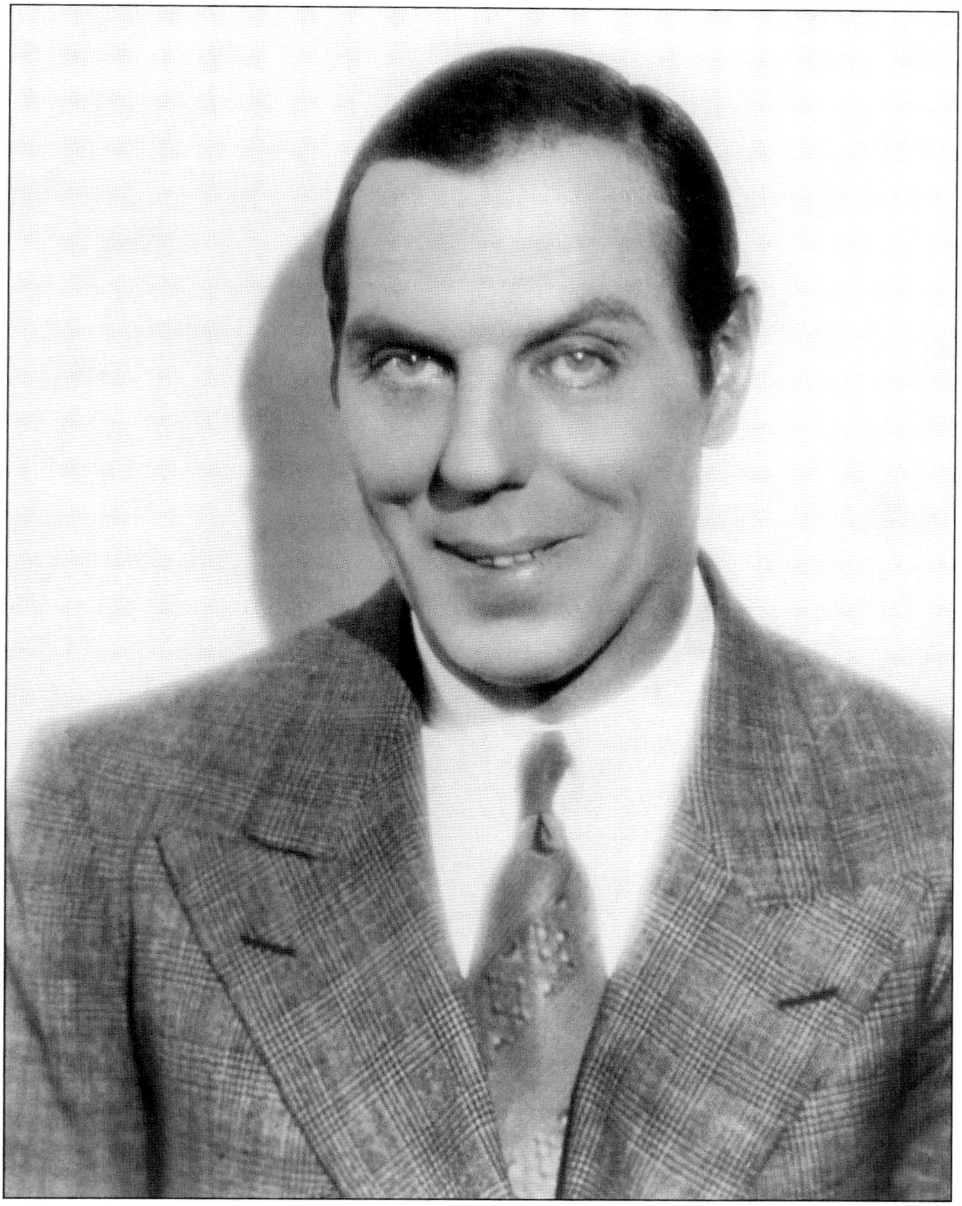

Karl Dane (1886–1934). Hollywood, like crocodiles, sometimes eats its own. Take, for example, the tragic story of actor and comic Karl Dane. Dane, born Rasmus Karl Therkelsen Gottlieb in Copenhagen in 1886, appeared in the silent blockbuster *The Big Parade* (1924), which starred John Gilbert and Renee Adoree. The film's success led to more work for the Danish immigrant alongside Rudolph Valentino in *The Son of the Sheik* (1926). MGM signed him to a long-term contract—and then came sound. Dane's heavily-accented voice did not translate well to American audiences, and he was cut by the studio. He soon found himself in the humiliating position of running a hot-dog stand outside the gates of MGM—the same studio where he had been a star a short time earlier. Former friends at the studio avoided his establishment, perhaps to save him embarrassment, and it failed a short time later. In April 1934, Dane killed himself with a revolver in his Hollywood apartment. His body lay unclaimed until fellow Danish actor Jean Hersholt convinced MGM to pay for his burial. (Garden of the Exodus, Single Space 203.)

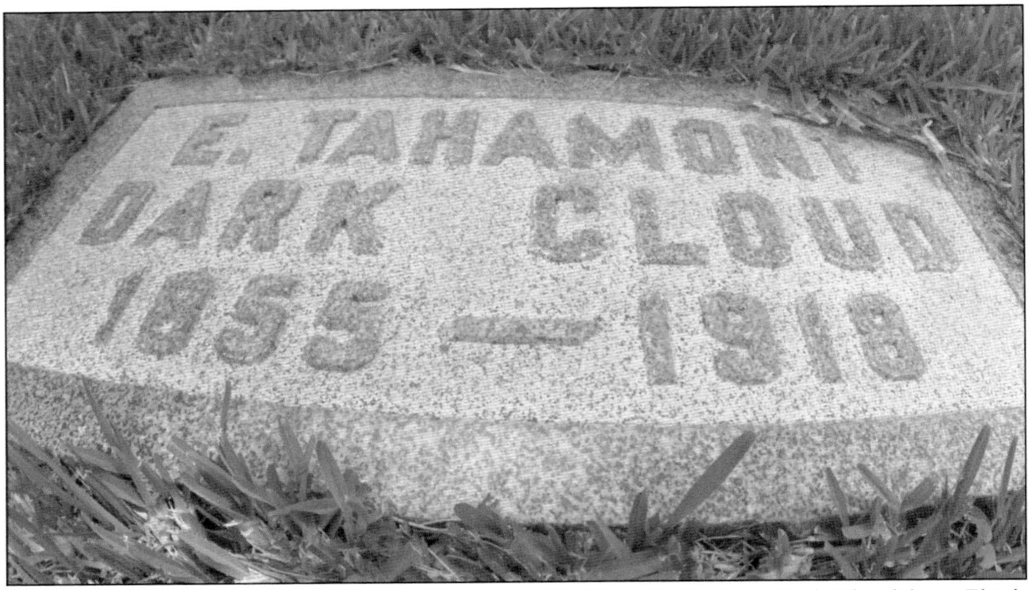

Chief Dark Cloud (1855–1918). An Algonquin chief born in Quebec, Dark Cloud, born Elijah Tahamont, was a model for Western sculptor Frederic Remington before commencing a career in silent films. He appeared in nearly three dozen features before dying in 1918 during the Spanish flu epidemic. (Section 10W.) (Courtesy of Pentax Forum.)

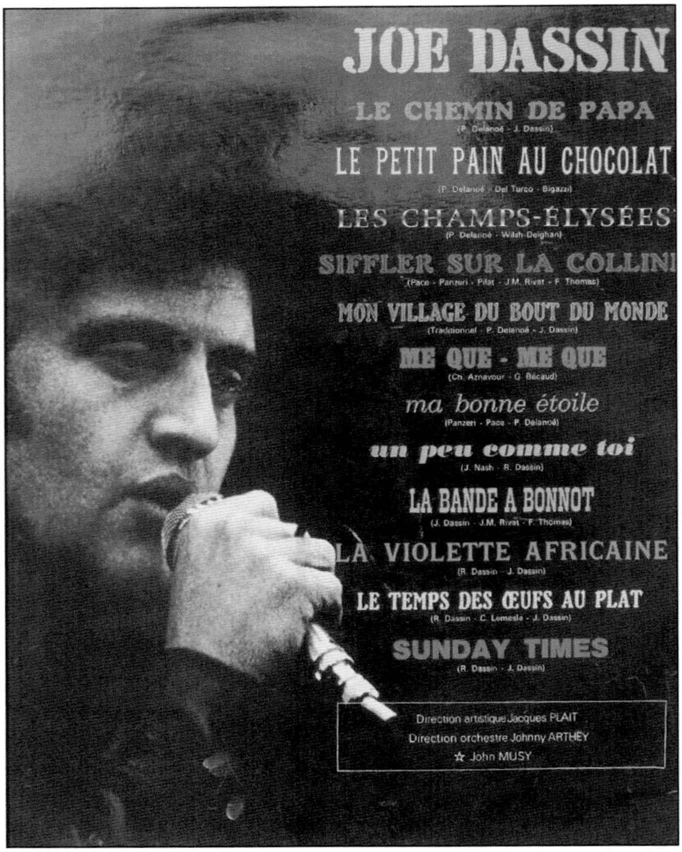

Joe Dassin (1938–1980). American French singer Joe Dassin was the son of American film director Jules Dassin. His father was blacklisted by Hollywood in 1950 for his political beliefs, prompting a move by the family to Europe. Joe Dassin became a French pop star, topping the charts in the 1960s and 1970s. He appeared in three of the films his father made in France, including *Topkapi* (1964). Dassin died at the age of 41 from a heart attack while on vacation in Tahiti. (Plains of Abraham, Row I, Space 79.)

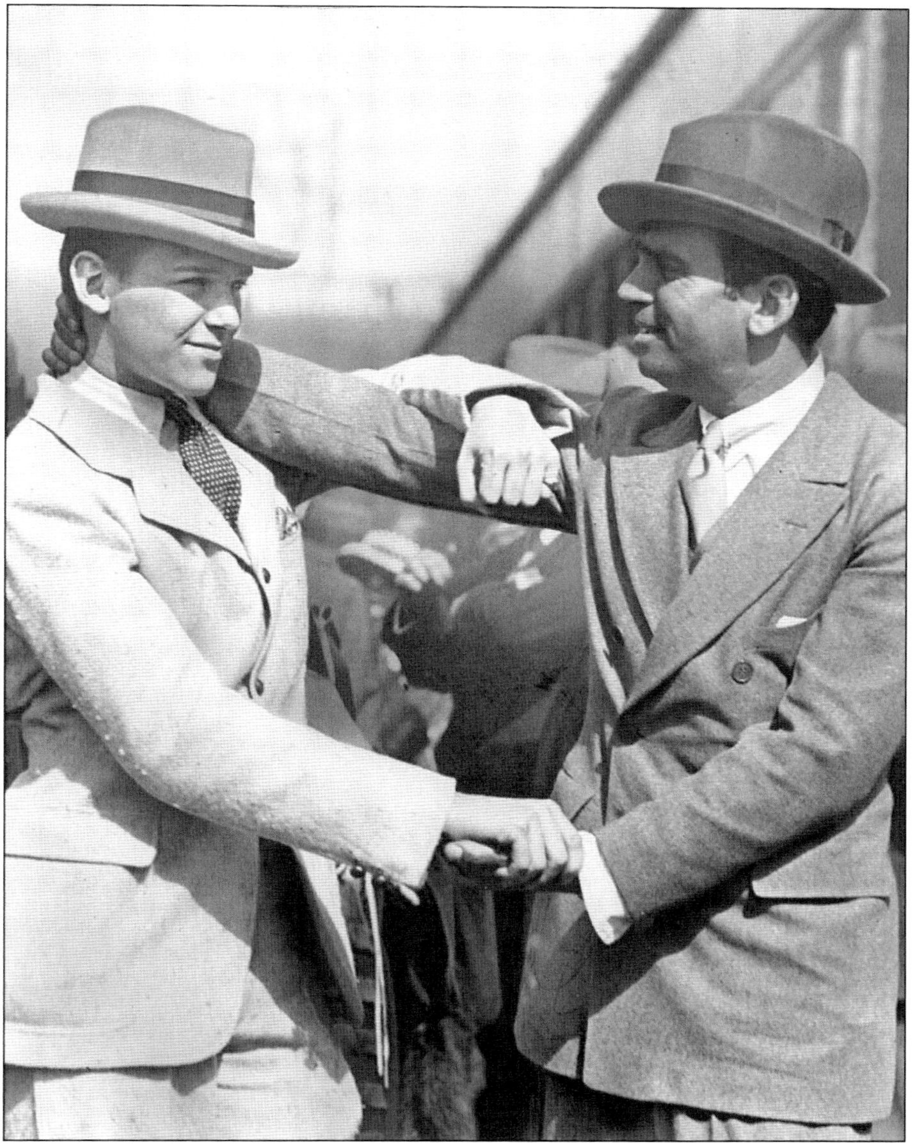

Douglas Fairbanks Sr. (1883–1939) and Douglas Fairbanks Jr. (1909–2000). The mere mention of the name *Douglas Fairbanks* conjures images of romantic silent swashbucklers and Hollywood glamour on a grand scale. Fairbanks's performances in *The Mark of Zorro* (1920), *Robin Hood* (1922), and *The Thief of Baghdad* (1924) were the stuff of legend, as was his longtime affair and later marriage to "America's Sweetheart," actress Mary Pickford. Born Douglas Elton Ulman in Denver, Fairbanks made his way to Broadway in 1902, where he married his first wife. They had a son they named Douglas Fairbanks Jr. Later in Hollywood, Fairbanks was catapulted to stardom. In 1919, Fairbanks and Pickford teamed up with D.W. Griffith and Fairbanks's good friend Charlie Chaplin to form United Artists. Fairbanks and Pickford lived in a renowned Beverly Hills mansion named Pickfair, the place to see and be seen. Fairbanks died quietly in 1939. His last words were, "I've never felt better." Douglas Fairbanks Jr., like his father, enjoyed a very successful film career and was a heavily decorated war hero in World War II. After his death in 2000, he was interred inside his father's crypt. The two men are pictured here in a 1924 photograph from the *Los Angeles Times*. (Fairbanks Lawn.)

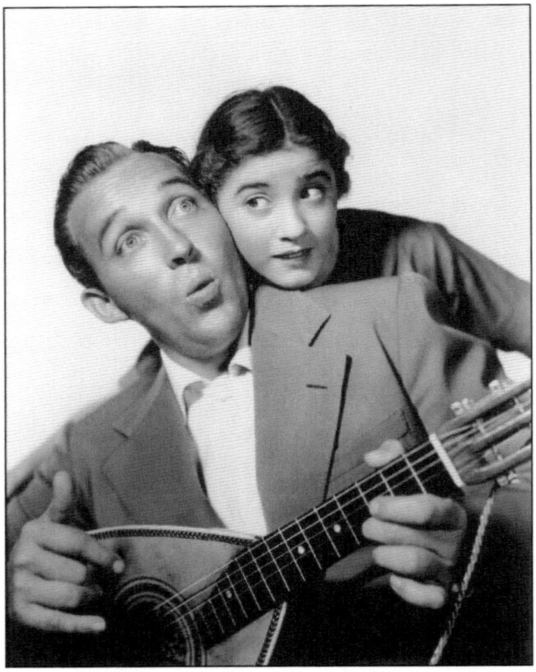

Edith Fellows (1923–2011). Edith Fellows was a child star in the 1930s whose talent for acting and singing earned her the first seven-year Hollywood contract ever offered to a child. As an adult, she suffered from drug dependency brought on by stage fright. After being away from acting for two decades, she overcame her affliction, appearing on several television shows. She is pictured here with Bing Crosby in a scene from *Pennies From Heaven* (1936). (Rose Garden.)

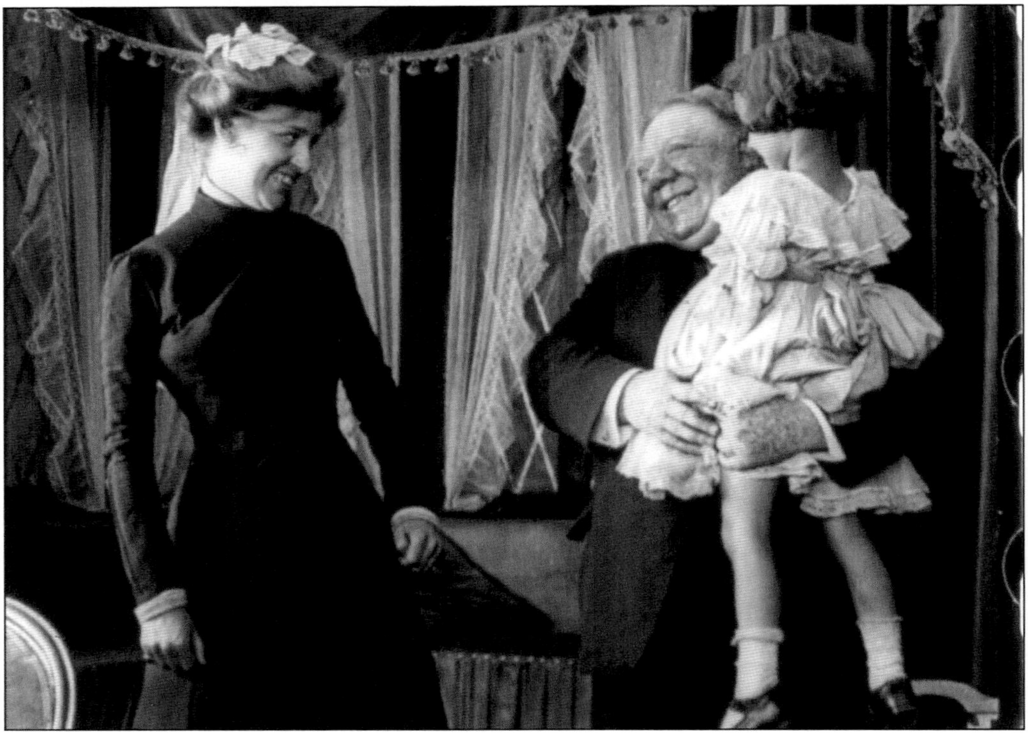

Flora Finch (1867–1940). Tall and paper-thin, British comedian Flora Finch made over 300 silent films during her career. She was successfully paired with comedian John Bunny (pictured here holding a child) between 1910 and Bunny's death five years later. The duo made 160 shorts, which were known as "Bunnyfinches." She made a handful of talkie films, including *Way Out West* (1937) with Laurel and Hardy. (Garden of Ancestors, Lot 416.) (Courtesy of Pentax Forums.)

CHARLES ROBERT FRANCIS (1875–1946). Marine private Charles Robert Francis was awarded the Congressional Medal of Honor for meritorious conduct in battle in 1900 in China during the Boxer Rebellion. (Garden of Eternal Love, Lot 737, Grave 5.)

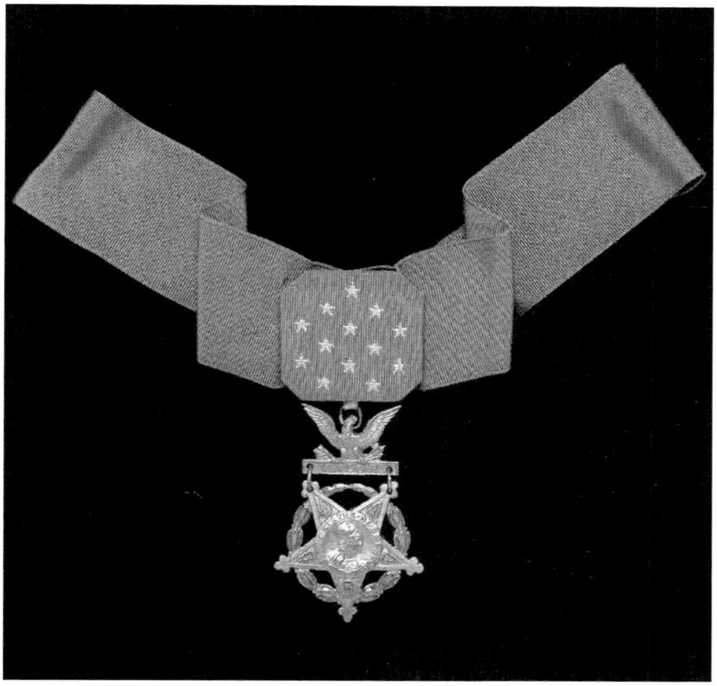

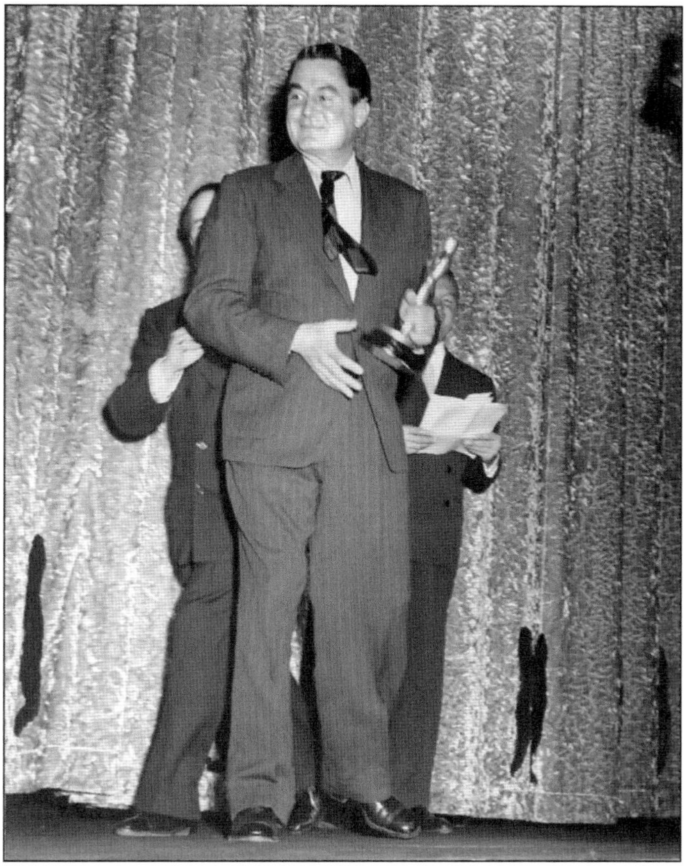

VICTOR GANGELIN (1899–1967). Victor Gangelin was an Academy Award–winning set decorator who won his Oscar for *West Side Story* in 1962. He worked for years for Warner Bros., where some of his most notable credits were for the John Wayne films *The Searchers* (1956) and *The Alamo* (1960). (Section 9.)

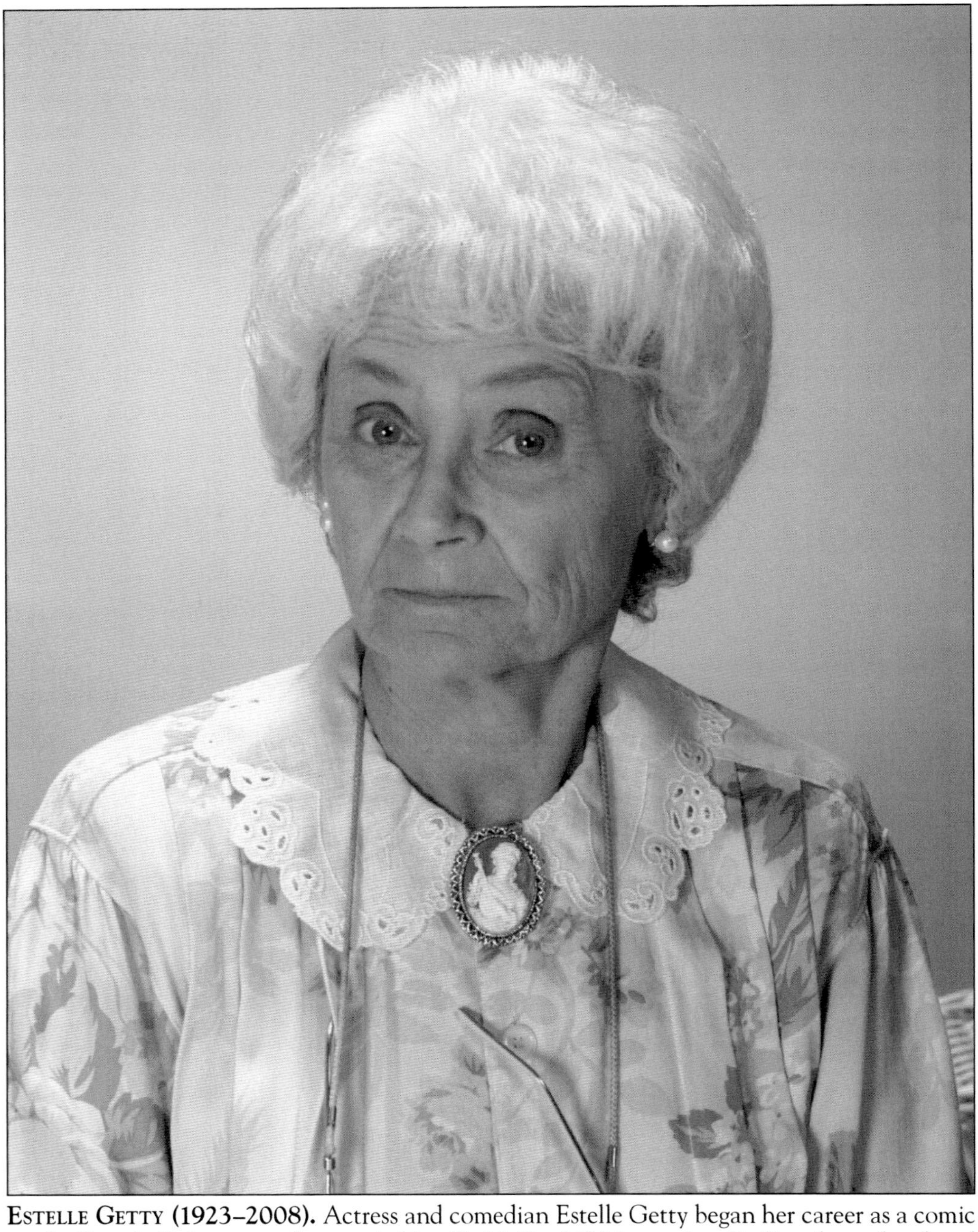

Estelle Getty (1923–2008). Actress and comedian Estelle Getty began her career as a comic on the Borscht Belt circuit of resorts in New York's Catskill Mountains. On Broadway, she played Harvey Fierstein's mother in *Torch Song Trilogy* during its initial run. Getty is best remembered today for her Emmy-winning role as Sophia Petrillo in the 1980s sitcom *The Golden Girls.* On that series, she played the mother of Bea Arthur's character, Dorothy Zbornak, even though the two actresses were separated in age by only one year. Getty was nominated seven times for Emmy Awards for the character, winning once in 1988. She also won a Golden Globe for the same role in 1985. She was frequently seen on other television shows during her career and made the occasional big screen appearance. Getty died of Lewy Body Dementia three days before her 85th birthday. (Plains of Abraham, Row CC, Space 88.)

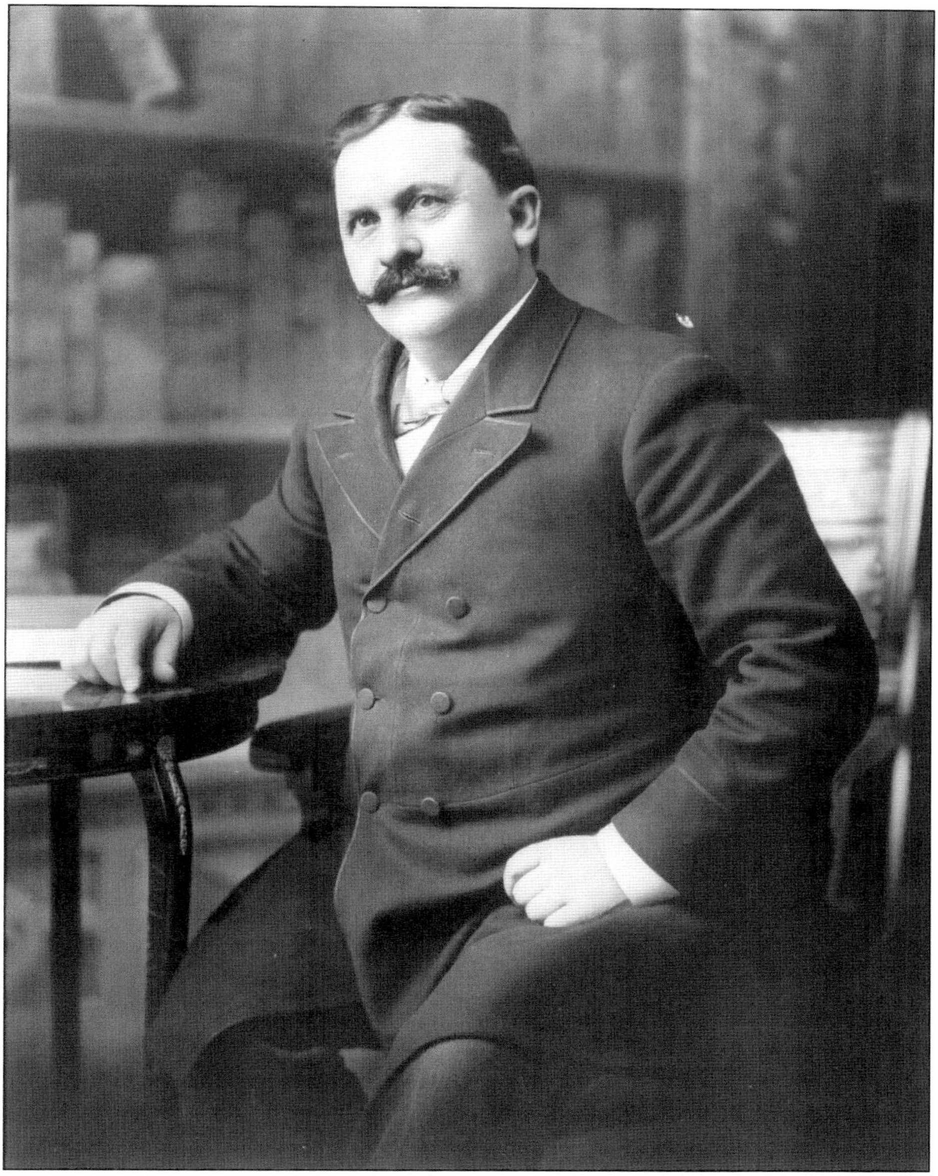

COL. GRIFFITH J. GRIFFITH (1850–1919). Col. Griffith J. Griffith was born in Wales and emigrated to the United States as a young man. As the mining correspondent for the *Alta California* newspaper, he became an expert at discovering gold and silver, which netted him a huge fortune. Griffith purchased a large parcel of land just north of Los Angeles and established an ostrich farm on the site. He later closed the farm, and the enraged and now-unemployed farm manager shot Griffith in the face before turning the gun on himself. Griffith survived, but the shooting proved to be a bad omen. In 1896, Griffith donated his property, now Griffith Park, to the city of Los Angeles. Afterwards, he became increasingly paranoid, believing that his Catholic wife was conspiring with the pope to poison him. In 1903, Griffith shot her in the face. She too survived, but Griffith ended up spending two years in San Quentin. After his release, the city spurned more of his gift giving. It was only following his death in 1919 that the city accepted a $1.5 million fund from his estate to build the Griffith Observatory and the Greek Theater. (Standing in the correct spot, Griffith's obelisk points directly toward the Griffith Observatory.) (Griffith Lawn.)

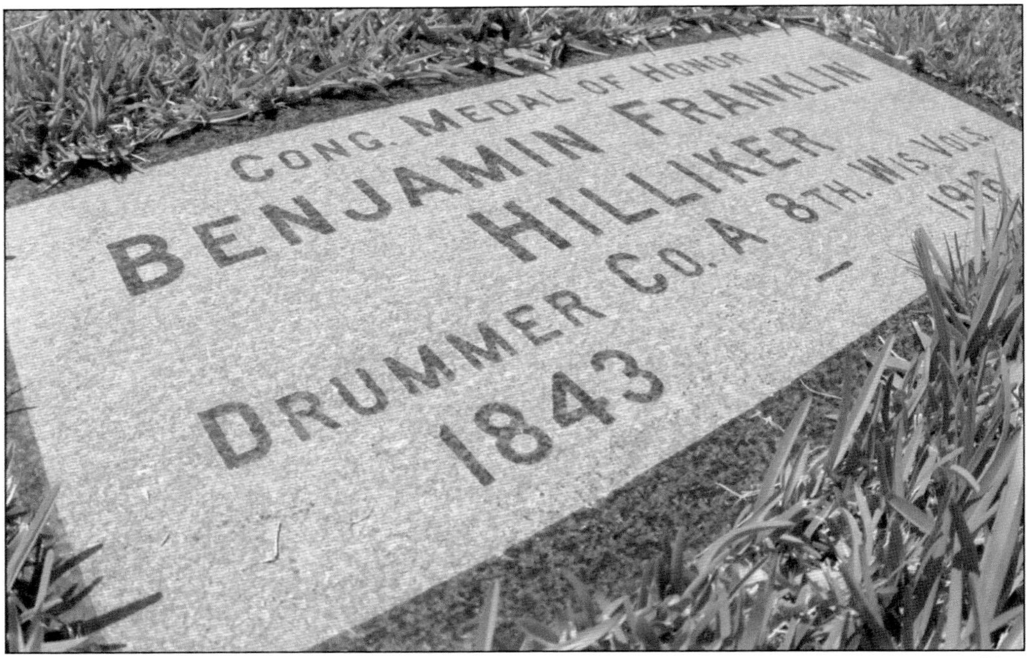

BENJAMIN FRANKLIN HILLIKER (1843–1916). In 1863, during the Civil War, Benjamin Franklin Hilliker, a drummer for Company A, 8th Wisconsin Infantry, sat down his drum, picked up a gun, and helped hold a shaky line in Mechanicsburg, Mississippi. He was shot in the head but recovered. Hilliker was later awarded the Congressional Medal of Honor for his gallantry. (Chandler Gardens.) (Courtesy of Pentax Forums.)

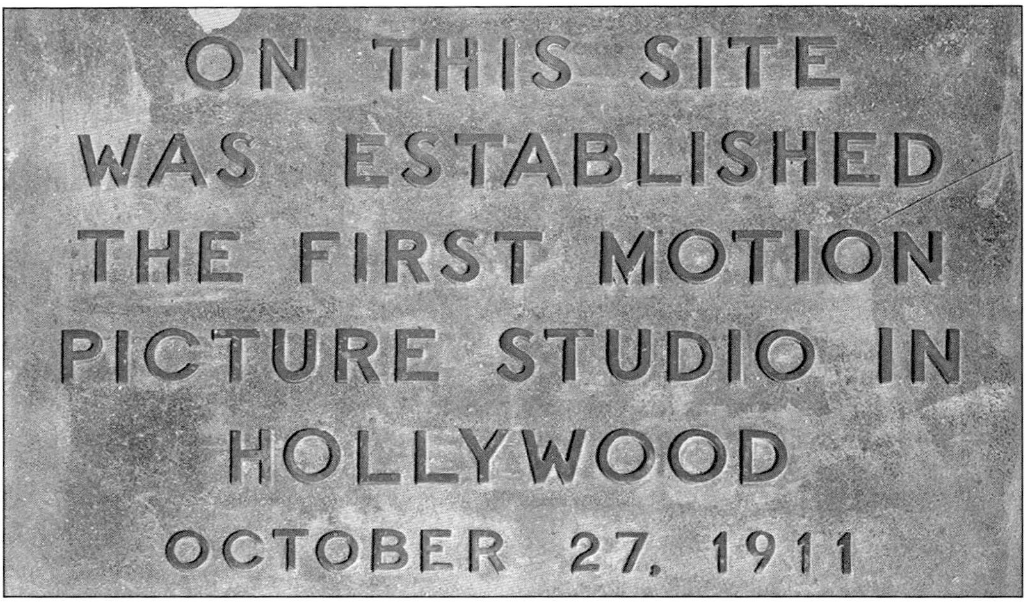

DAVID HORSLEY (1873–1933). In 1911, film pioneer David Horsley established Hollywood's first film studio, the Nestor Motion Picture Company, at the corner of Sunset Boulevard and Gower Street in what had previously been a tavern. A year later, Horsley merged his company with several other independent studios to form what is known today as Universal Studios. (Garden of Memory, Lot 218.) (Courtesy of The Hollywood Reporter.)

Herb Jeffries (1913–2014). Herb Jeffries, the "Bronze Buckaroo," was the first African American singing cowboy. Born Umberto Alexander Valentino in Detroit, Jeffries first made a name for himself as a singer. Louis Armstrong encouraged him to move to Chicago, where he worked with Earl Hines and Duke Ellington. His recording of *Flamingo* sold several million copies. In the 1930s, Jeffries filmed a series of Western-themed "race films" intended for black audiences. Jeffries died in 2014 when he was 100 years old. (Lake View East Columbarium.)

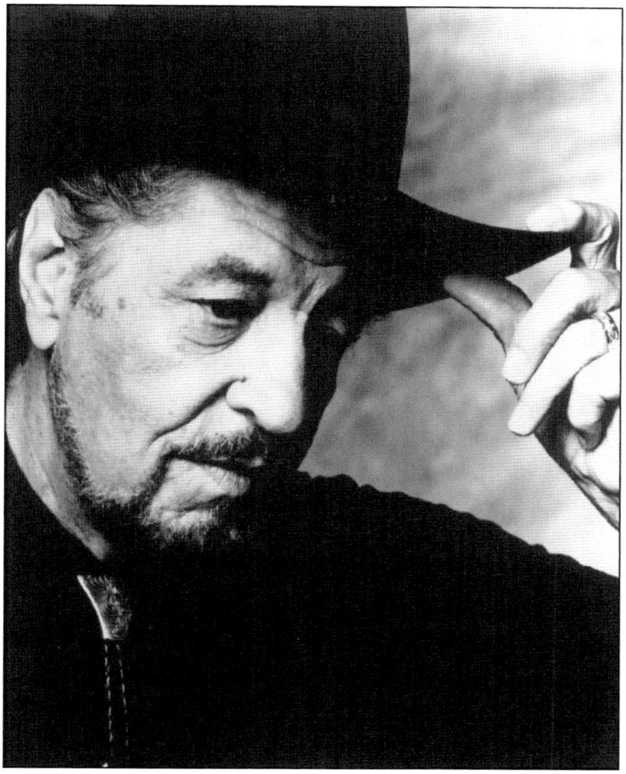

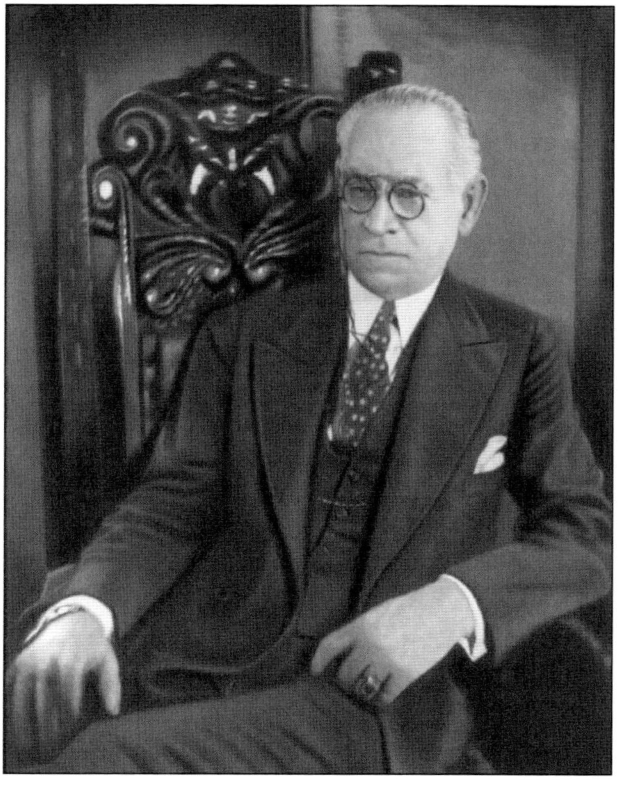

Frank Keenan (1858–1929). Frank Keenan was a celebrated Shakespearean actor on Broadway. He helped bring legitimacy to movies in the early days of the silent era at a time when many people considered them to be vulgar and unsophisticated entertainment. He was the grandfather of actor Keenan Wynn. (Garden of the Exodus, above-ground crypt.)

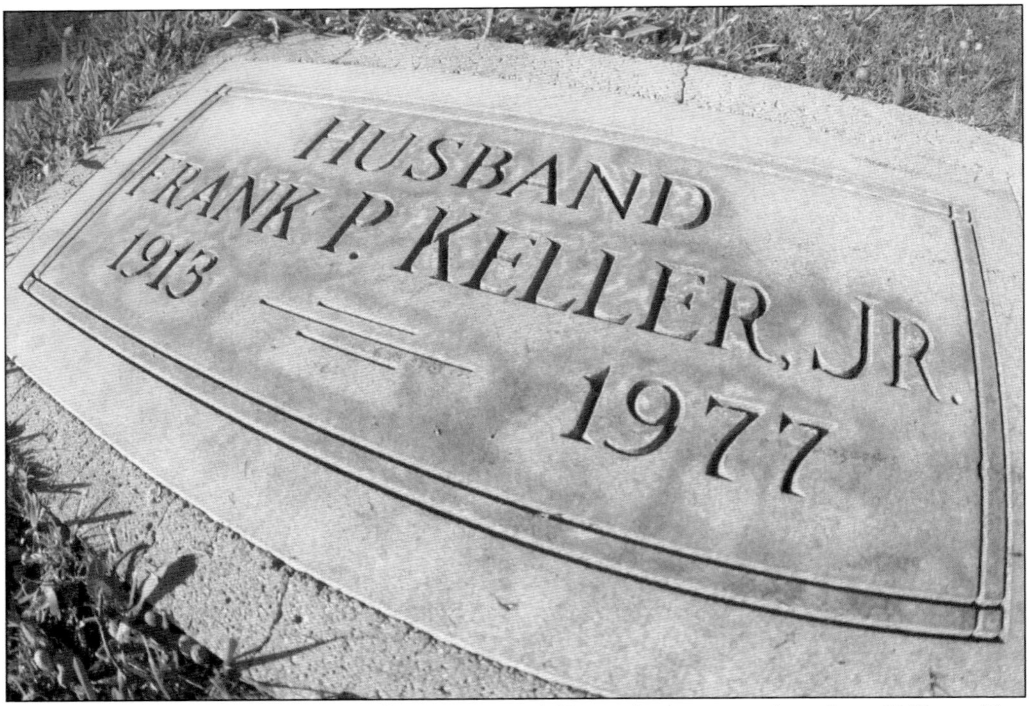

FRANK P. KELLER (1913–1977). Keller was a noted film and television editor from 1958 until his death. He left his lasting mark on film history with his Academy Award–winning work on Steve McQueen's car chase sequence through San Francisco in the movie *Bullitt* (1968). Keller died on the same day as Charlie Chaplin. (Garden of Eternal Love, East Side.) (Courtesy of Pentax Forums.)

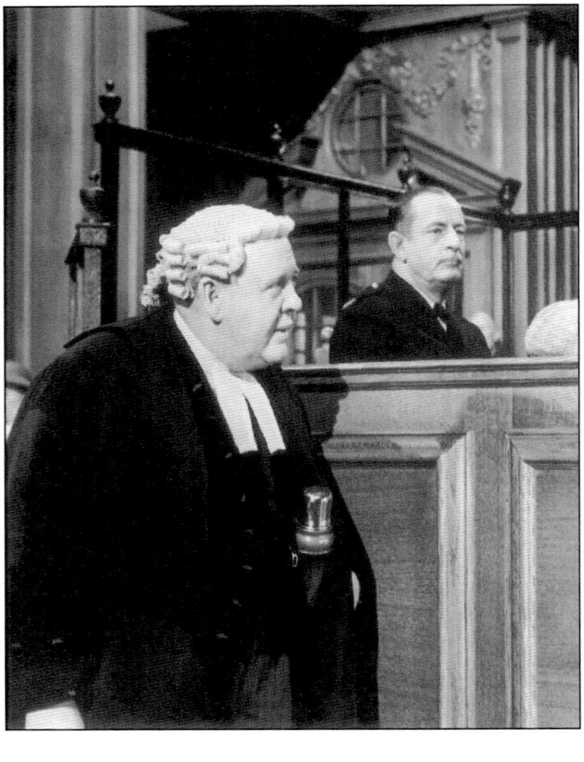

HARRY KURNITZ (1908–1968). Prolific screenwriter Harry Kurnitz wrote over 40 screenplays including *The Inspector General* (1949), *Witness for the Prosecution* (1957, pictured here), and *How to Steal a Million* (1966). Kurnitz created works across several genres with his comedies, dramas, swashbucklers, and mysteries. He even wrote a musical for the stage with Noel Coward. (Garden of Shalom, Section 16, Row K, Grave 22.)

DON LAFONTAINE (1940–2008). It is hard to think of the phrase "In a world . . ." without remembering the bass tones of Don "Thunder Throat" LaFontaine. LaFontaine began his career as a voice artist in 1964 and would eventually be known as "the King of the Movie Trailers" by recording more than 5,000 voiceovers for film advertisements. He died at age 68 from pneumothorax after having witnessed his catchphrase enter the American vocabulary. (Garden of the Exodus, Lot 747, Space 12.)

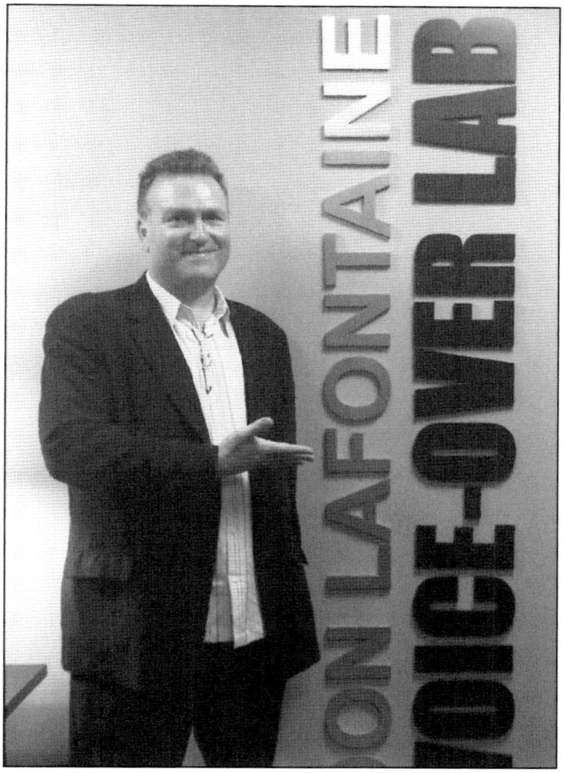

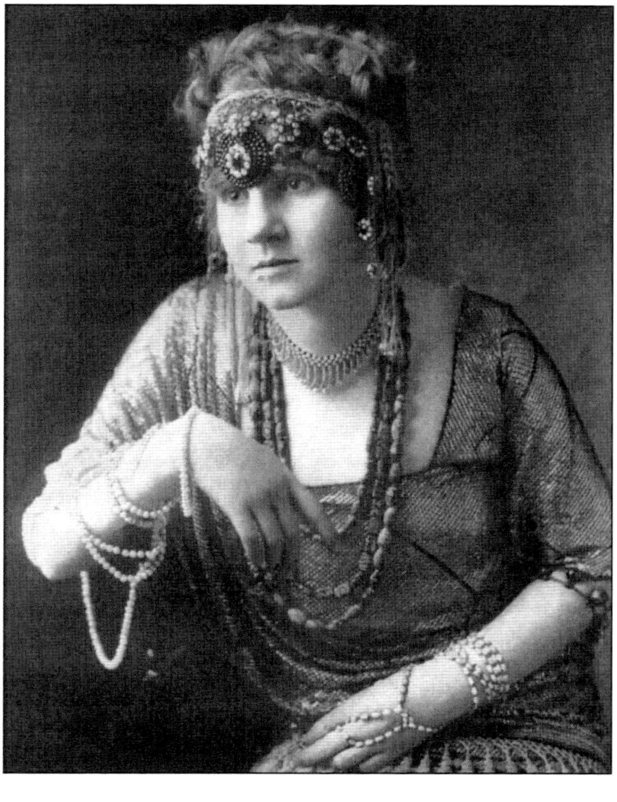

FLORENCE LAWRENCE (1886–1938). Canadian Florence Lawrence began her career making dozens of films for Biograph, listed in the credits only as "the Biograph Girl." Her bosses feared (correctly, as it turned out) that if the public knew actors by name, the players could demand higher salaries. Lawrence was later credited by name, making her the first movie star. In 1938, she committed suicide by swallowing ant poison. She was buried here in an unmarked plot until actor Roddy McDowall quietly purchased her a grave marker decades later. (Garden of Beginnings, Space 300.)

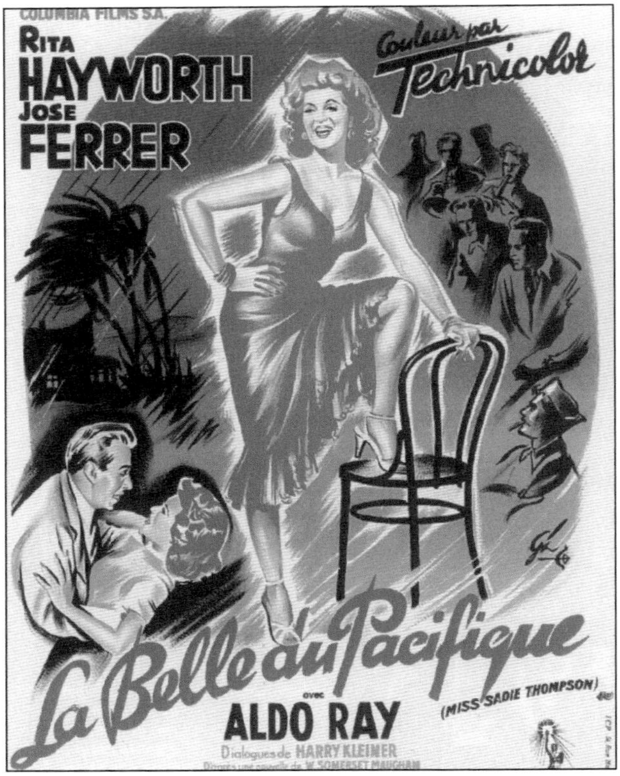

LESTER LEE (1903–1956). Composer Lester Lee scored films from the early days of talkies until his death in 1956. He penned dozens of songs, mostly for Universal and Columbia films, and was nominated for an Oscar for Best Song for "Blue Pacific Blues," from 1953's *Miss Sadie Thompson*, starring Rita Hayworth. (Garden of Eternal Love, Plot 838.)

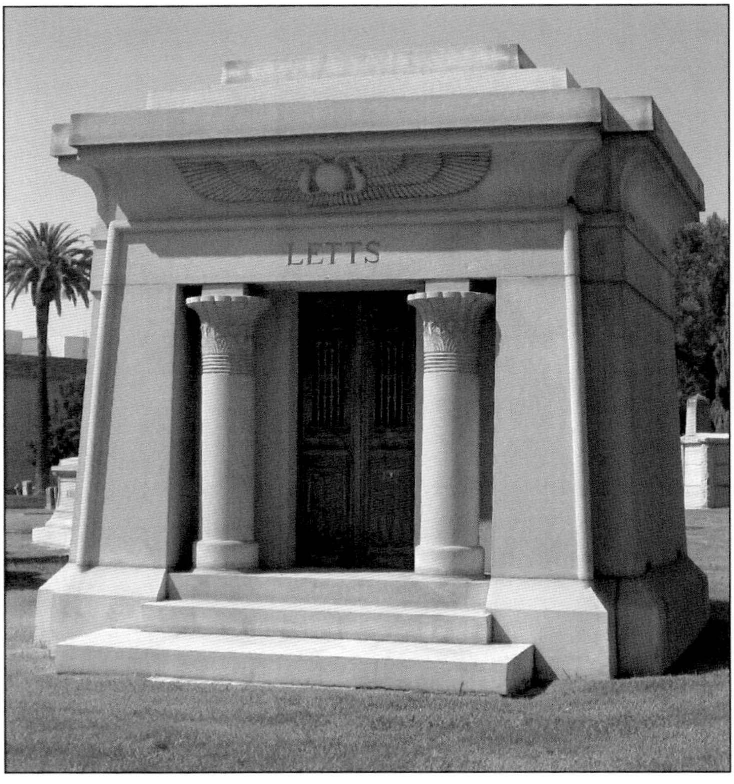

ARTHUR LETTS SR. (1862–1923). Arthur Letts turned a bankrupt dry goods store in Los Angeles into The Broadway and Bullocks. He also developed Westwood and Holmby Hills. His son Arthur Letts Jr. built the estate that is now the Playboy Mansion. (Chandler Gardens.)

Sonya Levien (1888–1960). Levien was a Russian-born Jewish woman who became one of the highest-paid female screenwriters of the 1930s. She began selling stories as a teenager while attending law school and earned her first screenwriting credit in 1921. She won an Academy Award for penning the script for *Interrupted Melody* in 1955. She also co-wrote the screenplay for *Oklahoma!* that same year. (Garden of Jerusalem, Plot 929.)

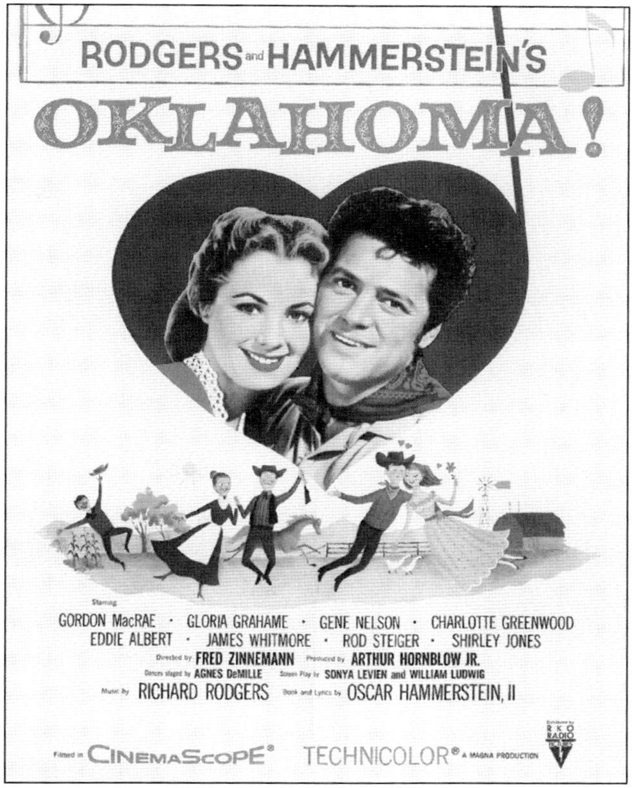

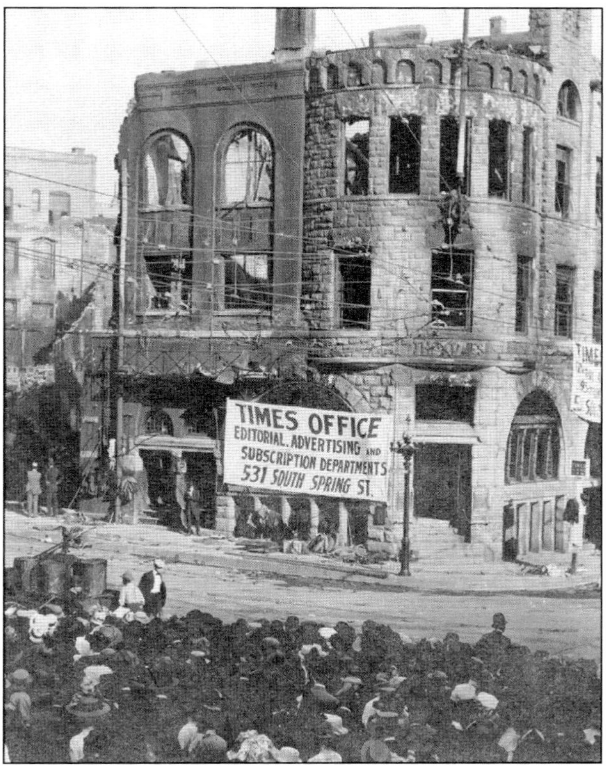

***Los Angeles Times* Bombing Memorial.** One of the bloodiest days in Southern California's history was October 1, 1910, when a bomb destroyed the *Los Angeles Times* building, killing 21 and injuring 100. Two brothers from the Iron Workers Union were convicted of the crime. At least 18 of the victims are interred at H4E. The memorial was placed here by Gen. Harrison Gray Otis, the publisher of the *Times*. Otis and his son-in-law Harry Chandler, who succeeded him as publisher, along with their families, are buried just steps away. (Chandler Gardens.)

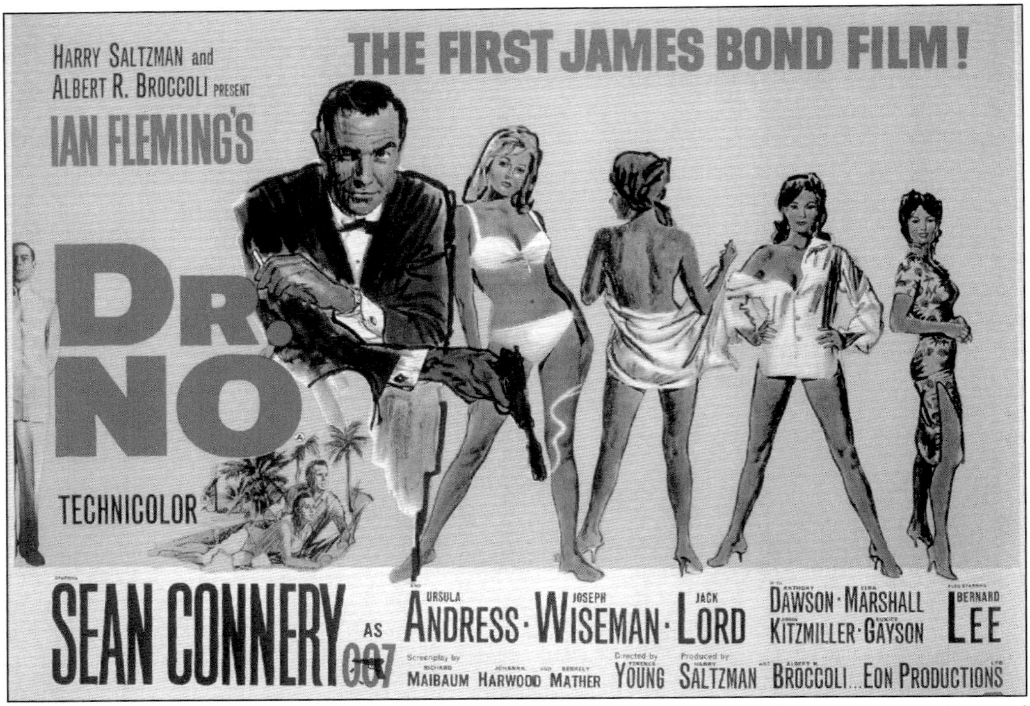

RICHARD MAIBAUM (1909–1991). Maibaum was an innovative producer, playwright, and screenwriter who penned several successful Broadway plays and Hollywood films during the 1930s. In his later years, he wrote 12 of the first 15 James Bond screenplays beginning with *Dr. No* (1962) and continuing through *License To Kill* (1989). (Plains of Abraham, Row A, Plot 76.)

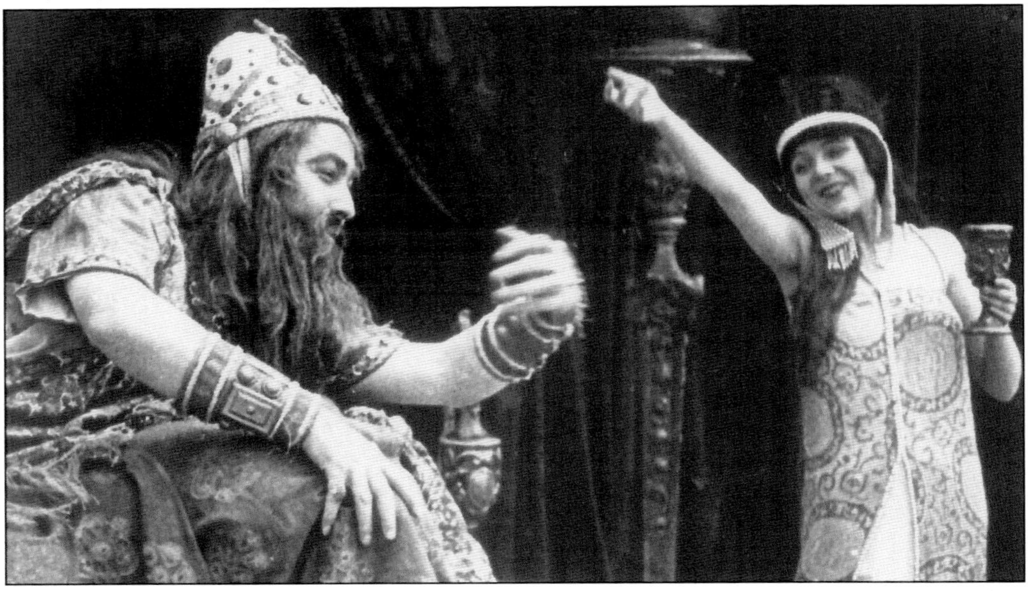

EMERY MCCARGAR (1888–1926). In 1912, cellist and pianist Emery McCargar became the first studio musician in history when D.W. Griffith hired him to provide mood music to help actors emote during the filming of *Judith of Bethulia* (1914). He worked in the career he pioneered until his death at age 37 from a brain tumor. Pictured here are Henry Walthall and Blanche Sweet in a scene from *Judith of Bethulia.* (Section 20B, Grave 65D.)

DARREN MCGAVIN (1922–2006). Darren McGavin starred in seven television series, most notably in *Kolchak: The Night Stalker* in the early 1970s (pictured here). On that show, he played a modern-day monster hunter. His most famous film role came in 1983's *A Christmas Story*, where he played the grumpy father with the kitschy leg lamp. McGavin died within 24 hours of Don Knotts and Dennis Weaver, giving credence to the notion that celebrities die in threes. (Griffith Lawn, Lot 203, Space 14.)

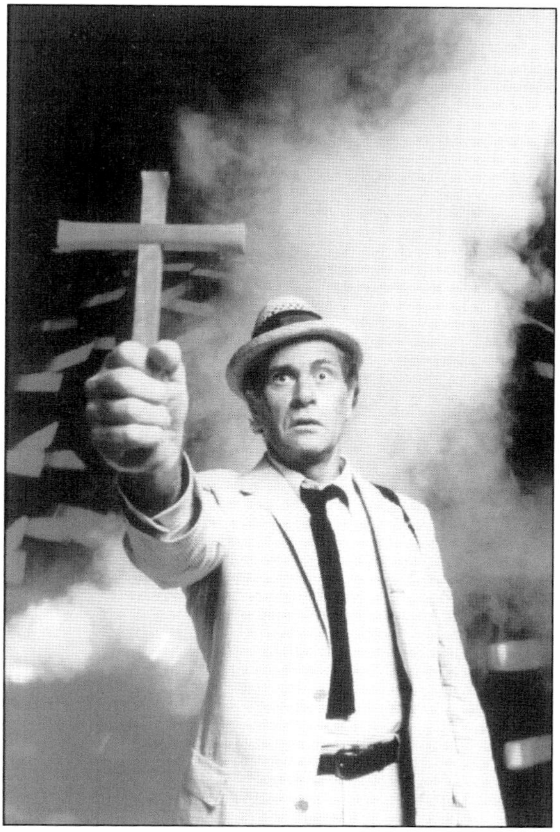

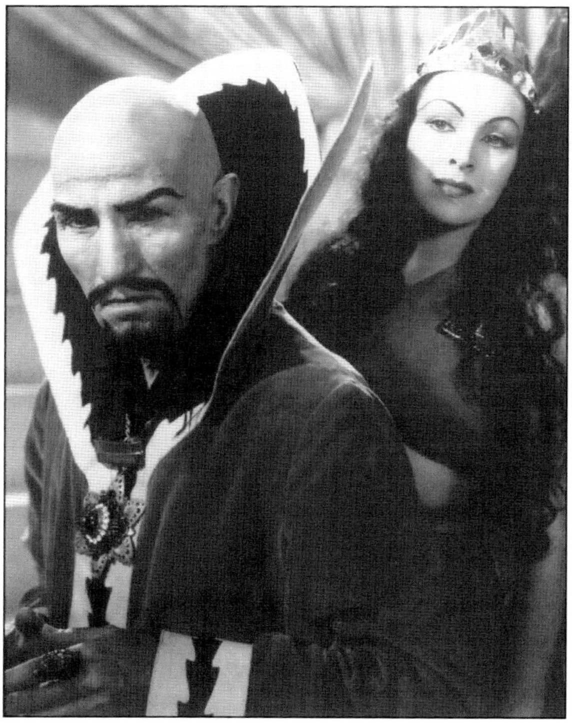

CHARLES B. MIDDLETON (1874–1949). Charles Middleton had a long stage career before turning to motion pictures in 1920 at the age of 46. Over the next three decades, he appeared in 200 films working with such talented performers as Harold Lloyd, Laurel and Hardy, and the Marx Brothers. But he is best remembered today for his role as evil emperor Ming the Merciless (seen here) in three different *Flash Gordon* serials in the late 1930s. (Garden of the Exodus, Lot 105.)

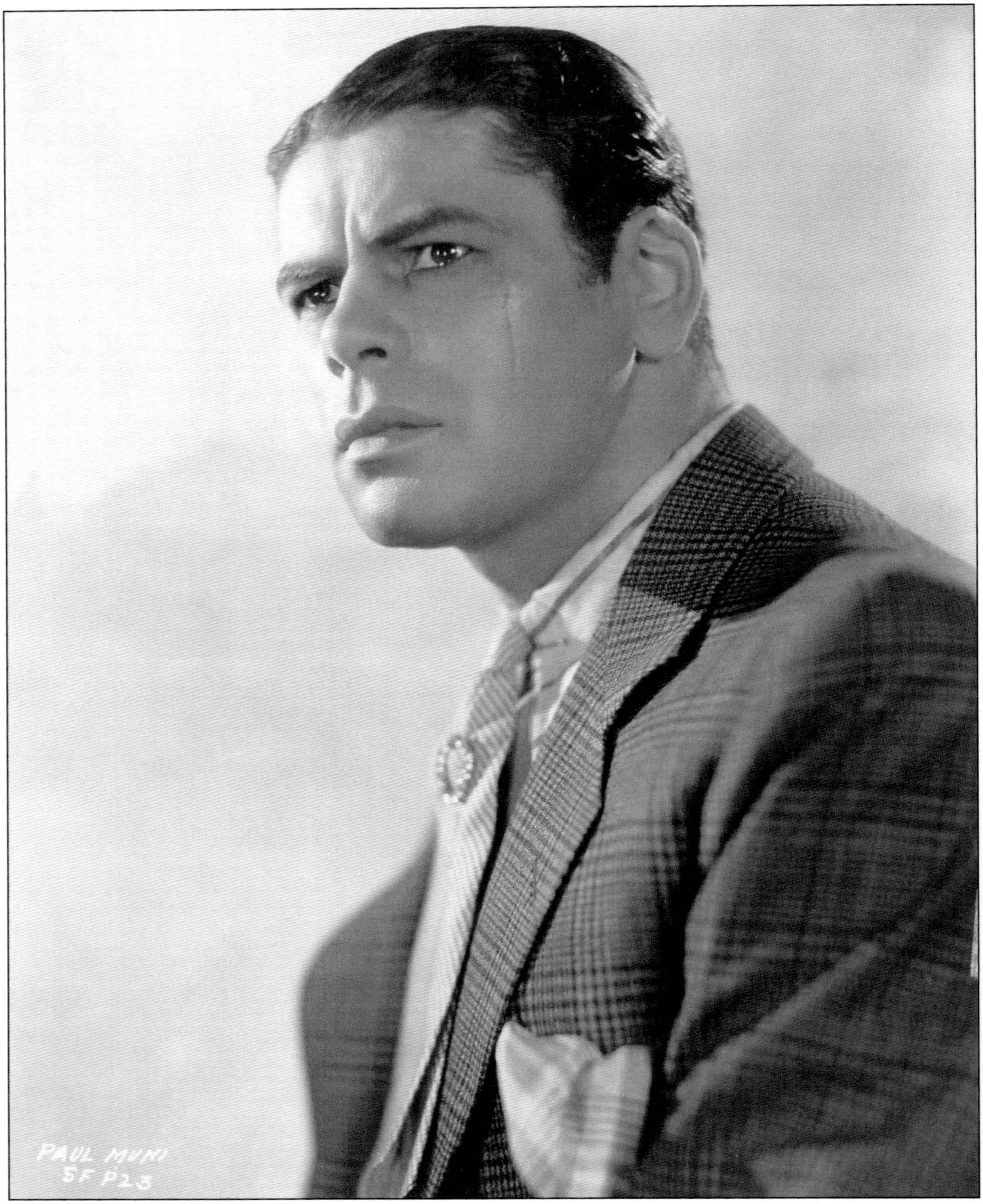

Paul Muni (1895–1967). One of the most talented actors of his era, Muni began his career in Yiddish theater in Chicago with his parents, who were both actors. Muni moved on to Broadway in 1926, where he performed for the first time in English (Yiddish was his first language). In Hollywood in 1929, Muni was nominated for an Oscar for his first film role. He starred in several biopics for Warner Bros. during the 1930s, winning the Academy Award for 1935's *The Story of Louis Pasteur*. Muni returned to Broadway for most of the remainder of his career but still made the occasional screen appearance, like in 1959's *The Last Angry Man*, for which he earned his fourth and final Academy Award nomination. Muni was married to Bella Finkel, an actress he met in Yiddish theater, from 1921 until his death in 1967. He is pictured here in a 1932 publicity photograph from the movie *Scarface*. (Plains of Abraham, Row OO, Space 57.)

Dudley Nichols (1895–1960). Dudley Nichols worked as a reporter in New York before moving west in 1929 to write screenplays. And write he did. He became one of the most successful screenwriters in Hollywood during the 1930s and 1940s, working with A-list directors like John Ford, George Cukor, Howard Hawks, Fritz Lang, and Jean Renoir. In 1935, Nichols became the first person to refuse an Oscar, which he won for the film *The Informer*, because of a conflict between the Academy and the Writers Guild. (Garden of the Exodus.)

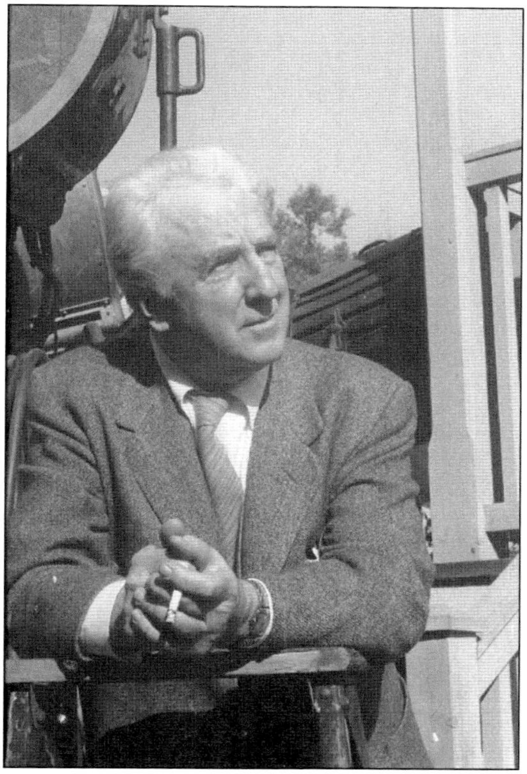

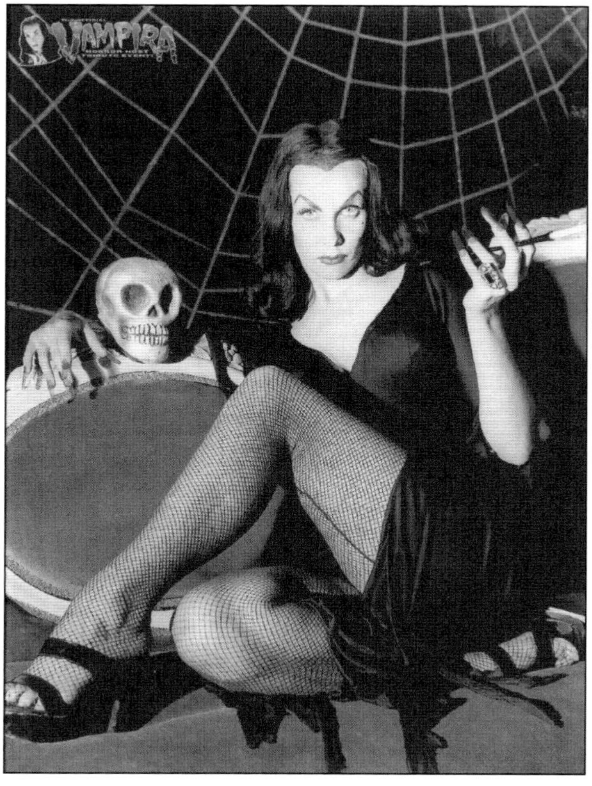

Maila Nurmi (1922–2008). Before Elvira, even before Morticia, there was Vampira, television's original ghoulish horror movie hostess, and familiar personality to Los Angeles late-night television viewers in the mid-1950s. Vampira was the gothic alter-ego of curvaceous actress, model, and chorus girl Maila Nurmi, who was born in Finland and moved to America when she was two. Nurmi migrated to Hollywood, where she worked as a dancer and as a model for acclaimed artists Alberto Vargas and Man Ray. Nurmi and James Dean became close friends but had a falling out shortly before Dean's death. Nurmi achieved lasting fame with her appearance in Ed Wood's *Plan 9 From Outer Space* (1959). She later unsuccessfully sued Cassandra Peterson, TV's Elvira, for cribbing her likeness. Nurmi passed away in 2008 at the age of 85, and fans pitched in to buy the marker for her grave. (Griffith Lawn, Lot 203, Space 1.)

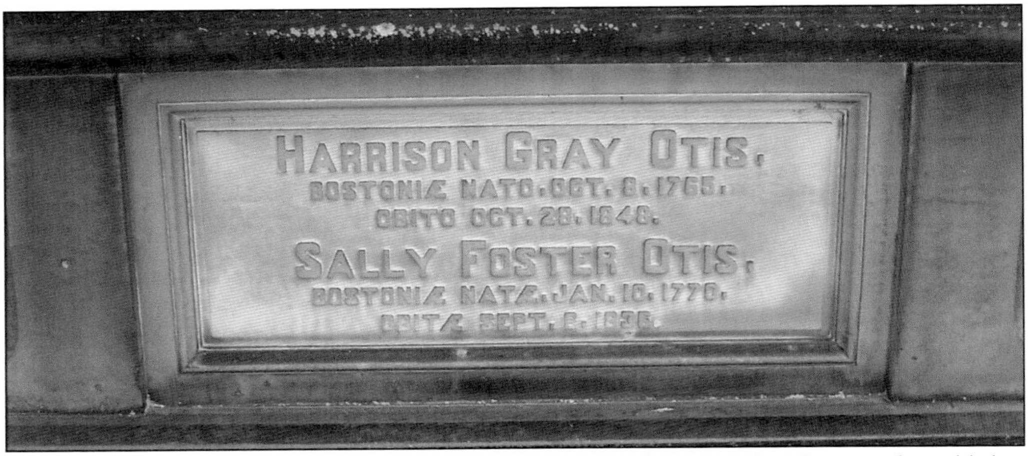

HARRISON GRAY OTIS (1837–1917). A giant in the history of Los Angeles, Otis was the publisher of the *Los Angeles Times*. Much of what Los Angeles became, good and bad, can be laid at his feet. He was the force behind relatively tiny Los Angeles's acquisition of the San Fernando Valley, helping create the megalopolis of today. His anti-union views made him a target of bombers who leveled the *Los Angeles Times* building in Downtown LA. in 1910. (Chandler Gardens, Lot 12, Space 6.)

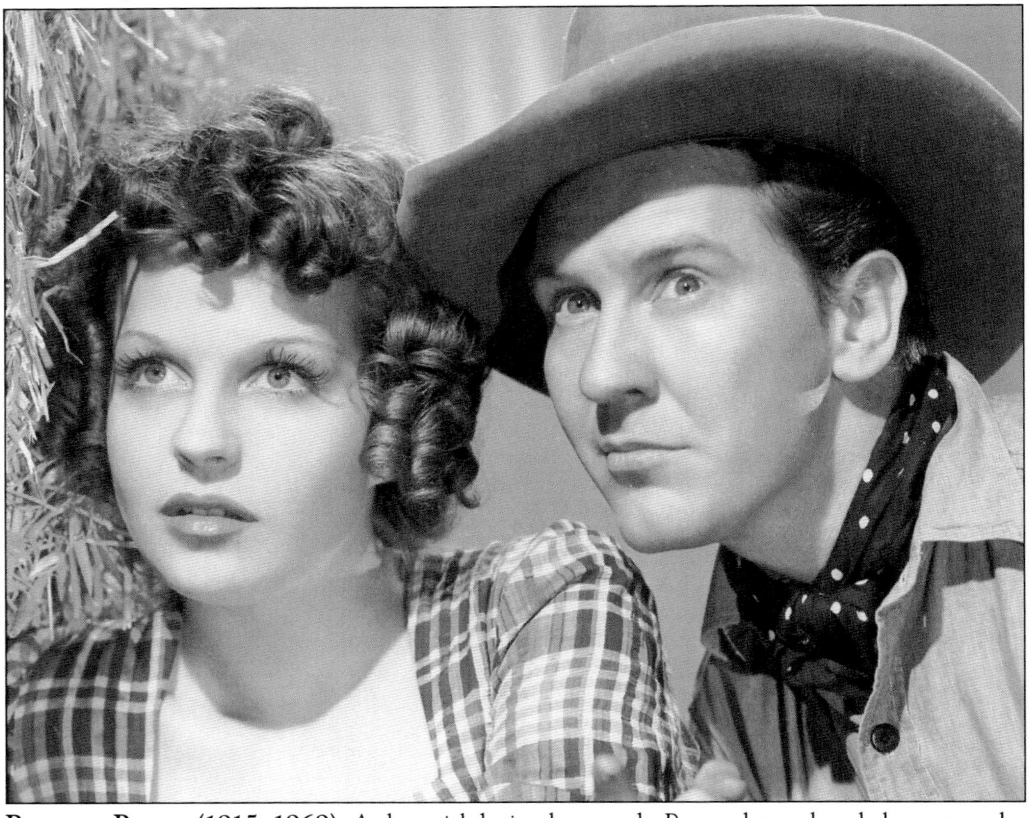

BARBARA PEPPER (1915–1969). A showgirl during her youth, Pepper later played character roles in comedies for the screen and on television. She is best remembered today as the first Doris Ziffel, the "mother" of pig Arnold Ziffel, on *Petticoat Junction* and *Green Acres*. Pepper was a lifelong friend of Lucille Ball. She is pictured here with Burgess Meredith in a scene from *Of Mice and Men* (1939). (Garden of Beginnings, Lot 12, Space 6.)

CARROLL RIGHTER (1900–1988). Righter was known as the "astrologer to the stars" and created charts for many of Hollywood's elite, including, controversially, Pres. Ronald Reagan and First Lady Nancy Reagan. At the height of his popularity, Righter's astrological column was syndicated in over 150 papers daily. (Chandler Gardens, Lot 222, Space 301.) (Courtesy of Pentax Forums.)

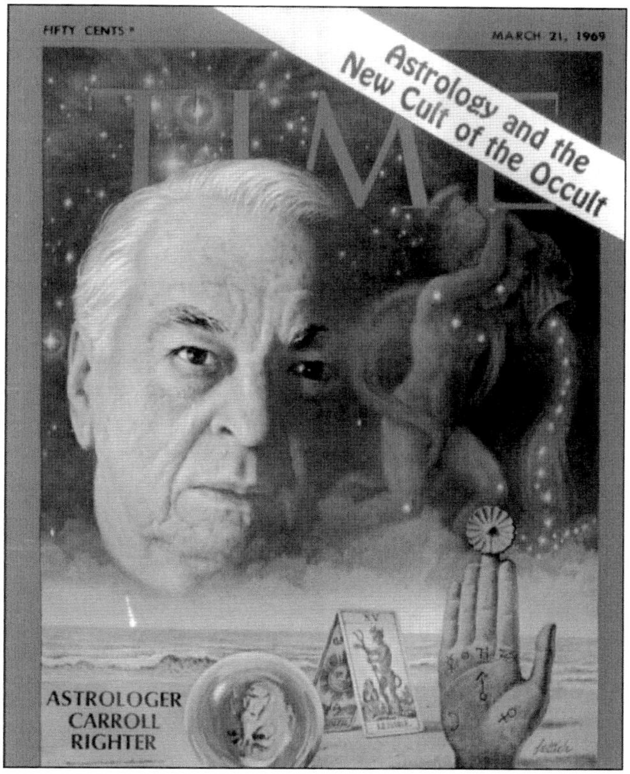

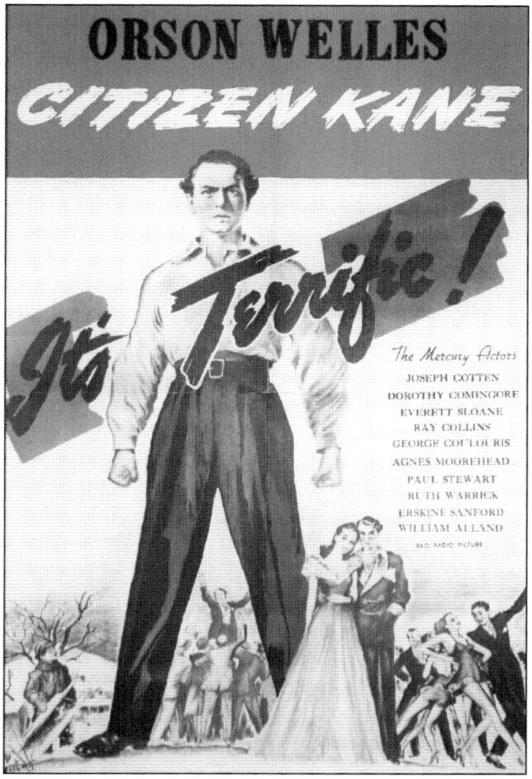

HERMAN RUBY (1892–1959). A Tin Pan Alley tunesmith, Herman Ruby wrote songs for Broadway shows during the 1910s and 1920s. Later in Hollywood, he wrote some screenplays and the music for films like *The Story of Vernon and Irene Castle* (1939), and *Citizen Kane* (1941). (Garden of the Exodus, Lot 153, Grave 210B.)

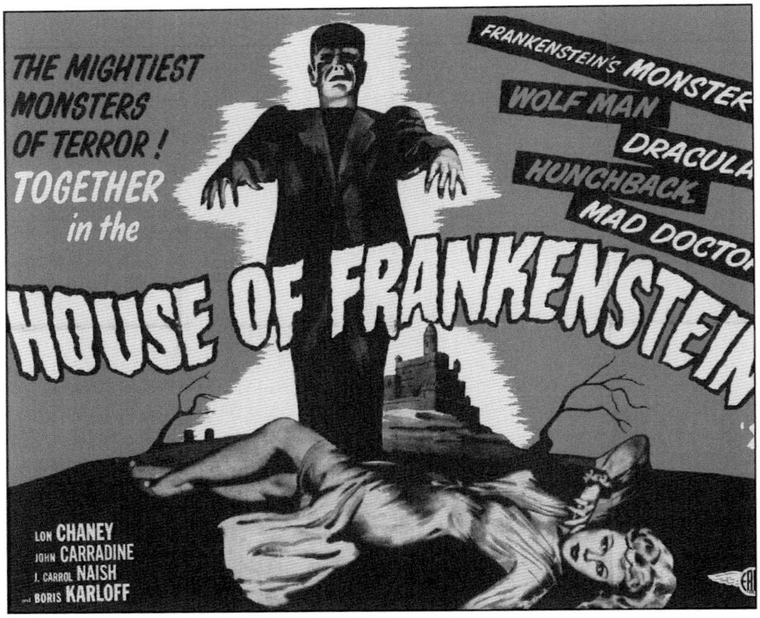

Hans Salter (1896–1994). American Hans Salter was a film composer who worked for many years for Universal, where he wrote music for many of the studio's classic horror films. He composed scores for *The Wolf Man* (1941), *Son of Dracula* (1943), *House of Frankenstein* (1944), *Creature From the Black Lagoon* (1954), and *The Incredible Shrinking Man* (1957). (Section 16, Lot 66B.)

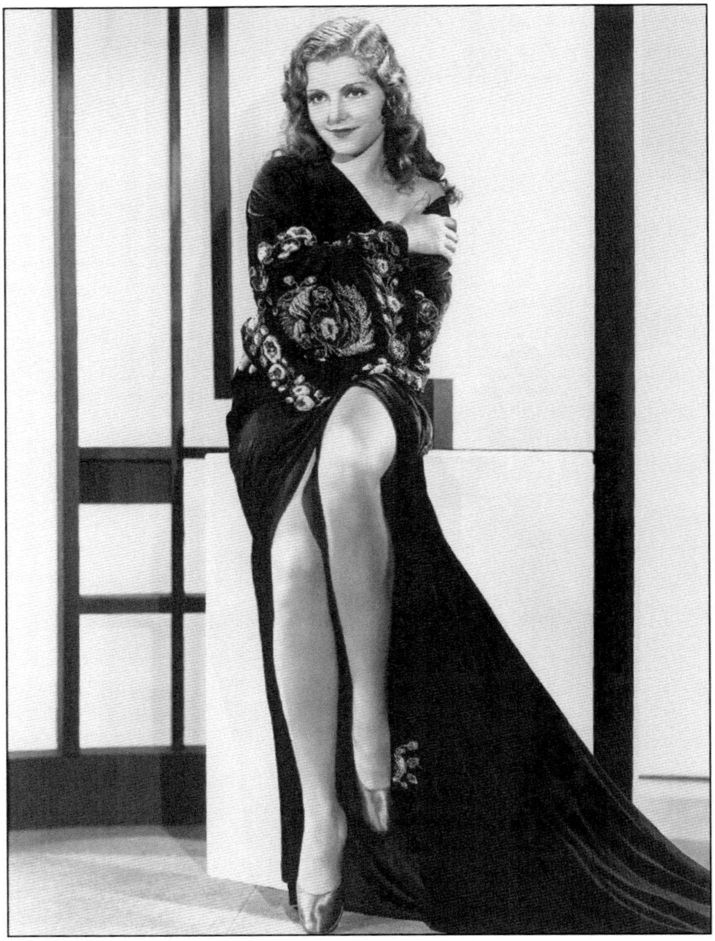

Peggy Shannon (1907–1941). Peggy Shannon was discovered on Broadway in the *Ziegfeld Follies* and came west, where she made her screen debut two days after arriving in Hollywood. She developed a drinking problem and earned a reputation for being difficult on set. She died of a heart attack brought on by alcoholism at the young age of 34. Three weeks later, her husband, Albert G. Roberts, shot himself in the same chair where Shannon's body was found. (Garden of Eternal Love, Plot 31, Grave 4.)

Chief Luther Standing Bear (1868–1939). Chief Luther Standing Bear was a Native American author, actor, and activist for Indian rights. Standing Bear was a member of Buffalo Bill Cody's Wild West Show and acted in several Westerns. He was buried here in 1939 after dying from influenza on the set of *Union Pacific*. (Garden of Beginnings, Plot 399.)

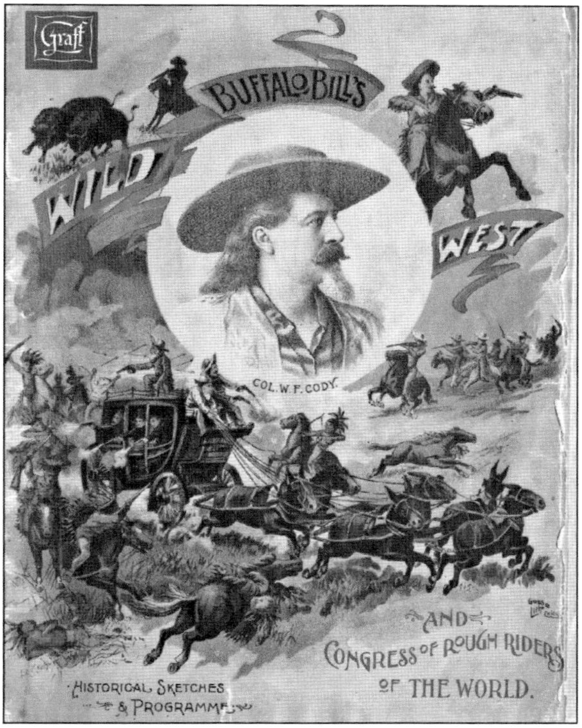

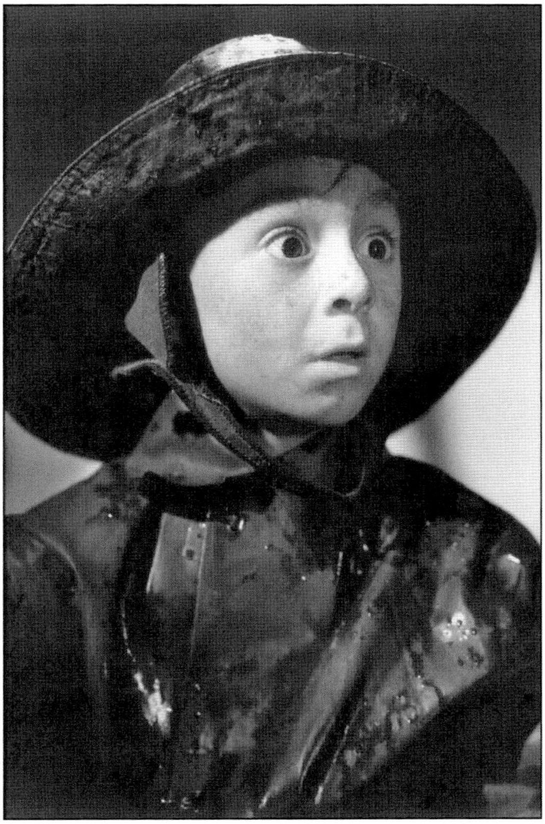

Carl "Alfalfa" Switzer (1927–1959). Child actor Carl Switzer made his name playing the perpetually cowlicked Alfalfa in the *Our Gang* comedies. He never found lasting success again in Hollywood. Switzer was shot and killed at age 31 during an argument over a dog. The death was ruled a justifiable homicide. His death and that of legendary director Cecil B. DeMille happened on the same day. DeMille's funeral dominated the trades, relegating the story of unlucky Alfalfa to the back pages. (Garden of Memory, Lot 26, Space 6.)

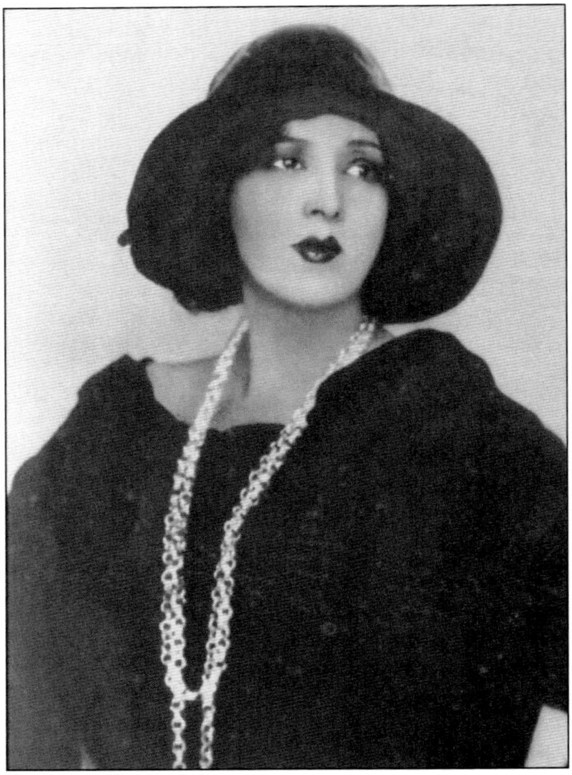

Estelle Taylor (1894–1958). Estelle Taylor was a film star during the silent era, appearing is such memorable hits as *The Ten Commandments* (1923) for director Cecil B. DeMille and *Don Juan* (1926), the first film with synchronized sound effects. She was married for a time to world heavyweight boxing champion Jack Dempsey. (Garden of Beginnings, Lot 9, Space 402B.)

Holly Woodlawn (1946–2015). Holly Woodlawn was born in Puerto Rico as Haroldo Santiago Franceschi Rodriguez Dankahl. Woodlawn came out as gay after moving to Miami and later migrated north to New York, where she became one of Andy Warhol's "superstars"—members of his entourage who he would put in his films. Holly made her mark in rock 'n' roll history in 1972 when Lou Reed referenced her in the lyrics of his hit song "Walk on the Wild Side." (Lake View East Columbarium.)

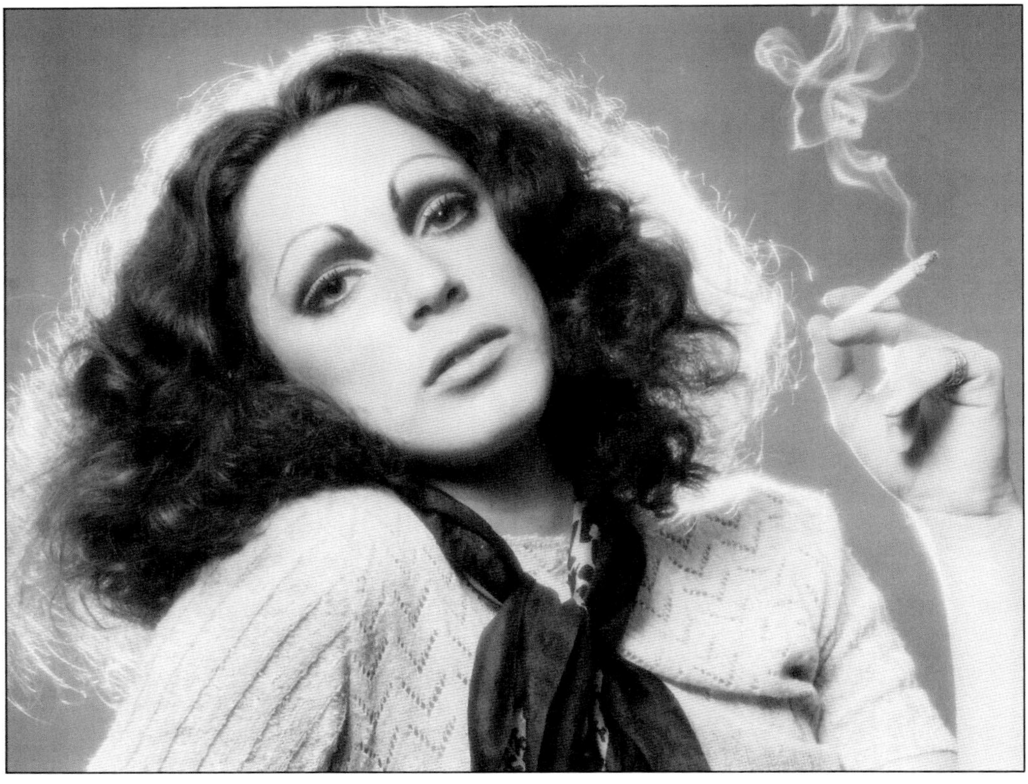

Five

Garden Of Legends

In *The Rocky Horror Picture Show,* Dr. Frank-N-Furter asks, "Whatever Happened to Fay Wray?" The answer is that she lived a long life and is now buried in the Garden of Legends in Hollywood Forever Cemetery.

The Garden of Legends is perhaps the most sought-after Hollywood location to make a permanent home after the limelights have gone out for the last time. It is an oval-shaped plot with a man-made pond in the center whose fake island houses one of the most elaborate tombs in America. There are few sights in Southern California more picturesque than the view of this monument, surrounded by its swan laden pond, against the background of the Hollywood Hills to the north, sporting the 50-foot white letters of the Hollywood Sign.

Garden of Legends is well named. Many of the residents here were deemed legends during life in their chosen fields. This includes directors John Huston, Cecil B. DeMille, Tony Scott, and Monta Bell; fashion designer Adrian; musicians Nelson Eddy, Erich Wolfgang Korngold, William Jurmann, and the Ramones; comedian Don Adams; choreographer Agnes de Mille; actors Tyrone Power, Marion Davies, Janet Gaynor, Adolph Menjou, Vera Sessions, Herman Bing, and Fay Wray; cinematographer Elmer Dyer; and producers like the Cohns, the Christies, Henry Lehrman, and Jack Laird. There is even a touch of royalty here, with the grave of Lady Sylvia Ashley.

Garden of Legends has other greats—and near-greats as well. The Rosson family, who made contributions to several aspects of filmmaking, are here. So is Hannah Chaplin, whose son Charlie is still one of the most recognizable humans on the planet. One can also find Eddie LeVeque, the last of the original Keystone Cops. Virginia Rappe, who was the unfortunate starlet who died during a party hosted by Roscoe "Fatty" Arbuckle, is here as well. So is one of Ernest Hemingway's wives and the grandmother of Carol Burnett, who Carol would signal to at the end of each of her shows by tugging on her left ear.

There is a certain north-south symmetry to Garden of Legends not found in other areas of H4E. On the south side of the pond is the pink cenotaph of Hattie McDaniel. It mirrors the pink cenotaph of Jayne Mansfield on the north side of the pond. The same is true for the matching white marble above-ground crypts that house the Cohns (on the south side) and the DeMilles (north side). Two of the Ramones are here: Johnny (south side) and Dee Dee (north side).

But by far, the grandest monument in Garden of Legends, if not all of America, is the massive limestone monument on the island in the center of the lake. While the name of its occupant, William A. Clark Jr., may not be recognized, the sheer excess and extravagance of his crypt is truly legendary.

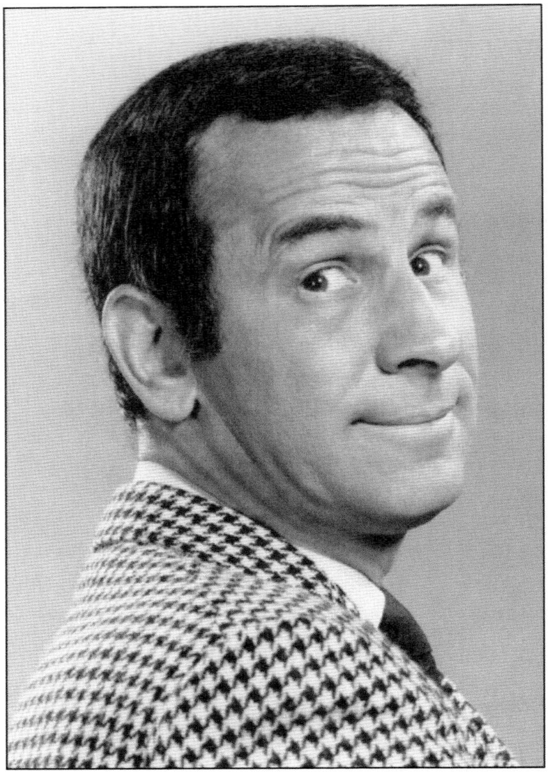

Don Adams (1923–2005). Comic actor Don Adams, born Don Yarmy in 1923, was once as military as it gets. Adams was the only member of his Marine platoon to survive the Battle of Guadalcanal. He later spent time stateside as a drill instructor. Turning to comedy, Adams landed the hilarious role of Maxwell Smart in *Get Smart* in 1965, which was on the air until 1970. (Lot 57, Space 20.)

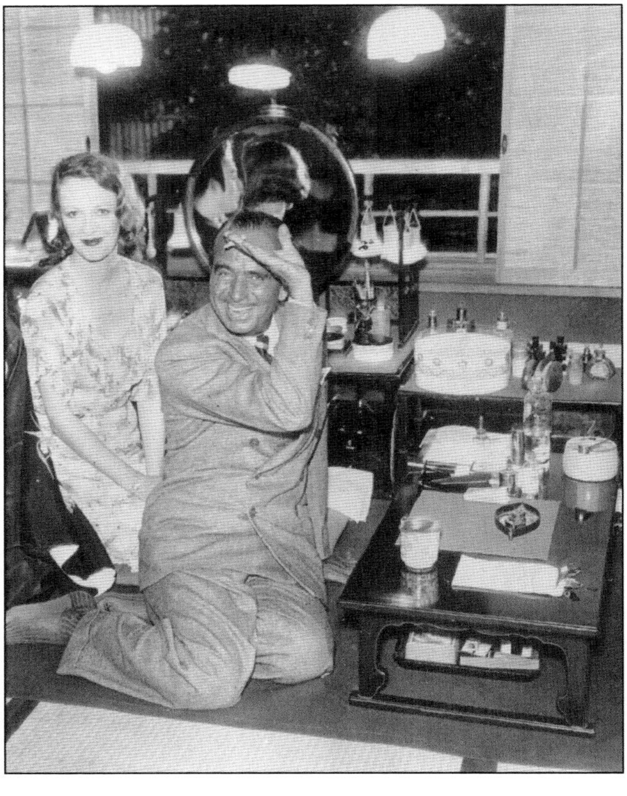

Lady Sylvia Ashley (1904–1977). Socialite Sylvia Ashley is remembered today for her husbands, who included a prince, a lord, a baron, and two "kings" of Hollywood. She wed Englishman Lord Ashley before marrying Hollywood star Douglas Fairbanks (the couple is pictured here). She then married an English baron, followed by actor Clark Gable, before becoming a princess by marrying the race-car driving prince Dimitri Djordjadze of the nation of Georgia. (Lot 53.)

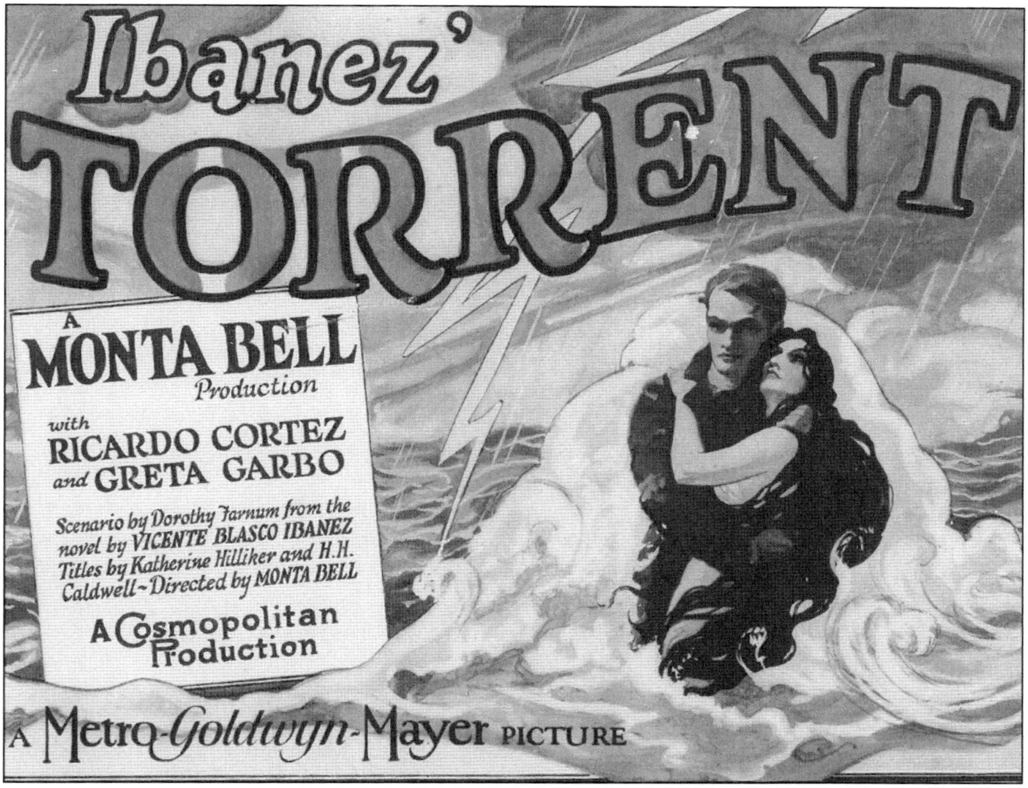

MONTA BELL (1891–1958). Monta Bell was a film editor and assistant director for Charlie Chaplin before becoming a full-time director. From then until the end of his career, Bell directed or produced 20 films, including Greta Garbo's first American movie. He also wrote nine screenplays. For years, Bell was the head of production at Paramount's Astoria Studios in New York. (Lot 88.)

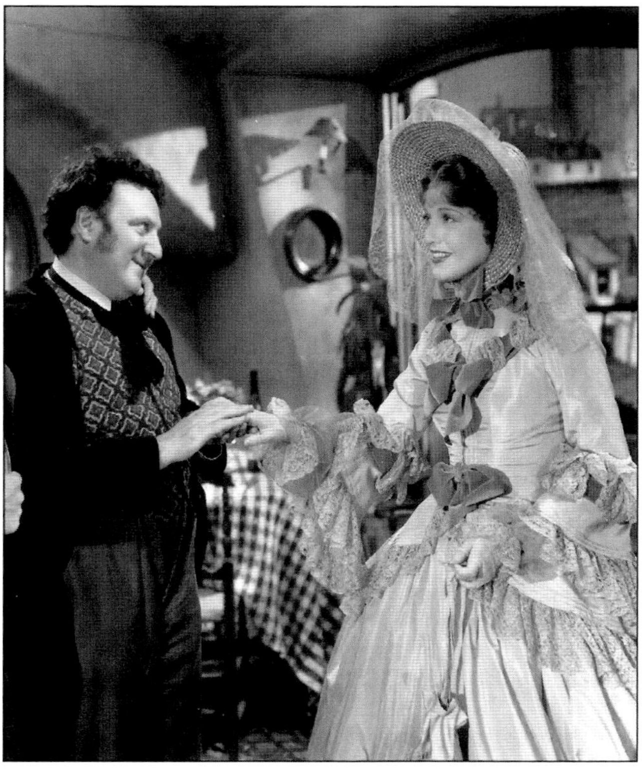

HERMAN BING (1889–1947). German-born Herman Bing acted in over 100 films during his time in Hollywood. His voice was also featured in cartoons for Disney and Warner Bros. In 1947, despondent over his inability to find work, Bing shot himself. He is pictured here with Jeanette Macdonald in a scene from *Maytime* (1937). (Lot 199.)

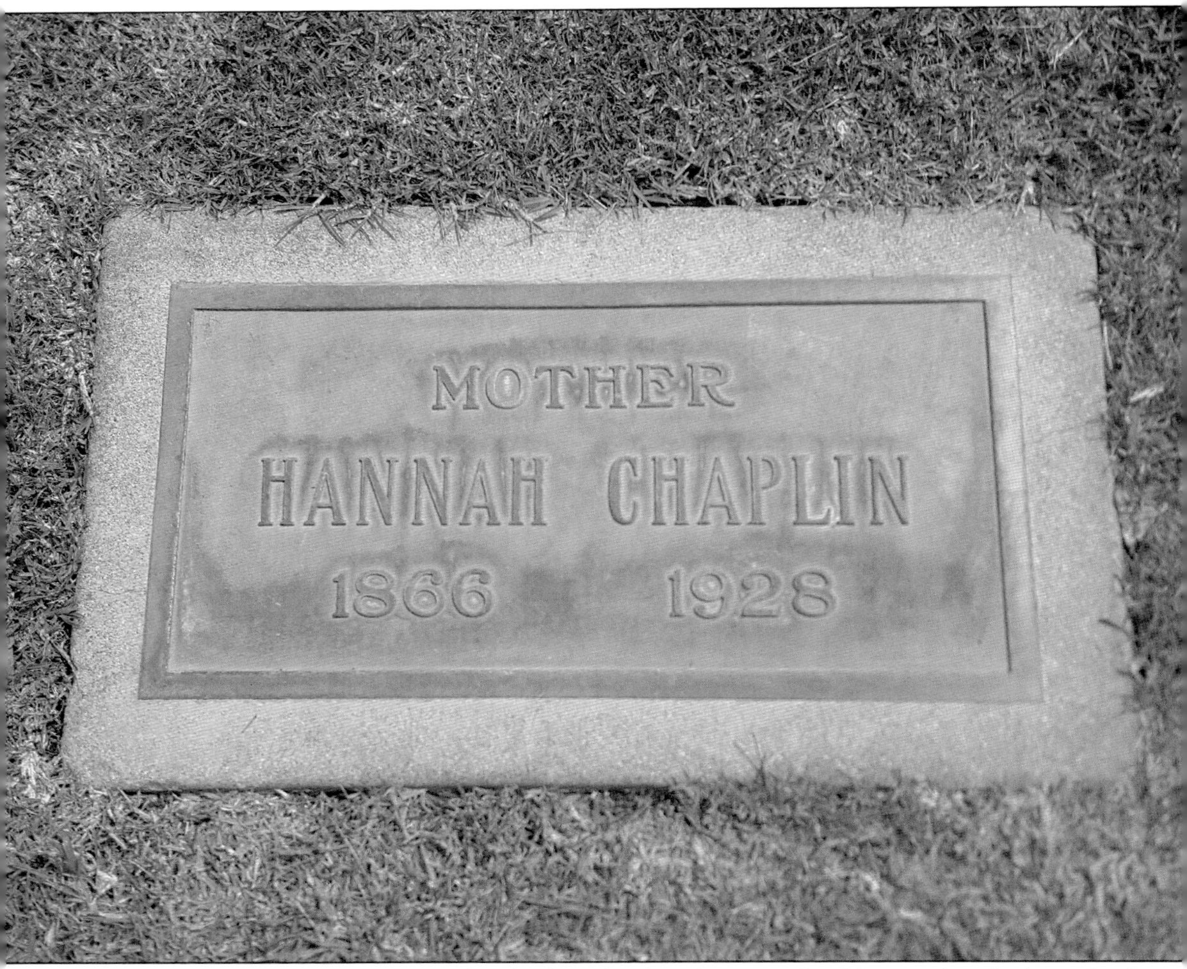

HANNAH CHAPLIN (1865–1928). Charlie Chaplin always credited his mother for his gift of pantomime. Hannah Chaplin, a British music hall performer for many years, was abandoned by her husband and forced to raise her two boys by herself in unforgiving Victorian London. The stress took its toll on her sanity, and she was in and out of asylums for much of the remainder of her life. After achieving fame in America, Charlie and his half-brother Sydney brought her to live in Southern California for the last seven years of her life. She was buried here in a plot given by Marion Davies, who is now entombed in a huge family mausoleum just steps away. Chaplin honored his mother by naming the heroine Hannah in *The Great Dictator* (1940). Hannah Chaplin's own granddaughter, Geraldine, played her in the movie *Chaplin* in 1992. (Lot 260.) (Photograph by E.J. Stephens.)

Al Christie (1881–1951) and Charles Christie (1880–1955). The Canadian film pioneering Christie brothers began their careers working for David Horsley's Centaur Film Company in New Jersey. They came to Hollywood to manage Centaur's West Coast operations, which was Hollywood's first studio. The two created Christie Comedies and, for years, churned out several one-reelers a month. They became two of the biggest moguls in early Hollywood before losing their fortunes during the Great Depression. (Lot 178.)

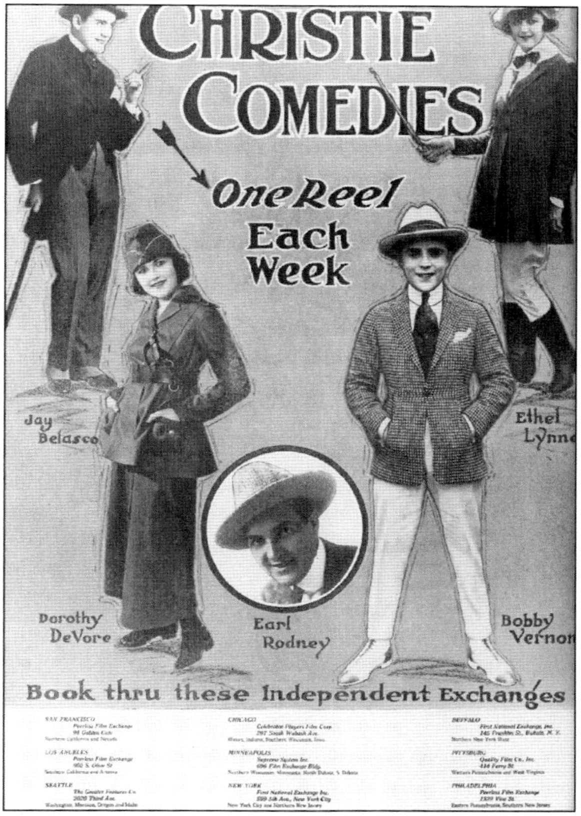

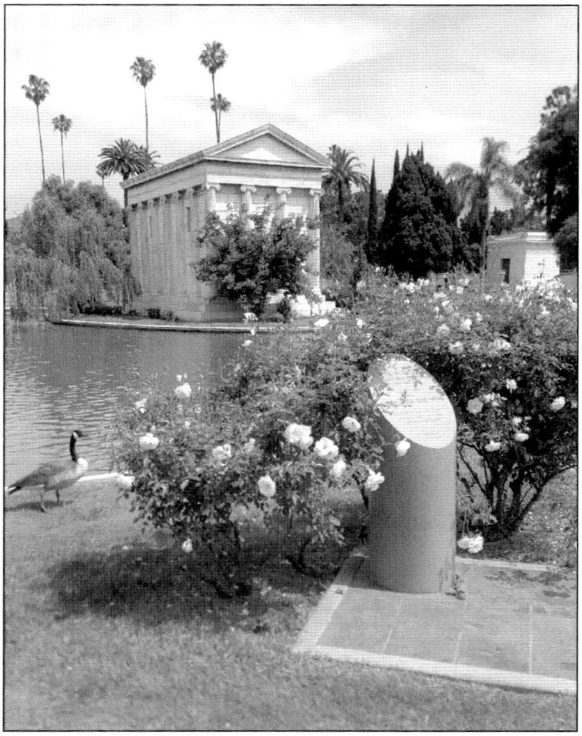

William A. Clark Jr. (1877–1934). While H4E is sprinkled liberally with the graves of some of the most famous entertainers in history, the cemetery's most imposing gravesite belongs to someone whose name many would not recognize. This massive afterlife estate, which graces the center of a man-made lake, houses the remains of William A. Clark Jr. His father made a fortune mining copper in the 1800s before becoming a US senator. Clark Jr. founded the Los Angeles Philharmonic Orchestra. His crypt is pictured here with Hattie McDaniel's cenotaph in the foreground. (Lake Island Mausoleum.) (Photograph by Kim Stephens.)

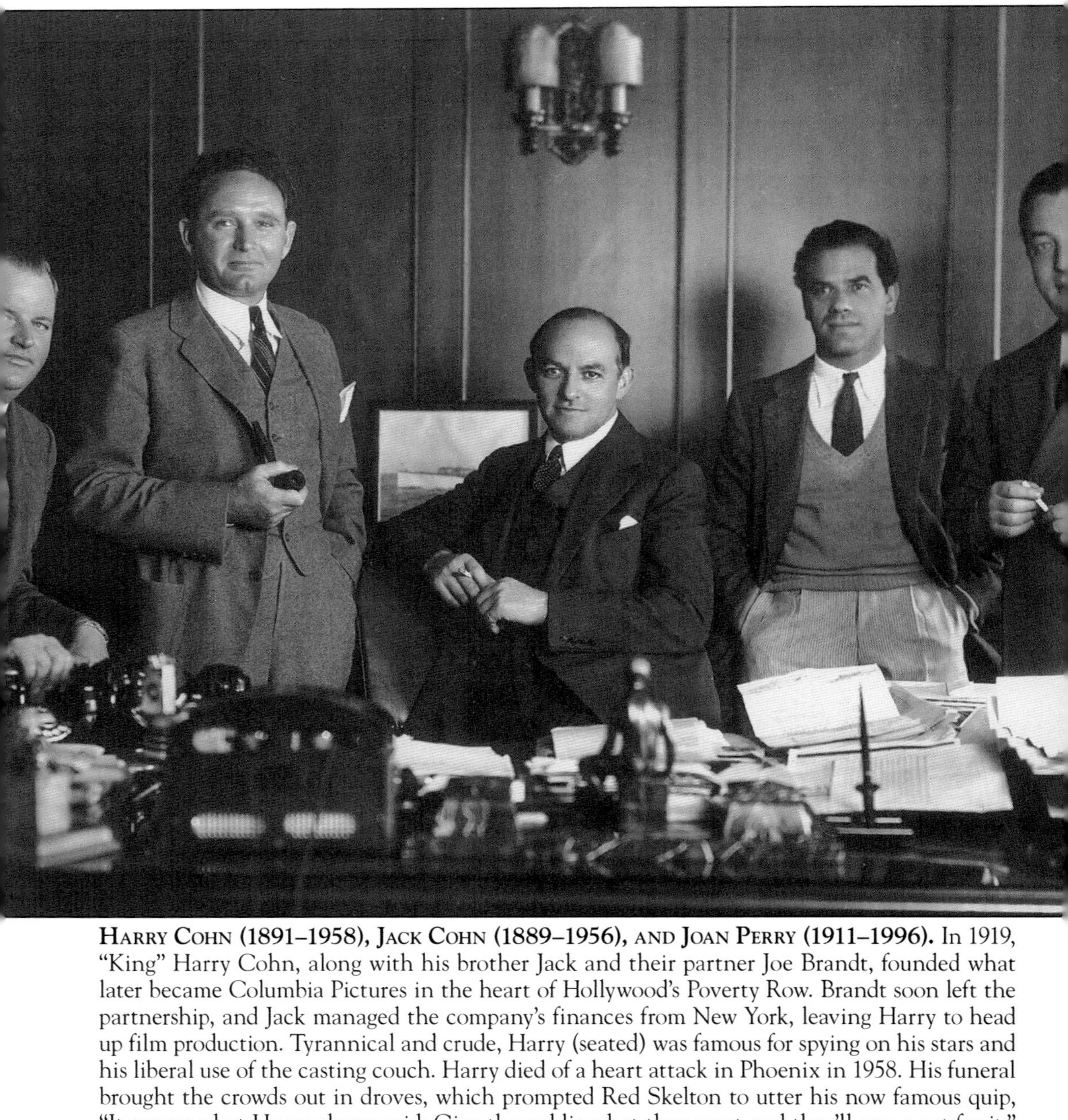

HARRY COHN (1891–1958), JACK COHN (1889–1956), AND JOAN PERRY (1911–1996). In 1919, "King" Harry Cohn, along with his brother Jack and their partner Joe Brandt, founded what later became Columbia Pictures in the heart of Hollywood's Poverty Row. Brandt soon left the partnership, and Jack managed the company's finances from New York, leaving Harry to head up film production. Tyrannical and crude, Harry (seated) was famous for spying on his stars and his liberal use of the casting couch. Harry died of a heart attack in Phoenix in 1958. His funeral brought the crowds out in droves, which prompted Red Skelton to utter his now famous quip, "It proves what Harry always said: Give the public what they want and they'll come out for it." Joan Perry, an actress during the 1930s, was married to Harry from 1941 until his death. They are interred in side-by-side crypts. Jack Cohn, Harry's older brother and partner in Columbia, is buried in the same plot, as is Jack's son Ralph, who founded Screen Gems, Columbia's television subsidiary. (Lot 86.)

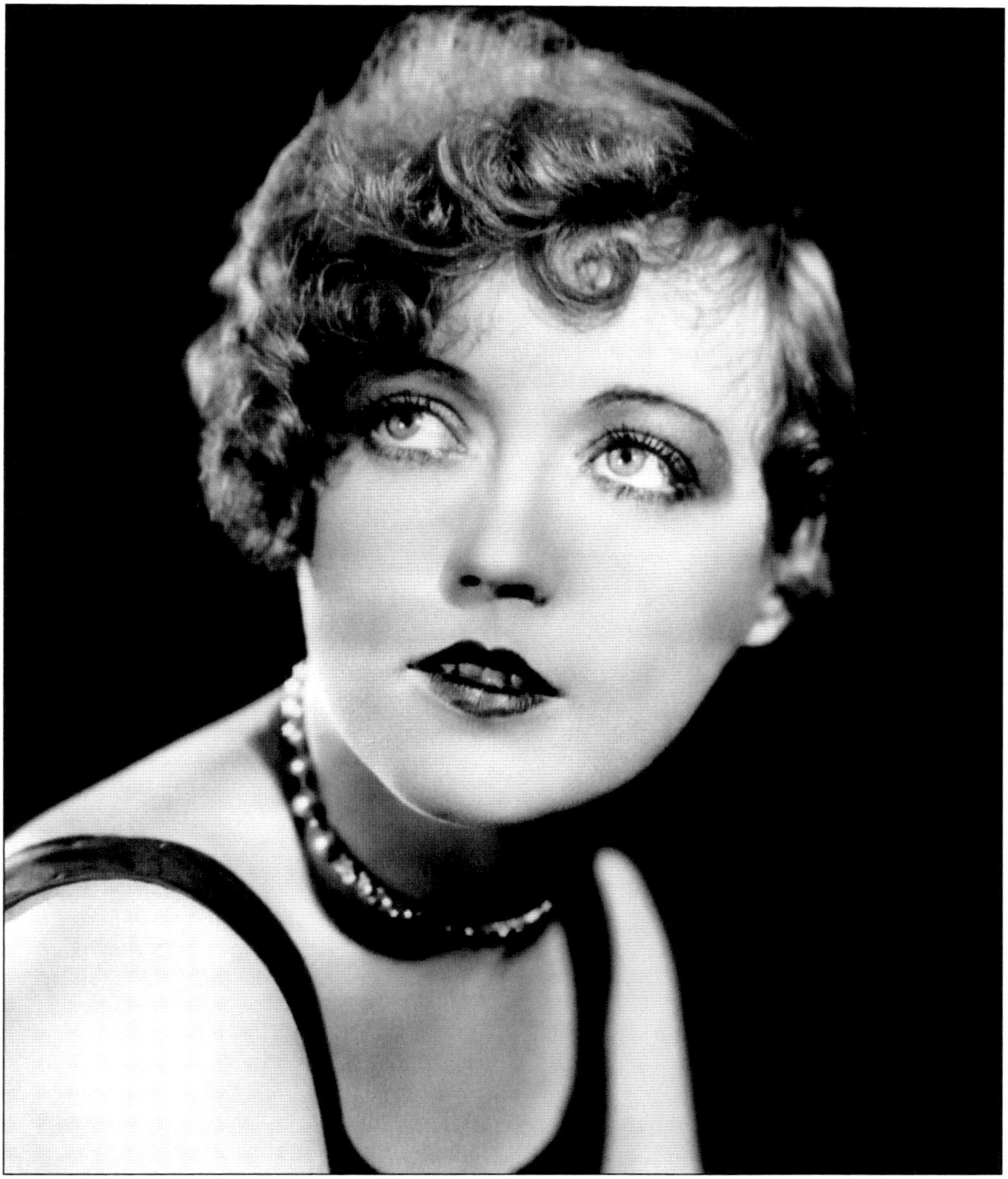

Marion Davies (1897–1961), Arthur Lake (1905–1987), and Patricia Lake (1919–1993). Marion Davies was born Marion Cecilia Douras. She had a 20-year film career, but is known more for being the mistress of newspaper mogul William Randolph Hearst. Davies caught the eye of the very rich, very powerful, and very married Hearst at the start of her career. They were companions for the next 30 years, lavishly entertaining Hollywood's glitterati in a string of palaces. Orson Welles mercilessly skewered the thinly veiled Hearst and Davies in 1941's *Citizen Kane*. Arthur Lake was born into a family vaudeville act and achieved fame as Dagwood Bumstead, *Blondie's* bumbling husband, on film, radio, and television. He married Patricia Lake, the "niece" of Hearst and Davies, who was long rumored to be their love child who had been given to Davies's sister to raise as her own. As it turned out, the rumor was true. Lake also had a career of her own on radio, voicing the character Blondie opposite her husband Arthur's Dagwood for many years. (Douras Mausoleum.)

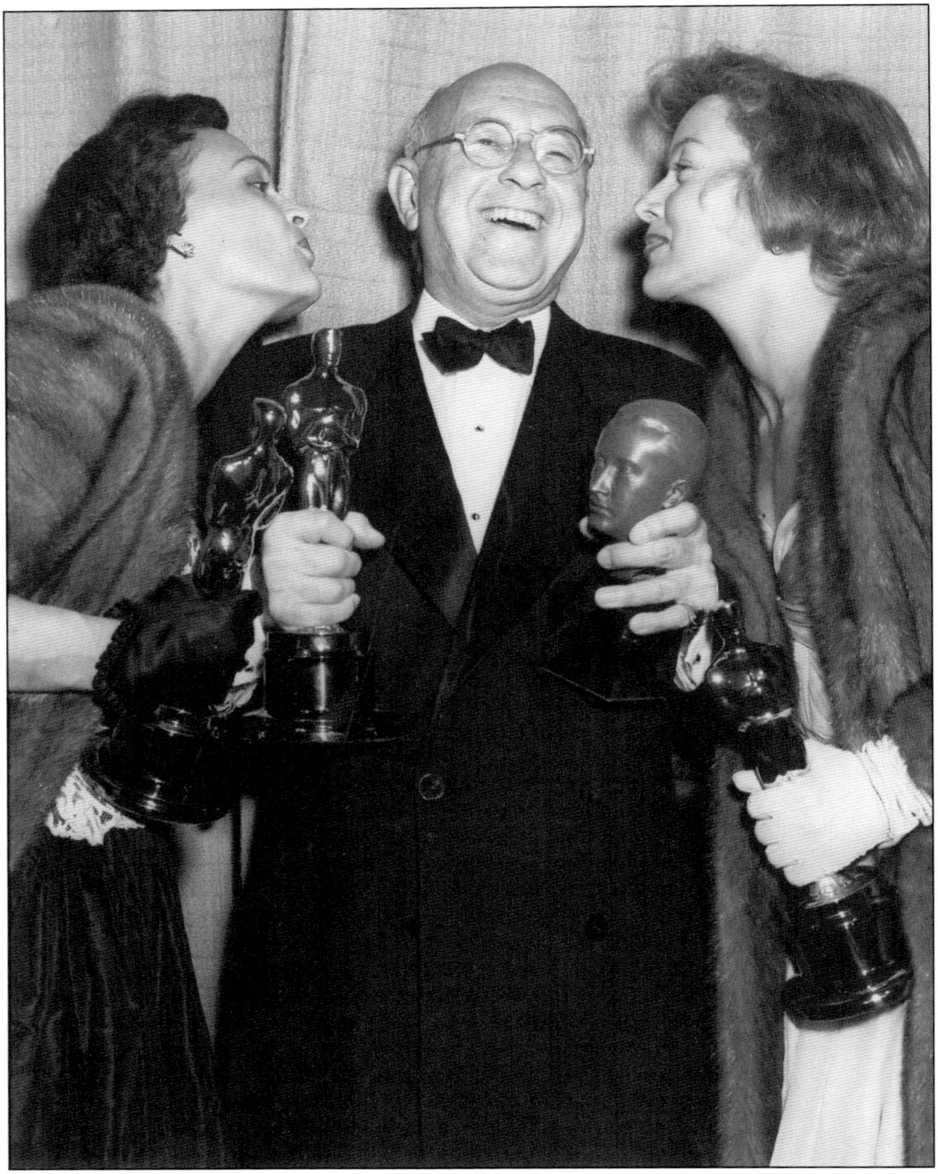

Agnes (1905–1993), Cecil B. (1881–1959), Clara (1886–1956), Matilda (1853–1923), and William DeMille (1878–1955). Cecil B. DeMille, the stereotypical epic-making, jodhpur-wearing, riding crop–smacking cinematic general, began his career as a Broadway actor. In 1913, he made *The Squaw Man*, the first full-length feature filmed in Hollywood. He spent the next 45 years bringing epic after epic to the screen, helping to create Paramount Pictures along the way, whose water tower can be seen from his grave. He and his wife, Clara, who was a screenwriter, are in matching above-ground white limestone crypts. When Cecil began his film career, he was less famous than his older brother William, who was a successful Broadway playwright and director, and is also buried here in the DeMille family plot. Their mother, Matilda, an agent and screenwriter, is also interred here, as is sister Agnes, who was a world-renowned choreographer. In the same plot is the headstone of two-year-old Christopher Quinn, who was the child of Cecil's adopted daughter Katherine and her husband, actor Anthony Quinn. Young Christopher wandered into next-door neighbor W.C. Fields's yard in 1941 and drowned in his fountain. (Lot 50.)

Elmer Dyer (1892–1970). Expert aerial photographer Elmer Dyer worked on Howard Hughes's *Hell's Angels* (1930) and Frank Capra's *Dirigible* (1931). He was nominated for an Oscar in 1944 for his work on *Air Force*. (Lot 53.) (Courtesy of Pentax Forums.)

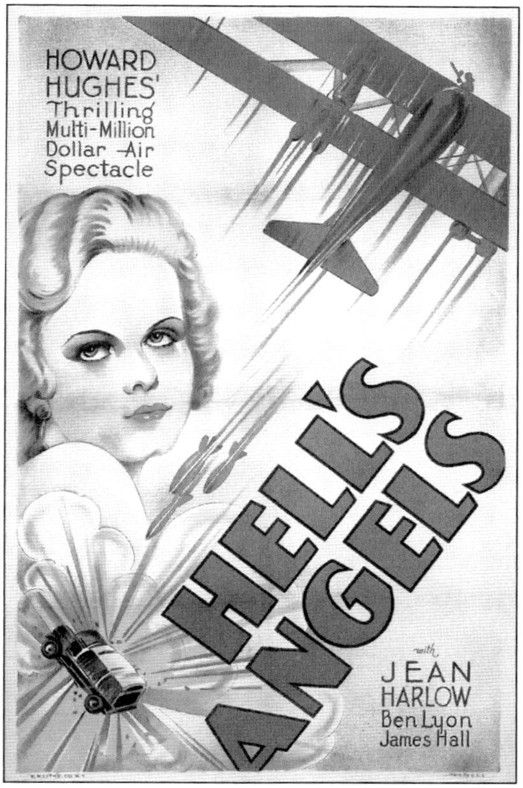

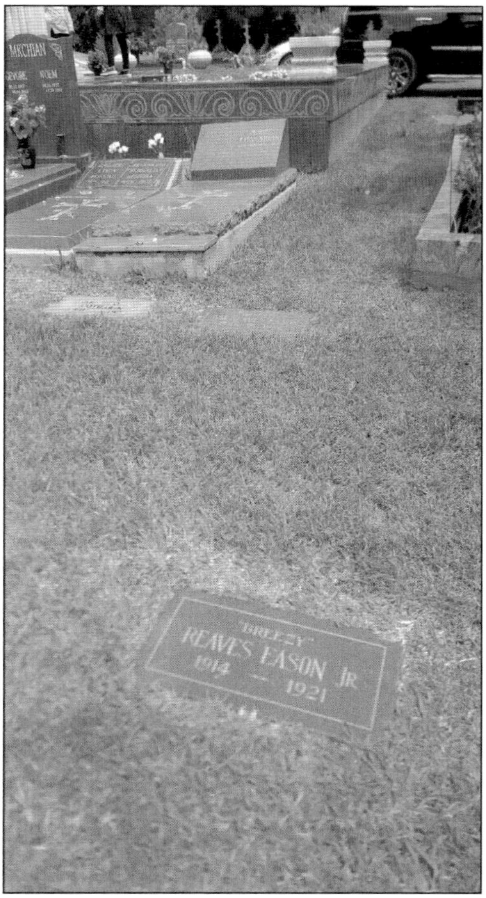

William Reaves Eason (1886–1956) and B. Reaves "Breezy" Eason Jr. (1914–1921). William Reaves Eason directed the burning of Atlanta scene for *Gone with the Wind* (1939). His son was child star Barnes Reeves "Breezy" Eason, who began his screen career when he was two. "Universal's Littlest Cowboy," as he was known, was tragically killed by a runaway truck when he was only six years old. He was one of the first actors interred in H4E. Breezy's grave is pictured here with his father's matching plaque above and to the left. (Lot 107.) (Photograph by E.J. Stephens.)

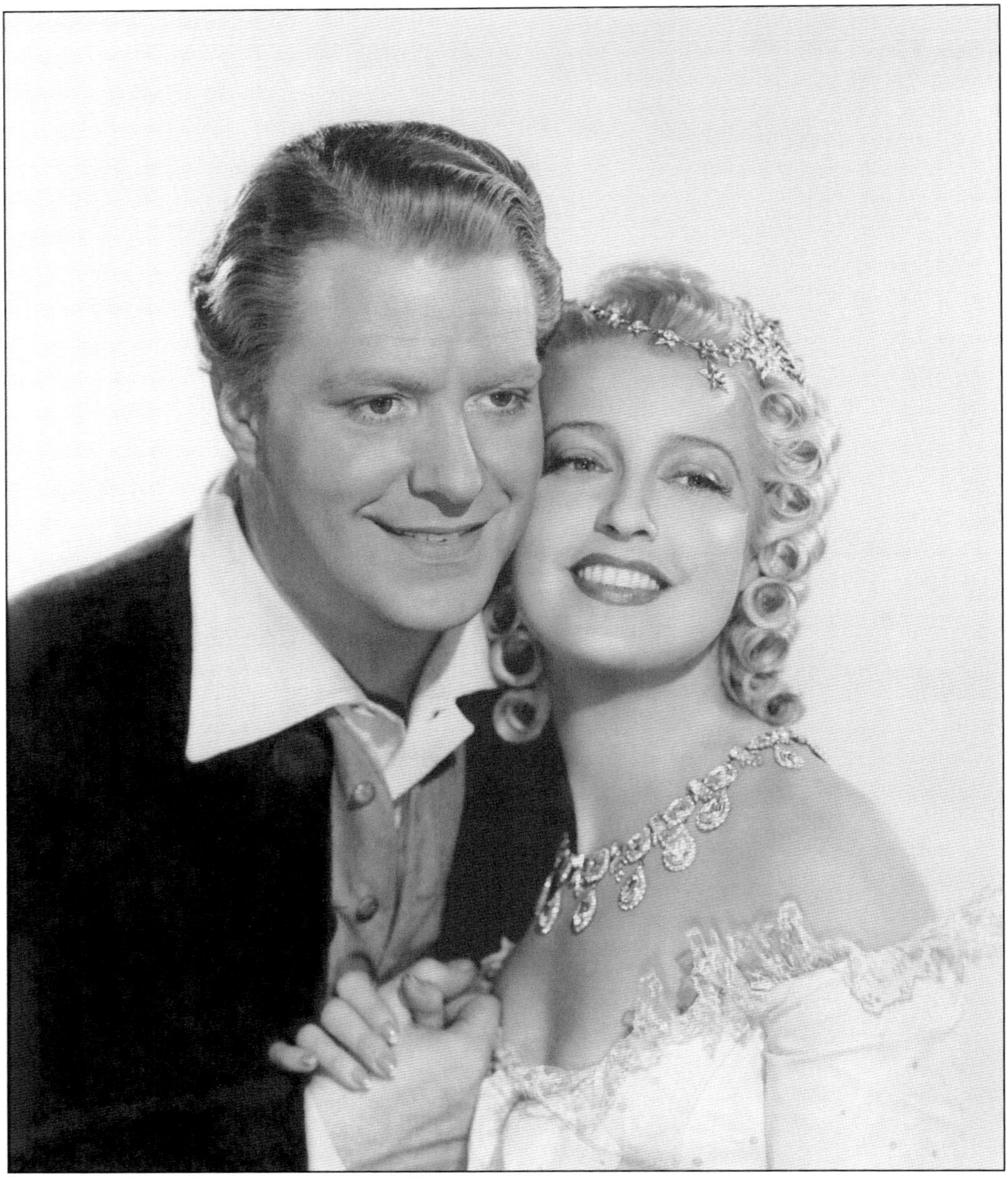

Nelson Eddy (1901–1967). Singing sensation Nelson Eddy had a 40-year career as a star of opera on stage and musicals on screen. He was born in Rhode Island and spent 10 years as a reporter in Philadelphia. He began his singing career in opera, first in Philadelphia and later in Europe. Eddy's film career began after a successful concert in Los Angeles brought him to the attention of talent scouts. He was paired with Jeannette MacDonald for the first time in 1935's *Naughty Marietta*. It proved to be a hit, and the couple went on to make seven more musicals for MGM. Eddy also performed in films with other leading ladies, like Eleanor Powell in *Rosalie* (1937). Between films, Eddy continued to record songs and perform in concert. He also appeared hundreds of times on radio, making him one of America's most popular singers. Eddy was singing on stage in a nightclub in Miami when he suffered a cerebral hemorrhage. He died a few hours later. He is buried here between his wife, Ann, and his mother Isabel. He is pictured here with Jeanette MacDonald in a scene from *New Moon* (1940). (Lot 89.)

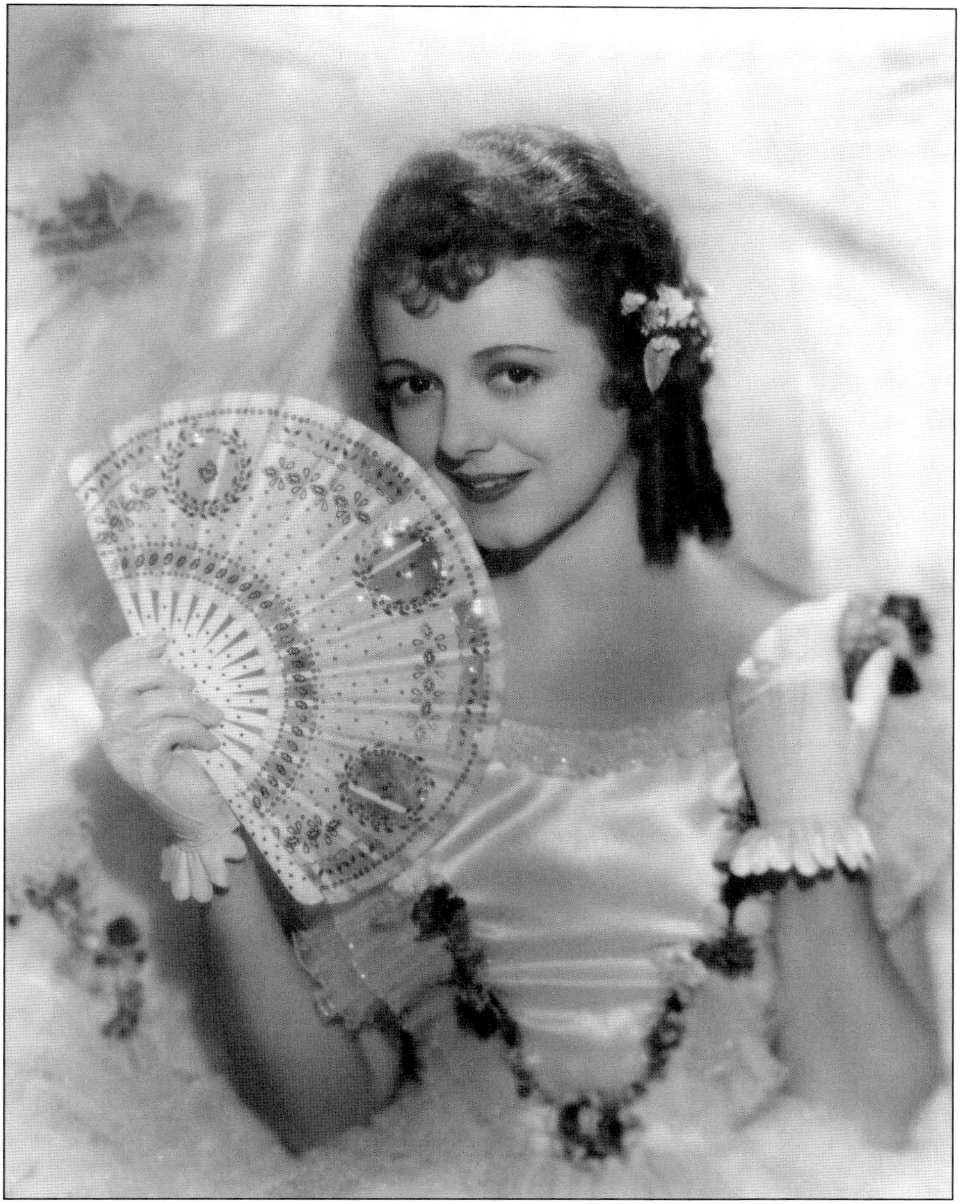

Janet Gaynor (1906–1984) and Adrian Gilbert (1903–1959). Standing only five feet tall, Janet Gaynor came to prominence at the end of the silent era, winning an Oscar in 1928 for three films. (In those days, actors were rewarded for their overall body of work for an entire year, rather than for a performance in a single film.) She successfully made the transition to talkies and was again nominated in 1937 for her performance in the original *A Star Is Born*. In 1982, Gaynor was riding in a taxi in San Francisco that was struck by a drunk driver. She never fully recovered from the crash, dying in September 1984. Gaynor is buried beside her second husband, the noted Hollywood fashion designer Adrian Gilbert, known to all simply as Adrian. During a career that spanned over 250 films in the 1930s and 1940s, Adrian worked with several of Hollywood's leading ladies, creating Joan Crawford's signature shoulder pads and Judy Garland's ruby red slippers for *The Wizard of Oz* (1939). He died suddenly at the age of 56 in September 1959. Gaynor died just one day past the 25th anniversary of the death of Adrian. (Lot 193.)

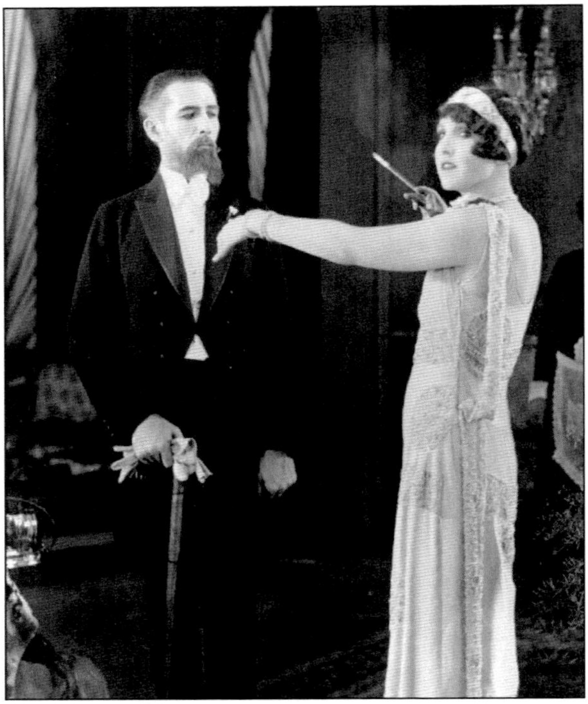

Carmelita Geraghty (1901–1966). Actress and artist Carmelita Geraghty had a 13-year career in film, bridging the silent and talkie eras. She appeared in *The Pleasure Garden* (1925), director Alfred Hitchcock's first film. She also had a role in the first big screen version of *The Great Gatsby* (1926). After retiring from acting, Geraghty had a successful career as an impressionist painter. She died from a heart attack at age 65. She is pictured here with Karl Falkenberg in a scene from *The Pleasure Garden*. (Lot 103.)

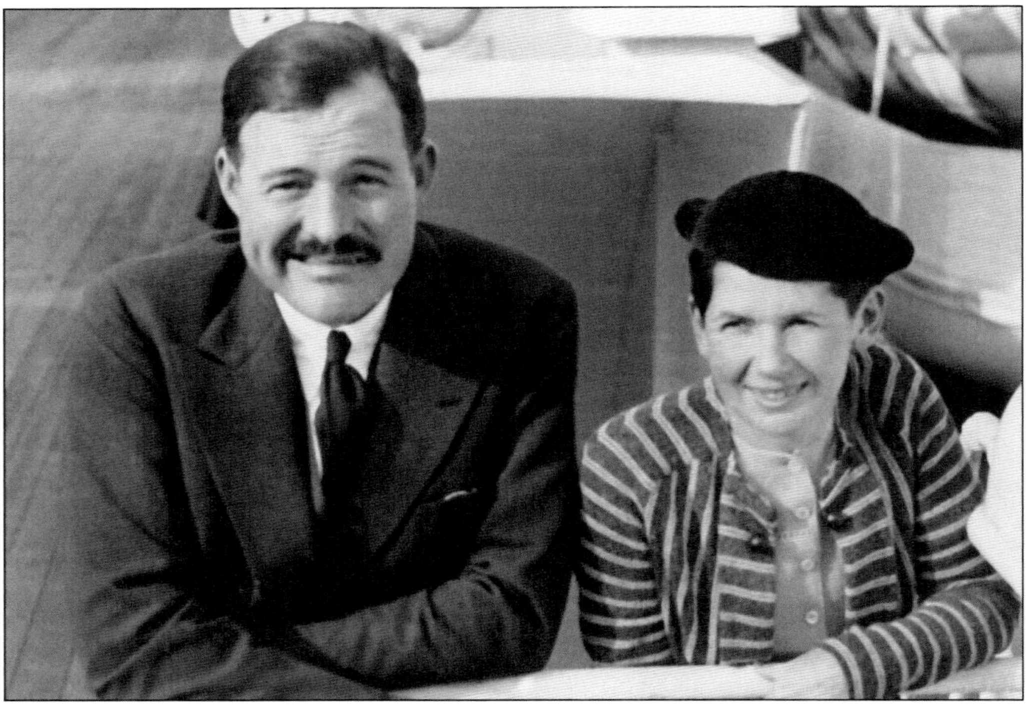

Pauline Pfeiffer Hemingway (1895–1951). Pfeiffer was an American journalist who crossed paths with author Ernest Hemingway in Paris in the mid-1920s. Hemingway, who was married at the time, had an affair with Pfeiffer, which led to his divorce and the couple's marriage. The Hemingways settled in Key West, Florida, where Pfeiffer continued to live after she divorced Hemingway in 1940. Pfeiffer's political and religious beliefs influenced Hemingway's novels. (Lot 12.)

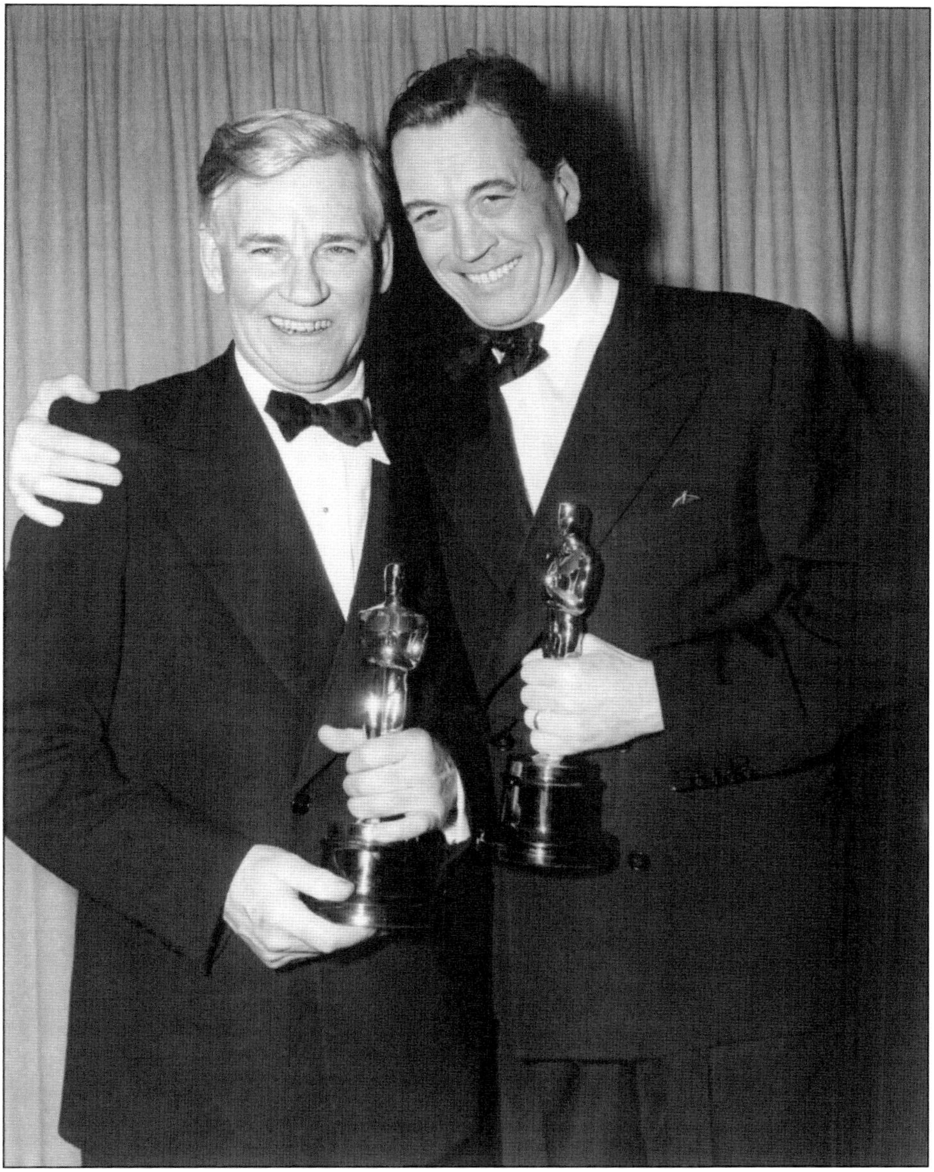

John Huston (1906–1987). It is hard to believe that Renaissance man John Huston lived only one lifetime. Among his directorial triumphs are *The Maltese Falcon* (1941), *The Treasure of the Sierra Madre* (1948), *Key Largo* (1948), *The Asphalt Jungle* (1950), *The African Queen* (1951), *Moby Dick* (1956), *The Misfits* (1961), *The Night of the Iguana* (1964), and *The Man Who Would Be King* (1975). He was nominated 15 times for Academy Awards, winning twice. He also directed both his father Walter and daughter Angelica to Oscar wins. Born in Missouri, Huston moved with his mother to Los Angeles after his parents divorced. He dropped out of school to be a boxer and then tried his hand at writing, finding success out of the gate. After penning a string of hit films for Warner Bros., he was awarded the directing duties for *The Maltese Falcon* (1941), one of Hollywood's finest achievements. Huston made films for the remainder of his life, often starring his friend Humphrey Bogart. He was also an accomplished actor, as was proven by his portrayal of Hollis Mulwray, the villain in the masterpiece *Chinatown* (1974). John and his father, Walter, are pictured here. (Lot 8, Space 21.)

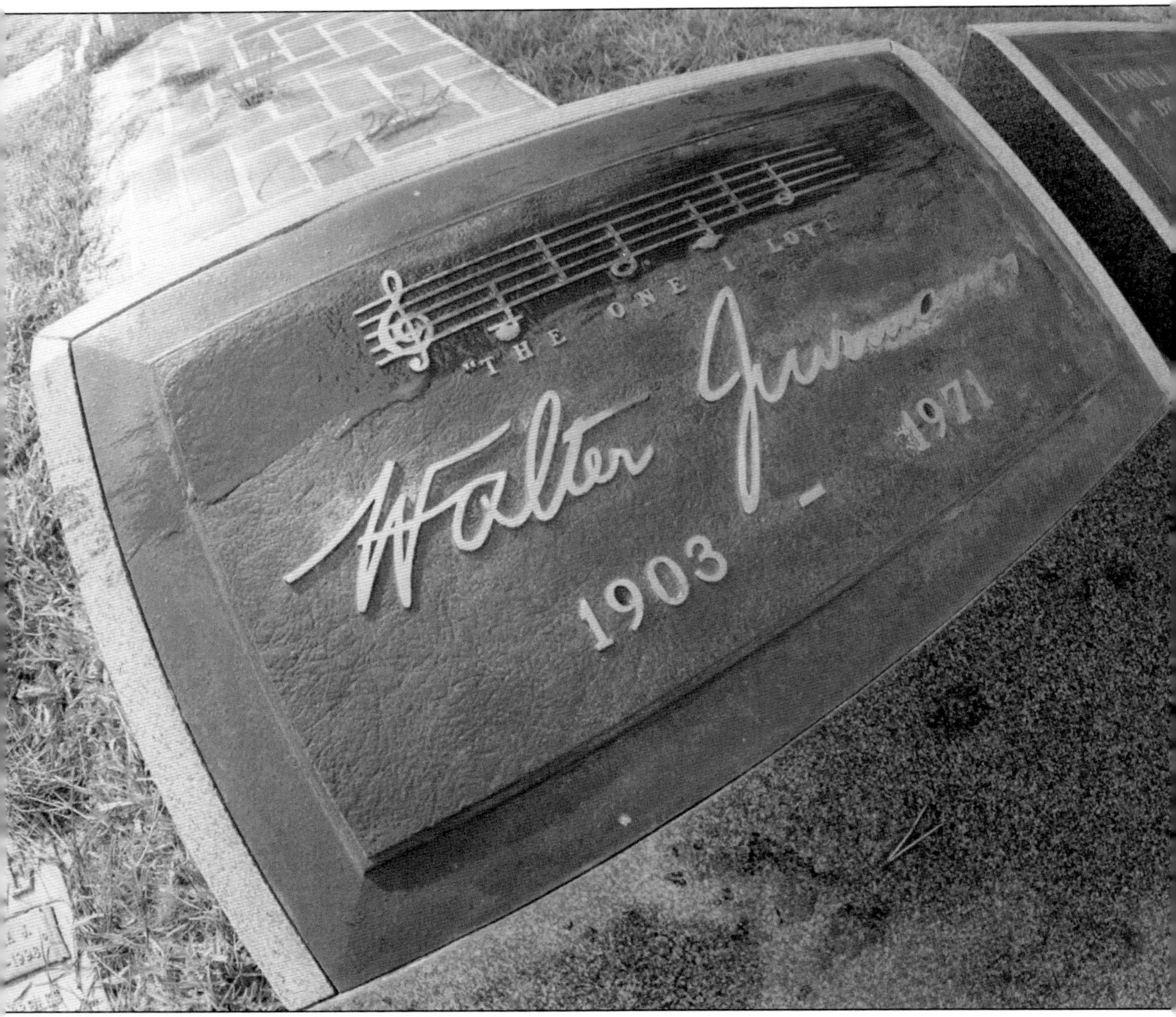

Walter Jurmann (1903–1971). Walter Jurmann was a Viennese composer who first made a name for himself writing catchy ditties in Berlin in the 1920s. He was forced to flee to Paris ahead of the Nazis in the early 1930s. There he met MGM head Louis B. Mayer, who offered Jurmann a seven-year contract in Hollywood. He came to America with his musical partner, and now H4E pal, Bronislaw Kaper. Once in Hollywood, Jurmann wrote music for such MGM hits as *Mutiny on the Bounty* (1935), *San Francisco* (1936), and the hilarious Marx Brothers classics *A Night at the Opera* (1935), and *A Day at the Races* (1937). Even after retiring from films, Jurmann continued writing catchy tunes for the rest of his life. (Lot 77, Space 5.) (Courtesy of Pentax Forums.)

Erich Wolfgang Korngold (1903–1971). Austrian composer Korngold is considered one of the true giants of film music. A child prodigy, Korngold wrote his first orchestral score when he was 14. Korngold came to America to score *The Adventures of Robin Hood* (1938), for which he won the Academy Award. While here, the Nazis invaded Austria, forcing Korngold, who was Jewish, to stay put. He continued scoring films for Warner Bros. until he retired from films to concentrate on composing concert hall music. Korngold died in North Hollywood at age 60. (Lot 15, Space 403.)

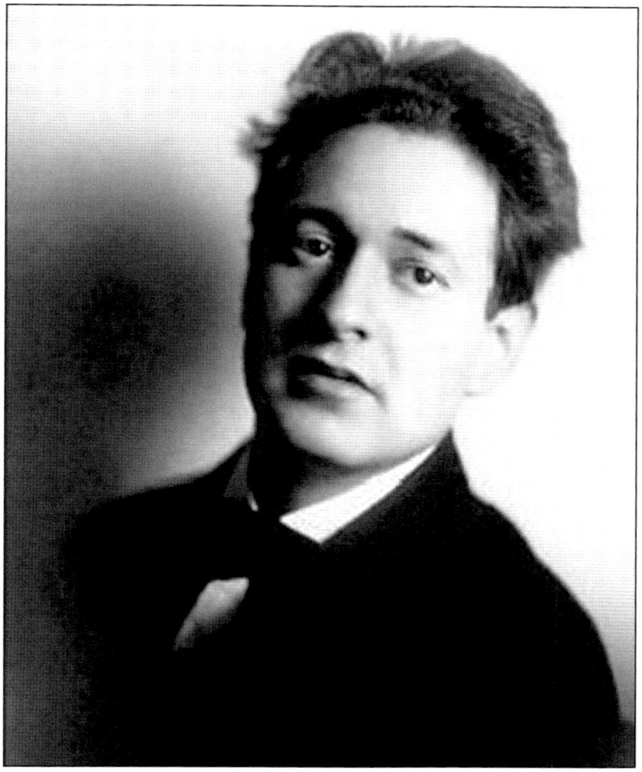

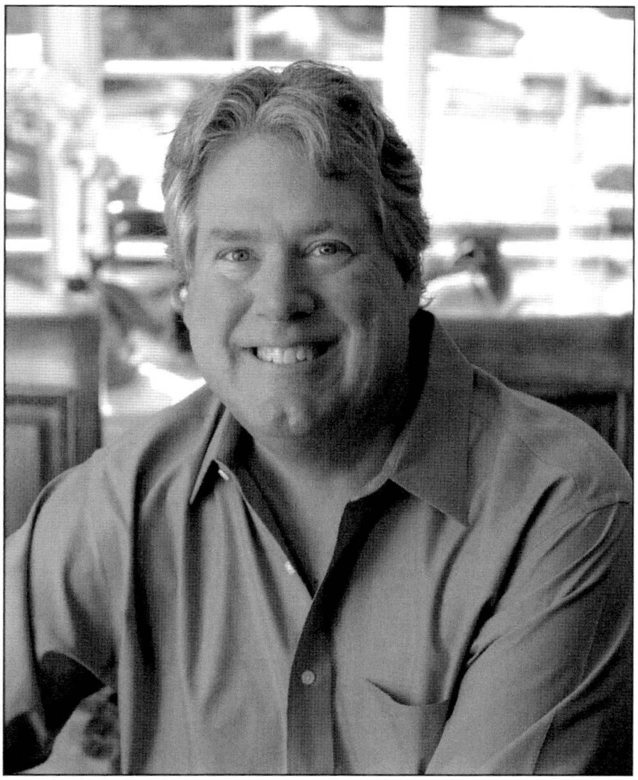

Jack Laird (1923–1991). Jack Laird was a major television writer/producer during the 1960s and 1970s. He produced the hit shows *Ben Casey*, Rod Serling's *Night Gallery*, and *Kojak*. Laird died from cancer at age 68. (Lot 218.)

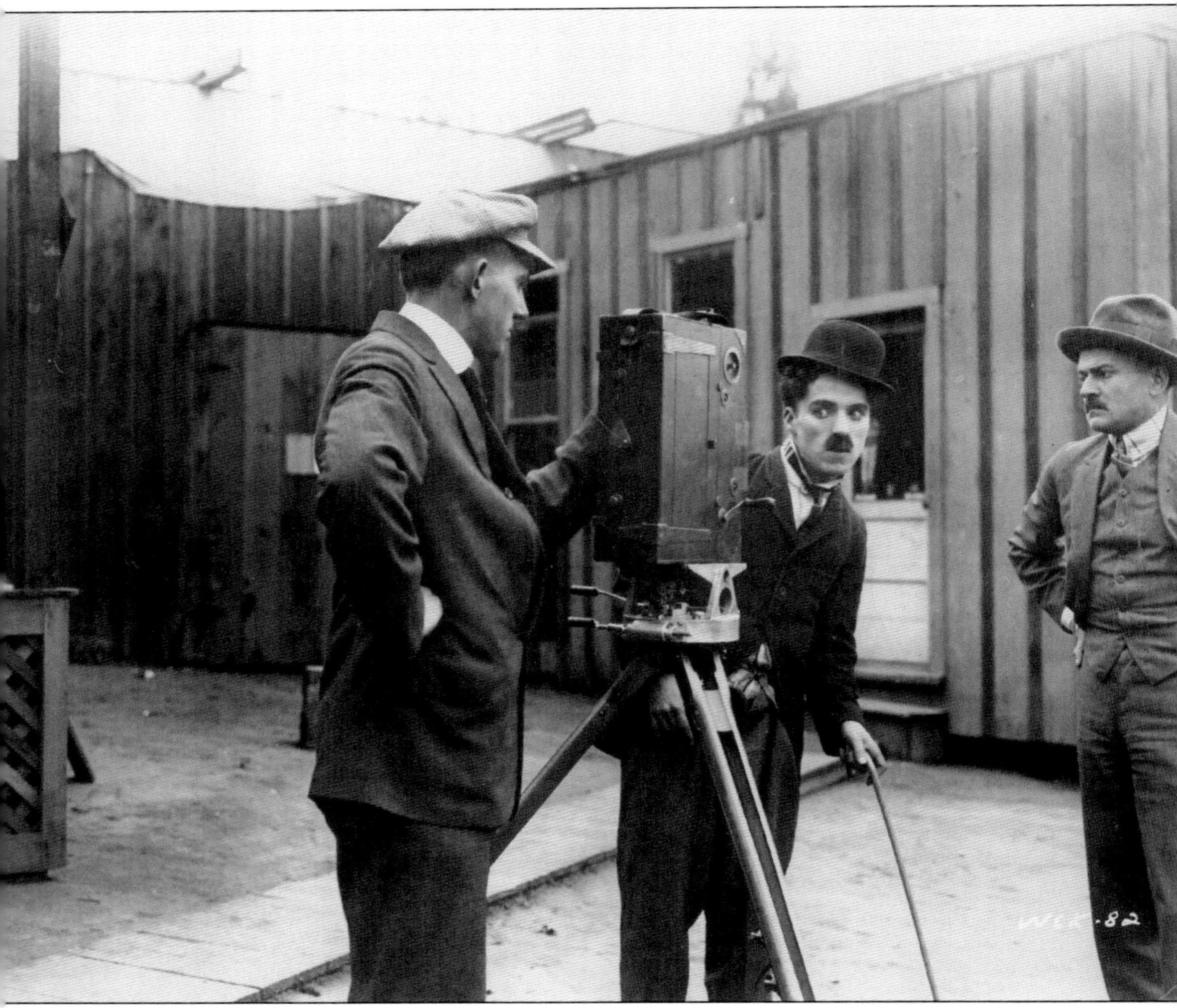

Henry Lehrman (1886–1946). Hollywood pioneer Henry "Pathe" Lehrman, pictured here at far right directing Charlie Chaplin, was seemingly everywhere in Hollywood during the 1910s. An immigrant from Vienna, Lehrman got his first job in motion pictures by claiming he was from Pathe studios in France. Whether his employers believed him or not is questionable, but he did land the job and earned the nickname Pathe. Lehrman acted for D.W. Griffith and then worked as an actor, screenwriter, and director for Mack Sennett at Keystone Studios. It was here in 1914 that Lehrman became the first director for an English newcomer named Charlie Chaplin. Lehrman later formed his own studio called the L-KO (Lehrman-Knock Out) Kompany in the heart of Hollywood's Poverty Row. Lehrman claimed to be engaged to Virginia Rappe (see page 106) at the time of her death and screamed the loudest for Fatty Arbuckle's head. Lehrman's career ended with the arrival of talkies. He died of a heart attack at the age of 60, twenty-five years after Rappe, who he now rests beside. (Lot 257.)

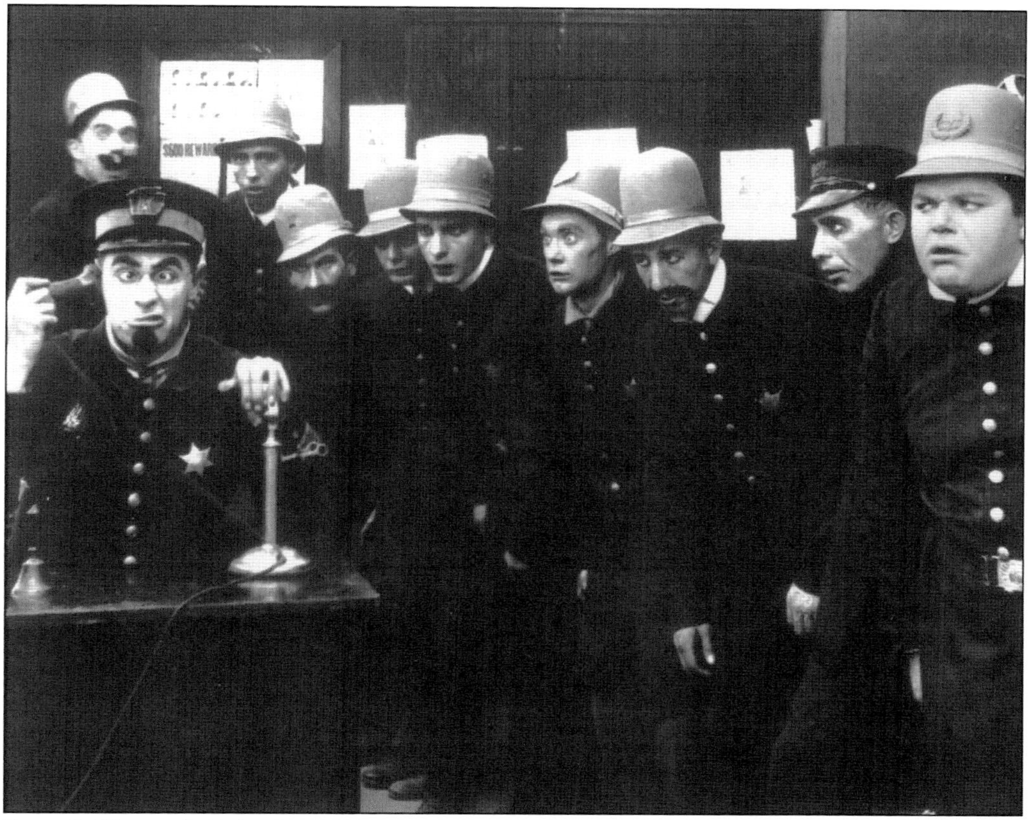

Eddie LeVeque (1896–1989). The last of the original Keystone Cops, Mexican-born Eddie LeVeque came to Los Angeles in 1914 and landed a job in D.W. Griffith's *Intolerance* (1916). Later, at Keystone, he became one of the manic "cops." LeVeque returned from fighting overseas in World War I to work with fellow H4E-ers Rudolph Valentino in *The Four Horsemen of the Apocalypse* (1921) and Douglas Fairbanks Sr. in *The Black Pirate* in 1926. (North of Lake.)

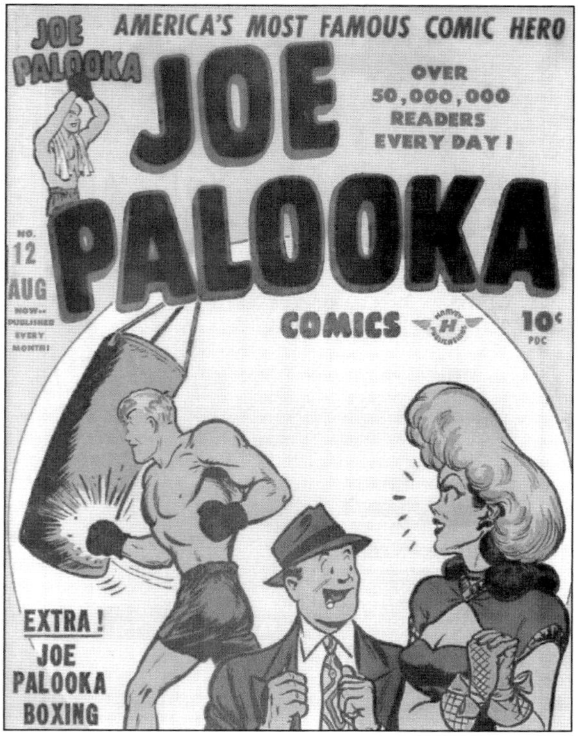

Edward Mann (1922–1995). Talented in many disciplines of stage production and filmmaking, Edward Mann began as a cartoonist in the 1940s for Andy Gump and Joe Palooka comics. He became a writer and director and cofounded the original Circle in the Square Theatre in New York. (North of Lake.)

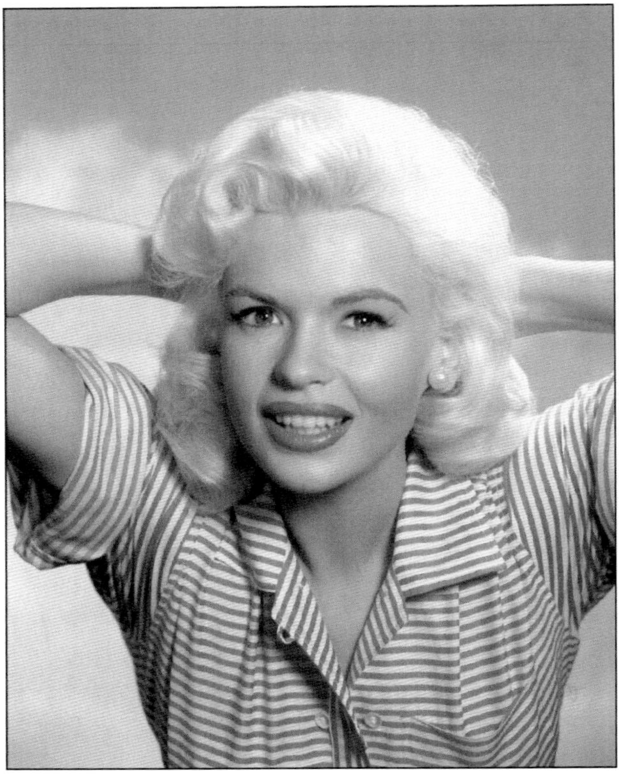

Jayne Mansfield (1933–1967). Blonde and busty, Jayne Mansfield had a steady career in the 1950s playing the quintessential dumb blonde, despite reportedly having an IQ of 160. Her popularity waned in the 1960s, but she still maintained a solid career as a nightclub performer. In June 1967, Mansfield was killed in an automobile accident and her body was buried in Pennsylvania. Her fans, who wanted a memorial for Mansfield in Hollywood, purchased a cenotaph here. Mansfield's daughter is actress Mariska Hargitay of *Law & Order: Special Victims Unit.* (Lot 218 [cenotaph].)

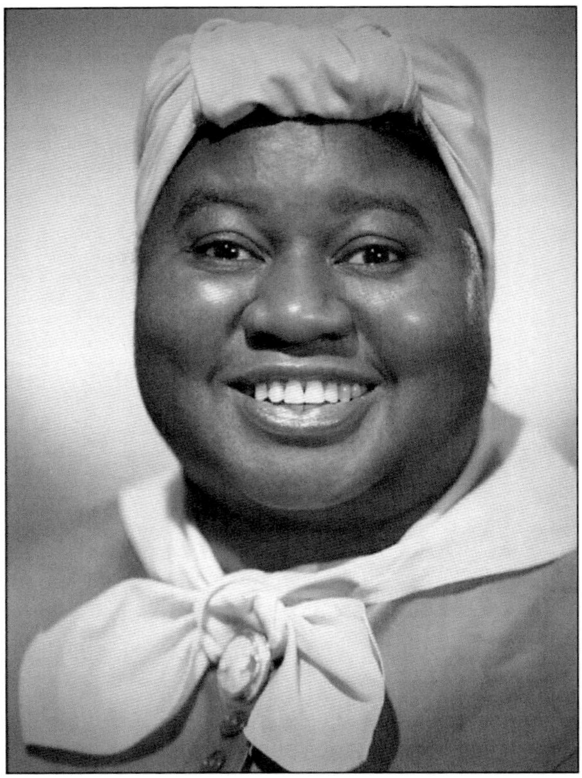

Hattie McDaniel (1895–1952). When Academy Award–winning African American actress Hattie McDaniel died of breast cancer in 1952, the owner of the Hollywood Memorial Park Cemetery at that time barred her burial here because of her race. After Tyler Cassity purchased the cemetery in 1998, he attempted to right an old wrong by offering to re-bury McDaniel at H4E free of charge. Her family chose not to disturb her remains, so instead, Cassity erected a cenotaph here in her honor. (Lot 306, Space 9 [cenotaph].)

ADOLPHE MENJOU (1890–1963) AND VEREE TEASDALE (1903–1987). Adolphe Menjou was one of the busiest actors in Hollywood during the 1920s and 1930s. He appeared in silent classics like *The Sheik* (1921) with H4E neighbor Rudolph Valentino, and was nominated for an Oscar for *The Front Page* 10 years later. His right-wing political views alienated him from many other members of the Hollywood film community. He is interred with actress Veree Teasdale, his wife of many years. (Lot 11, Space 14.)

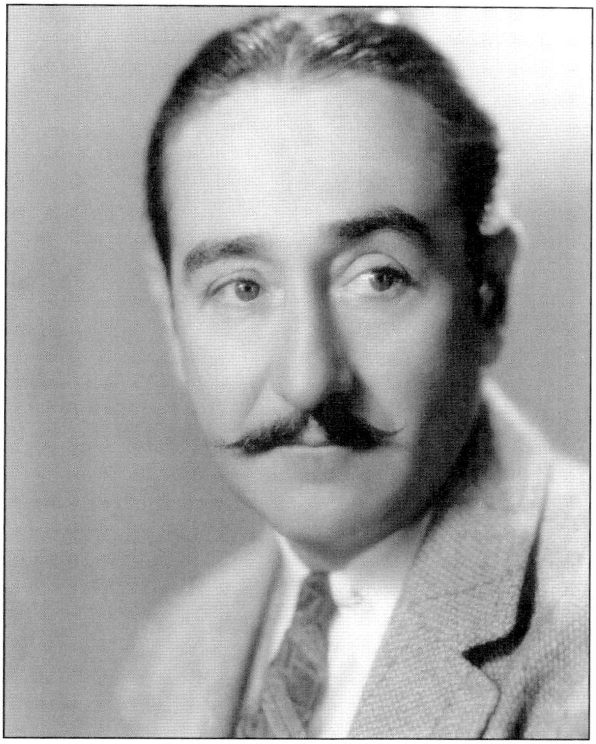

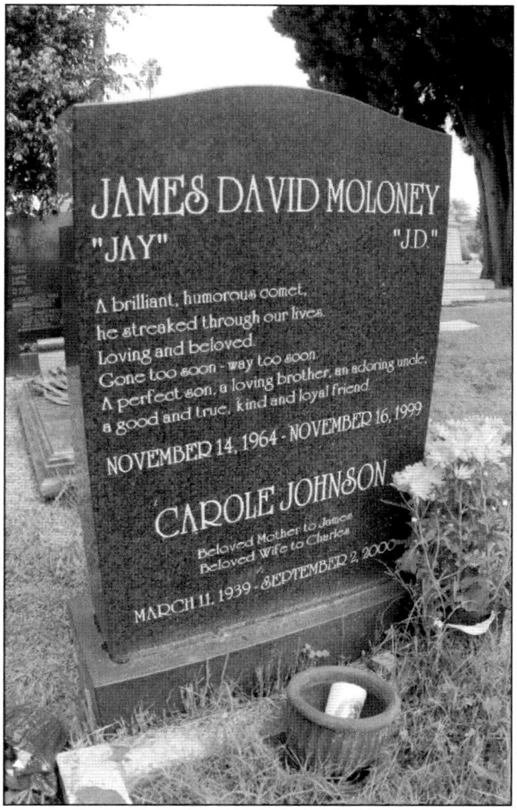

J.D. MOLONEY (1964–1999). Super-agent J.D. Moloney represented such A-listers as Uma Thurman, Leonardo DiCaprio, and Steven Spielberg during his short career. Drug dependency plagued him for several years. Moloney committed suicide by hanging himself in his home. (Lot 115.)

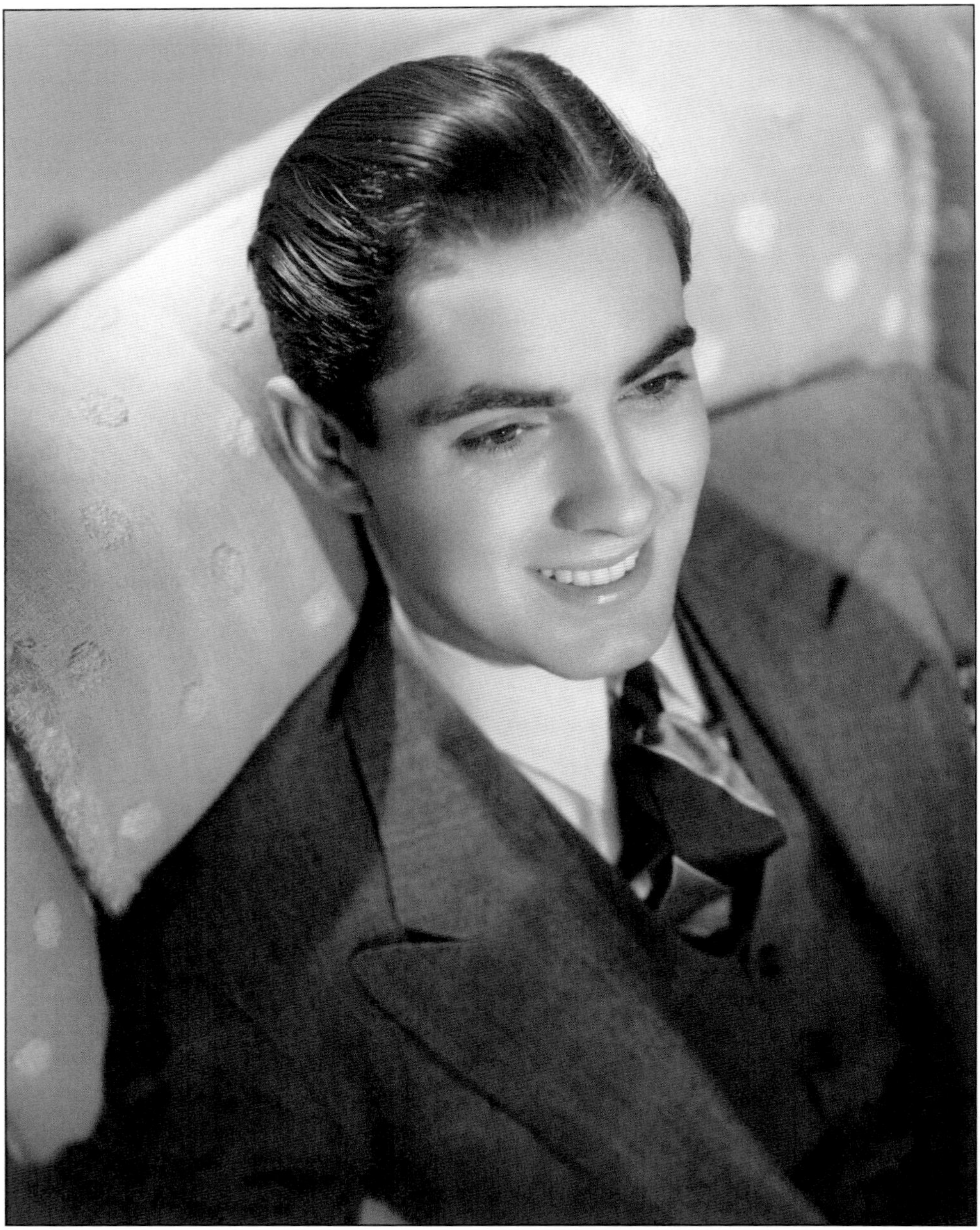

TYRONE POWER (1914–1958). One of Hollywood's most popular leading men, handsome Tyrone Power Jr. packed a lot of living into only 44 years of life. With matinee-idol good looks and enormous talent, Power got his big break in the lead role of *Lloyd's of London* (1936), which made him a star. As one of Fox's most popular actors, Power scored hit after hit, mostly in dramas and swashbucklers. He joined the Marines during World War II and served as a pilot during the Battles of Okinawa and Iwo Jima. After his release from the military, Power made *The Razor's Edge* (1946), opposite Gene Tierney. His final completed film was *Witness for the Prosecution* (1957). The following year, Power was filming a dueling scene in Spain for *Solomon and Sheba* when he suffered a major heart attack and died a few hours later. Nearly a decade after his death, Power was one of the personalities immortalized on the cover of the Beatles' *Sgt. Pepper's Lonely Hearts Club Band* album. (Lot 265.)

Dee Dee Ramone (1951–2002). Born Douglas Glenn Colvin, Dee Dee Ramone was the bass player for the seminal punk rock group the Ramones. He wrote many of the band's best-known songs and was originally the band's lead singer. Dee Dee died of a heroin overdose in 2002, just months after the band was inducted into the Rock & Roll Hall of Fame. His grave is only 100 yards from that of bandmate Johnny Ramone. (Lot 2003.)

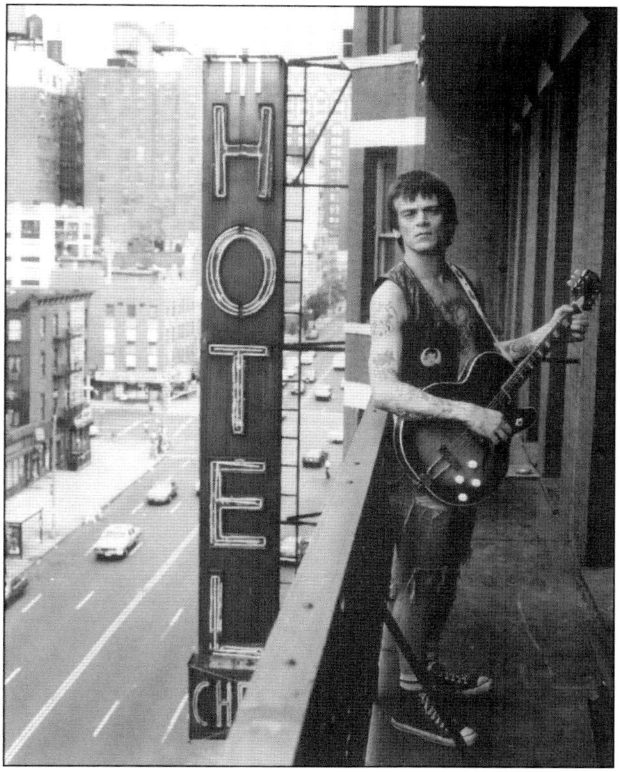

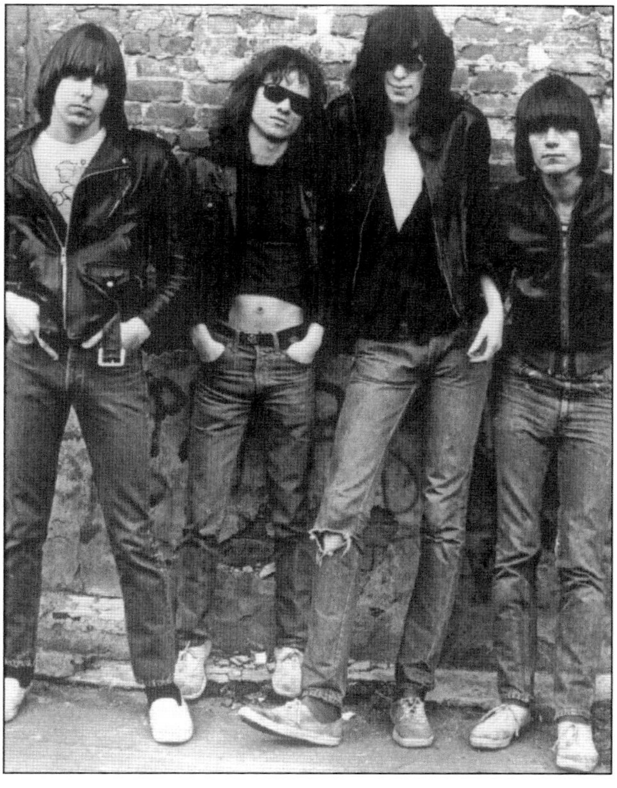

Johnny Ramone (1948–2004). The rarest of rockers, Johnny Ramone, pictured here on the far left, was born John Cummings in Queens and was a politically conservative NRA supporter. Choosing a career that lends itself to excess, Johnny also proved exceptional in that he was known as a "straight-edge punk," shunning the vices that would eventually kill bandmate and H4E neighbor Dee Dee Ramone. While never scoring a Top-40 hit, the Ramones were hugely influential, landing the faux brothers in the Rock & Roll Hall of Fame in 2002. (Lot 2067.)

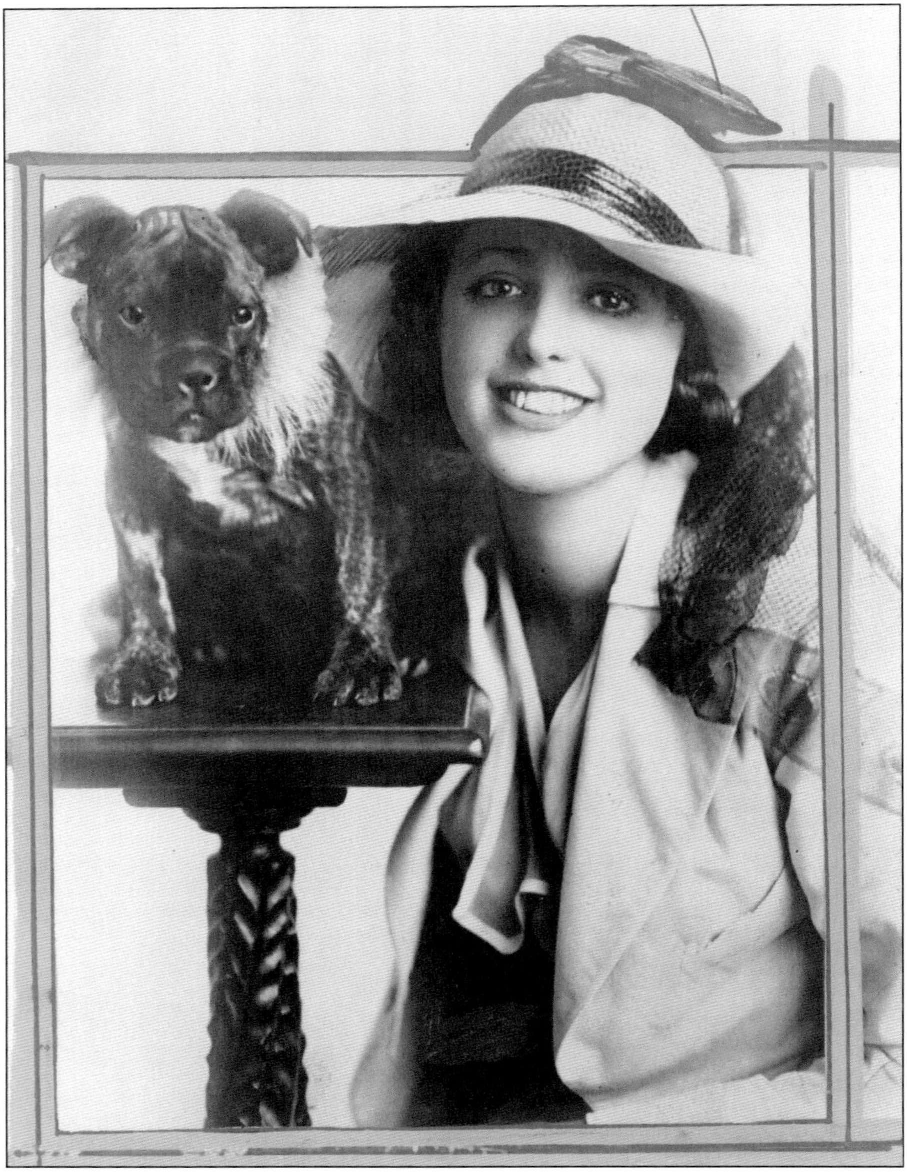

Virginia Rappe (1891–1921). Roscoe "Fatty" Arbuckle was one of the biggest comedians of the silent era, both literally and figuratively. As gregarious as he was rotund, Fatty liked to tip the bottle along with his Prohibition-ignoring friends, which is what he was doing on Labor Day weekend 1921 in San Francisco's St. Francis Hotel. Actress Virginia Rappe (pronounced rap-PAY) arrived at the party and sometime later took ill. Arbuckle called for a doctor, who led her to a separate room to sleep it off while the party continued. Arbuckle left money to cover Rappe's doctor's expenses and drove back to Los Angeles, believing that Rappe would recover. It was not to be. Three days later, she died from a ruptured bladder and peritonitis, and Arbuckle was arrested after Rappe's friend claimed that Virginia had been raped by Arbuckle. After three trials, Fatty was exonerated by the courts, but not with the movie viewers, and his career was over. As a result of this scandal and others, Hollywood was increasingly seen by the public as a place that could not police itself. Will Hays, the Harding administration's postmaster general, was brought in to be Tinseltown's "czar of morality." (Lot 257.)

Arthur Rosson (1886–1960), Hal Rosson (1895–1988), Richard Rosson (1893–1953), and Vera Sisson (1891–1954). The Rossons were a family of filmmaking siblings from New York. Arthur Rosson directed over 60 films over a 30-year career. Hal Rosson was an Academy Award–nominated cinematographer who filmed *The Wizard of Oz* (1939) and *Singin' in the Rain* (1952). He was married for a time to actress Jean Harlow (the couple are pictured seated at right). Brother Richard acted in nearly 100 films before becoming a director. He committed suicide when he was 60. Vera Sisson, Richard's wife, was a silent star who appeared in nearly 80 films. Born in Utah before it was a state, Sisson died from a barbiturate overdose when she was 63. (Lot 44.)

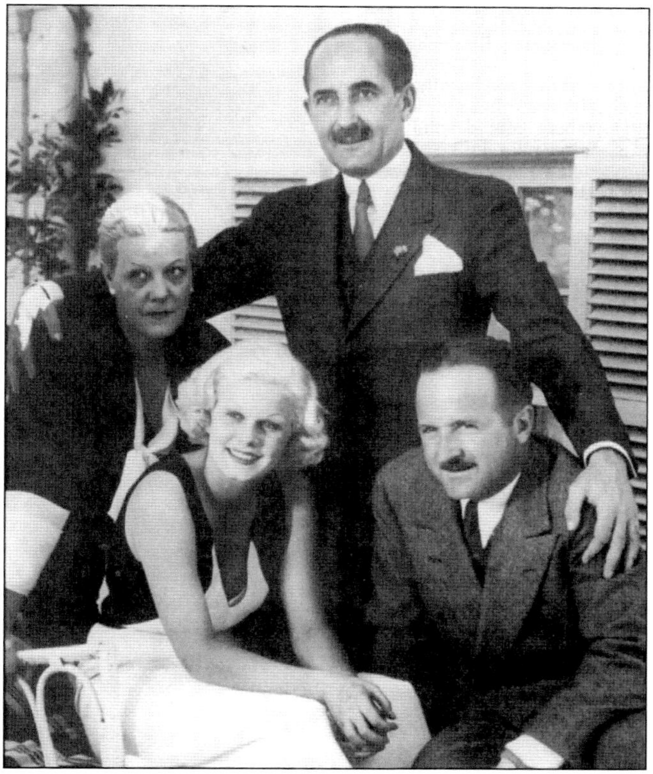

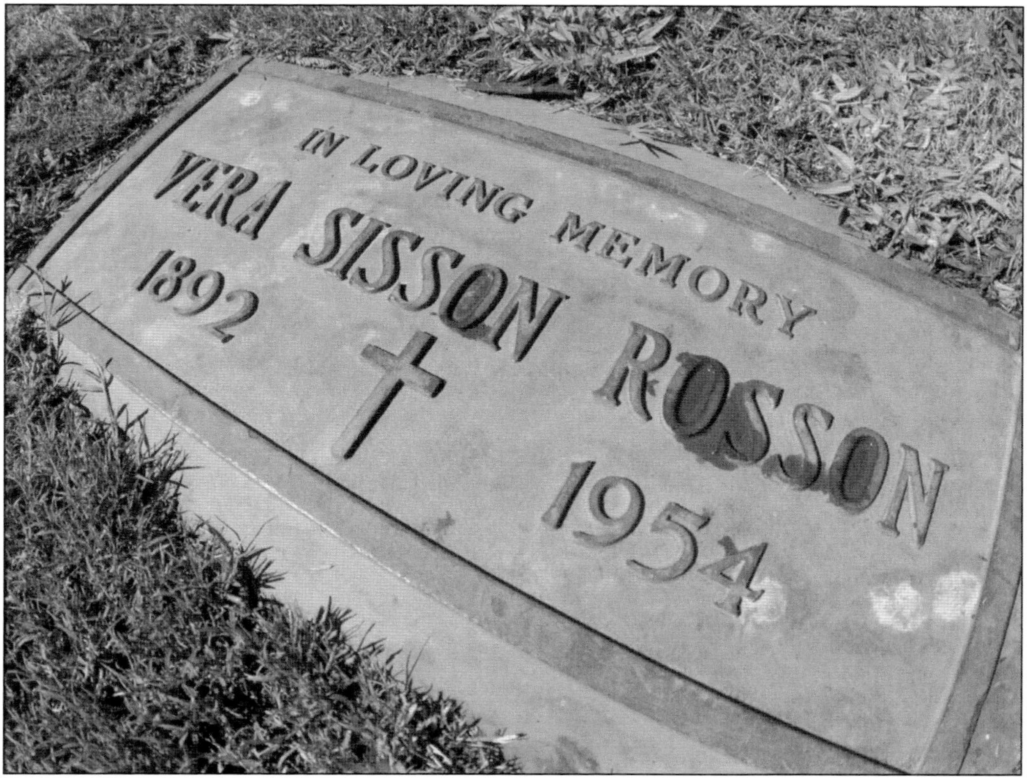

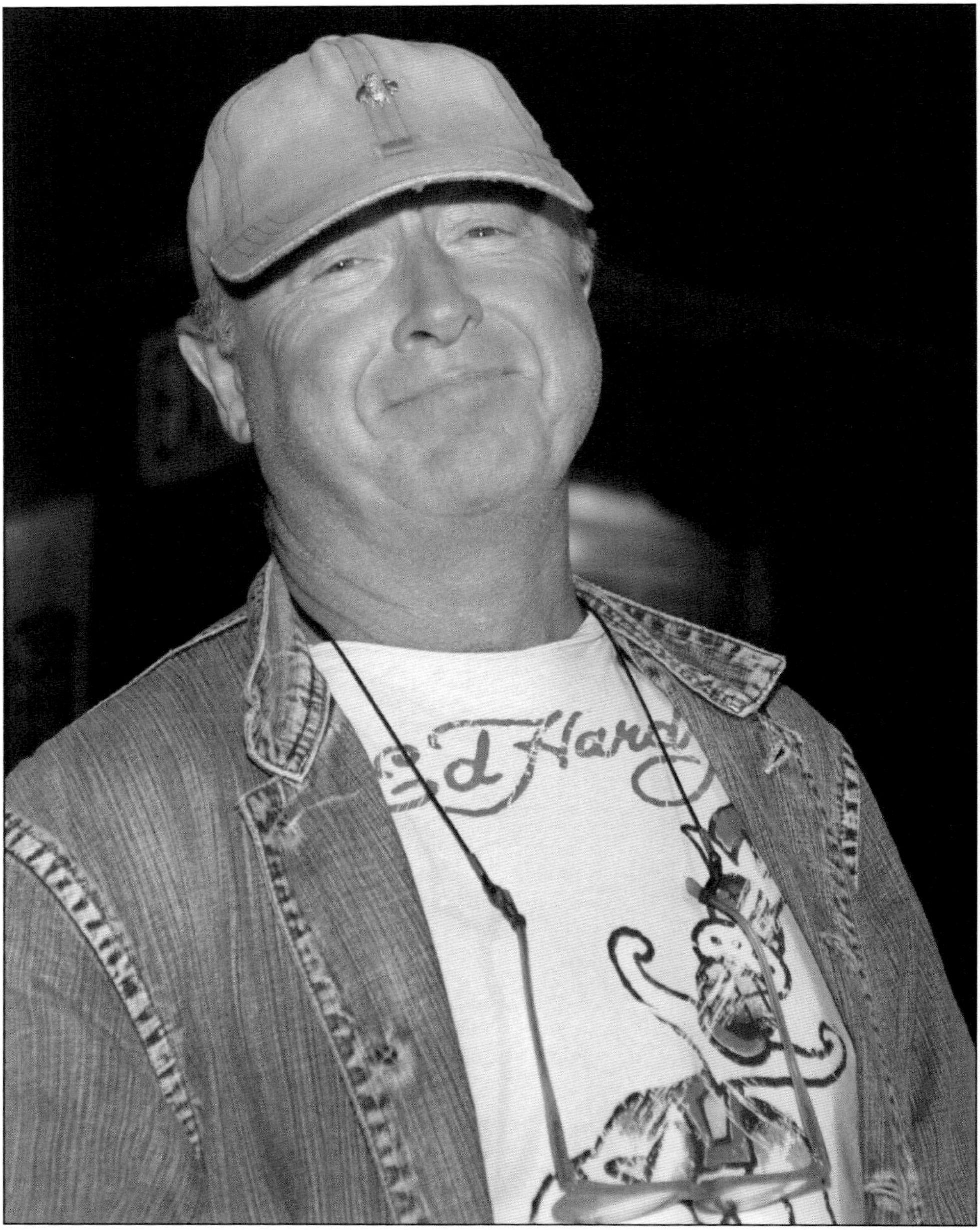

Tony Scott (1944–2012). The film world was shocked and saddened by the suicide of English film director and producer Tony Scott in August 2012. Tony, the younger brother of director Ridley Scott, helmed hugely successful action films including *Top Gun* (1986), *Beverly Hills Cop II* (1987), *Days of Thunder* (1990), *Crimson Tide* (1995), *Enemy of the State* (1998), *The Taking of Pelham 123* (2009), and *Unstoppable* (2010). He also coproduced *Numb3rs* for television with his brother. One of the era's most influential directors, as well as one of the least loved by critics, Tony began his career working with his brother making commercials. He was able to bring techniques he employed in commercials into his action films, initially for Don Simpson and Jerry Bruckheimer. Tony, who may have had cancer, jumped to his death from the Vincent Thomas Bridge in Long Beach. A gathering of Hollywood luminaries, many who he helped to put on the A-list, turned out for his funeral. (South of Lake, near the McDaniel Cenotaph.)

"Nanny" Mae Eudora White (1885–1967). Anyone who ever saw *The Carol Burnett Show* during its long run remembers how Burnett would tug her left ear at the closing of each show. This gesture was a show of love to her grandmother "Nanny" Mae White, who rescued young Carol from her alcoholic parents and raised her in an impoverished Hollywood neighborhood. Even after White died during the run of the show, Burnett continued the practice. (Lot 78, Grave 8.)

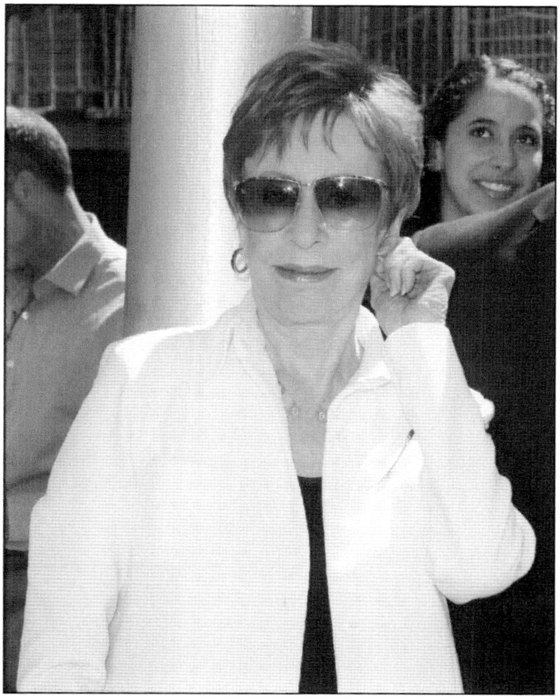

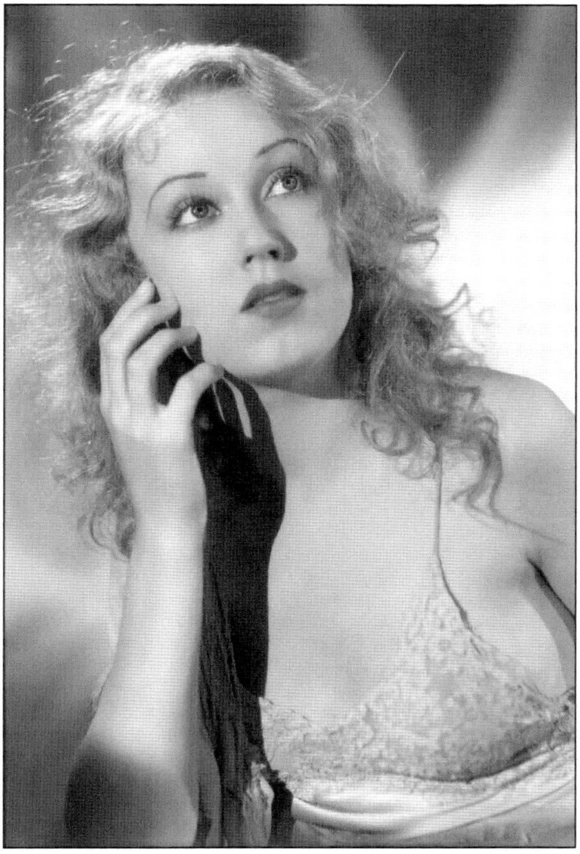

Fay Wray (1907–2004). Fay Wray, the heroine of 1933's classic *King Kong*, was born in Alberta, Canada, to Mormon parents. When she was 14, her family moved to Hollywood where she landed a major role in *The Coast Patrol* (1925) while still in her teens. Wray secured her first lead role in 1928 in Erich Von Stroheim's *The Wedding March*. After talkies emerged, she had her most memorable role at RKO in 1933's *King Kong*, where she became one of cinema's first scream queens. While she was shooting *King Kong* during the day, she was busy filming another movie on the same sets at night. The success of *King Kong* reportedly saved RKO from bankruptcy. Wray passed away at the age of 96, shortly before she was to make a cameo appearance in Peter Jackson's remake of *King Kong*. (Lot 2300, Space 7.)

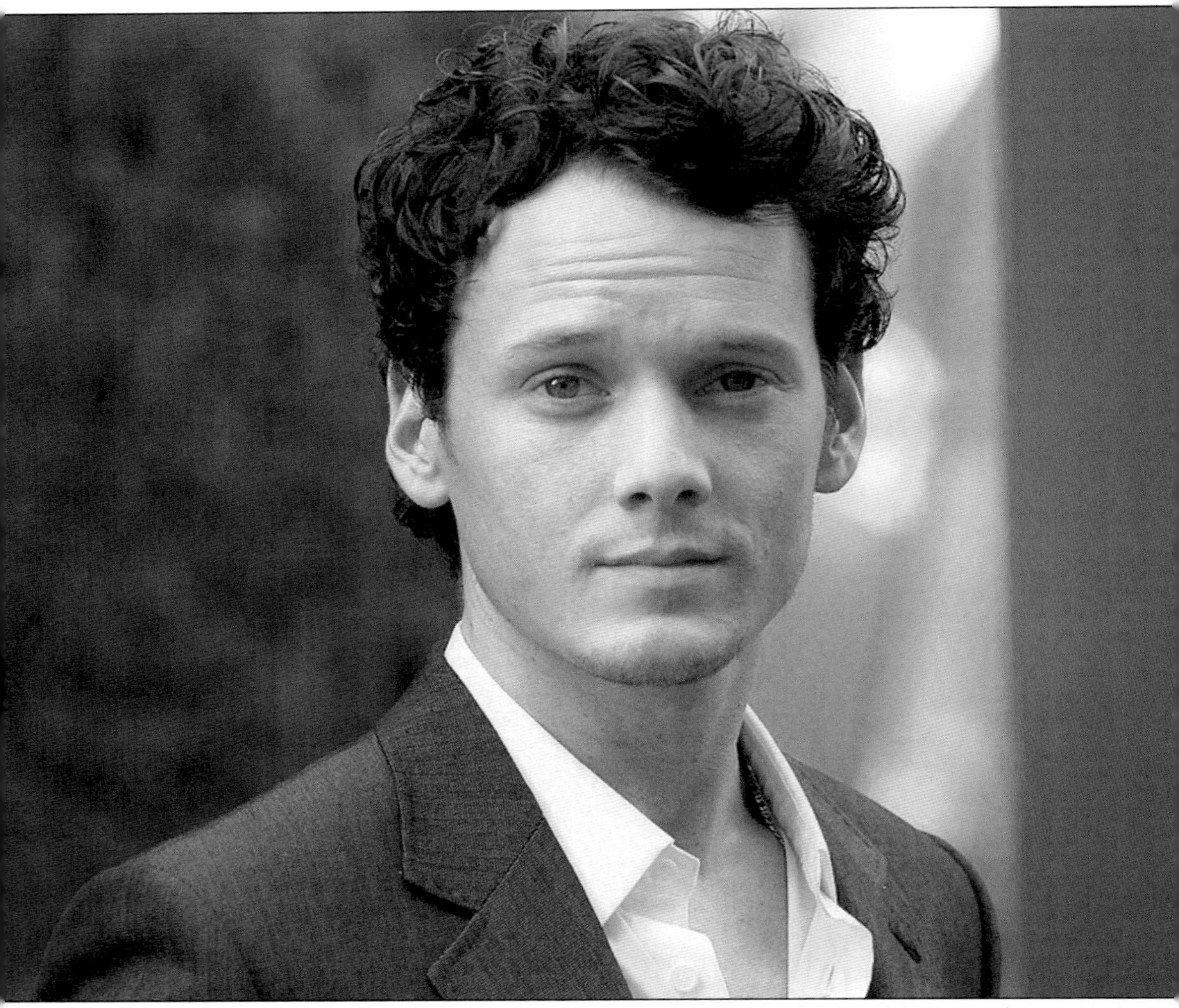

Anton Yelchin (1989–2016). One of the most tragic celebrity deaths of the many during 2016 was that of young actor Anton Yelchin, who died in a freak automobile accident in Studio City, California. Yelchin was well on his way to stardom thanks to his breakout role as Ensign Pavel Chekov in the rebooted *Star Trek* film series. Chekov's Russian accent came naturally to Yelchin, who was born in St. Petersburg, Russia, to parents who were professional figure skaters. His family moved to Southern California while he was an infant. Yelchin made his acting debut at the age of nine. His final film, *Thoroughbred*, wrapped just two weeks before his death. (Lot 8485.)

Six

Cathedral Mausoleum

The Cathedral Mausoleum is so associated with its most famous resident, Rudolph Valentino, that many taphophiles refer to it as the "Valentino Mausoleum." It's understandable, because Valentino is probably the most famous person in Hollywood Forever, which is interesting considering that the vast majority of people living today have never seen a Valentino film.

Valentino's crypt is in an alcove at the end of a corridor at the mausoleum's southeast corner. He is entombed next to his friend June Mathis, in what was supposed to be a temporary crypt. It turned out that Valentino was broke at the time of his death, and his estate could not afford a better location, so he has been housed in this "temporary" crypt now for 90 years.

The Cathedral Mausoleum has lots of other famous people as well, like actor Peter Finch, who won an Academy Award for Best Actor posthumously. Peter Lorre is here, and so is one of his wives, actress Cilia Lovsky, who once played the leader of Vulcan on *Star Trek*. Dancer extraordinaire Eleanor Powell's cremains are behind glass in the main vestibule.

There is a bust of David White here. He gained fame in the 1960s in the role of Larry Tate on *Bewitched*. Actress Barbara La Marr, a victim of the flapper era, is here too. She was known as "The Girl Who Was Too Beautiful" during her brief life. Theresa Dorris's crypt is in the mausoleum. The mother of actors Wesley and Charles Ruggles, she was shot and killed in an apparent murder-suicide.

Speaking of murder, William Desmond Taylor, the victim of one of Hollywood's greatest unsolved crimes, is interred here under his real name, William Deane-Tanner, which he jettisoned after he abandoned his wife and daughter.

Conman Jules Roth, who owned the cemetery for 60 years, is here. So are Daeida and Harvey Wilcox, the founders of Hollywood. The town they initially created did not allow alcohol or film people inside the city limits. With the way things turned out in Hollywood, visitors may want to listen for the sound of spinning bodies coming from inside their crypts

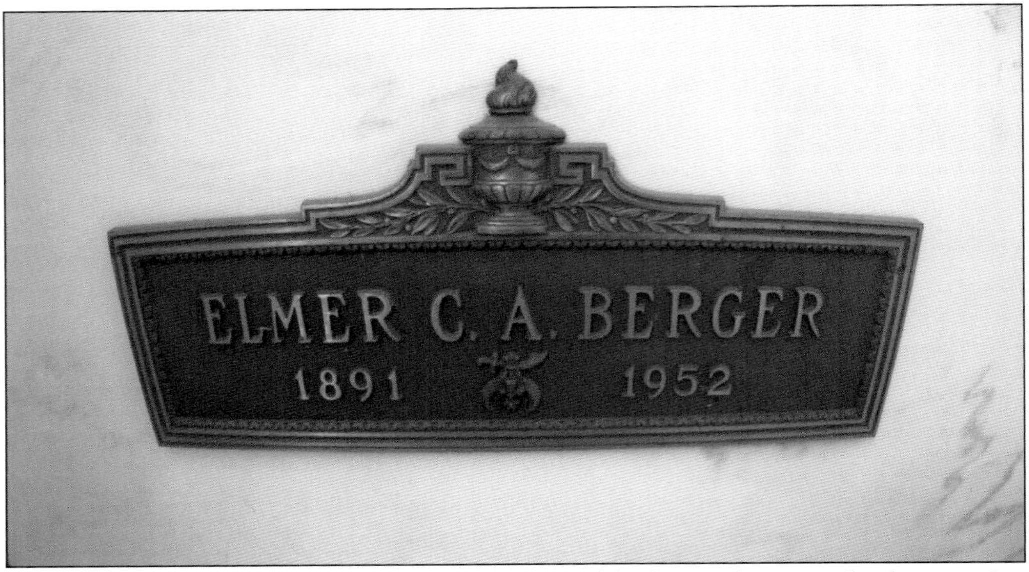

Elmer Berger (1891–1952). Every time someone safely changes lanes on the freeway after using their indicator, they can thank Elmer Berger, the inventor of the turn signal. He called his invention the "Cop-Spotter." (Cathedral Mausoleum, Corridor A, Crypt 1405.)

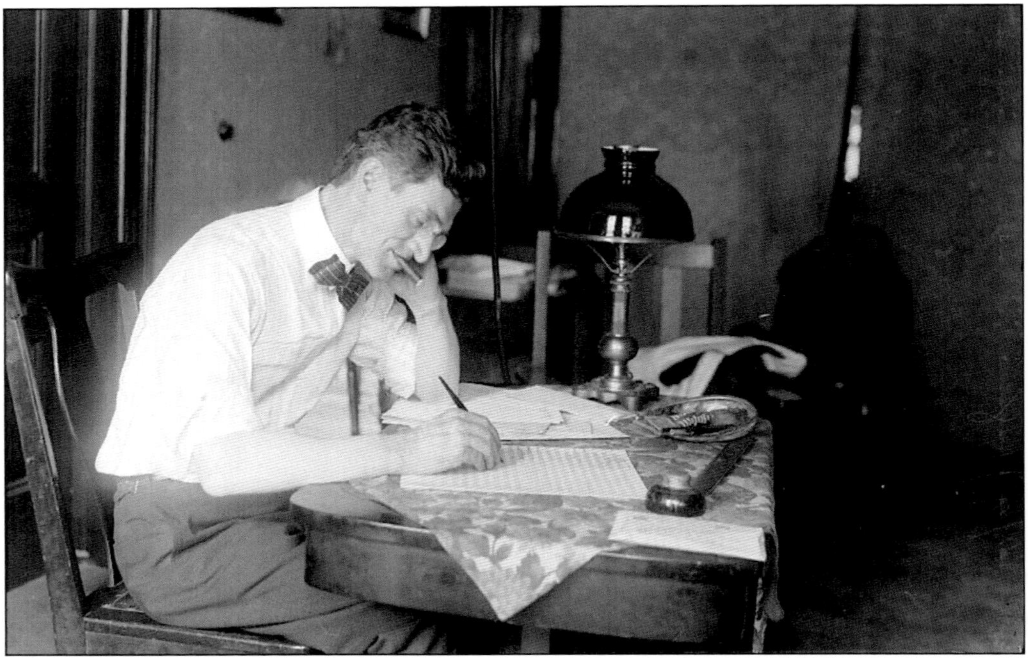

Joseph Carl Breil (1870–1926). Self-taught American composer Joseph Carl Breil was the first to show Hollywood that through the use of an orchestra playing classical music interspersed with original compositions, film music could be elevated to the same level of importance as the pictures on the screen. Breil composed the scores for D.W. Griffith's twin epics *The Birth of a Nation* (1915) and *Intolerance* (1916), which gave legitimacy to the entire art form. (Cathedral Mausoleum, Alcove of Reverence, Tier 10, Niche 7.)

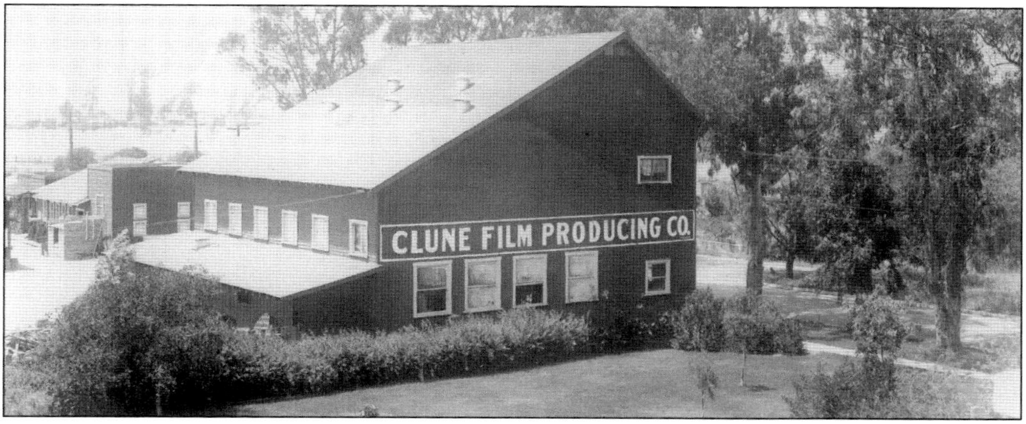

William H. Clune (1862–1927). William Clune owned a chain of theaters around Los Angeles before buying his own studio in Hollywood. Known today as Raleigh Studios, Clune made two pictures here before leasing the studio out to independent producers. Over the years, companies such as the Paralta Corp., Douglas Fairbanks Productions, United Artists, Paramount, Tec-Art, Prudential, Sherman, Schulberg, California, and Producers Studio have hung out a shingle on Clune's old lot. (Cathedral Mausoleum, Crypt 994.)

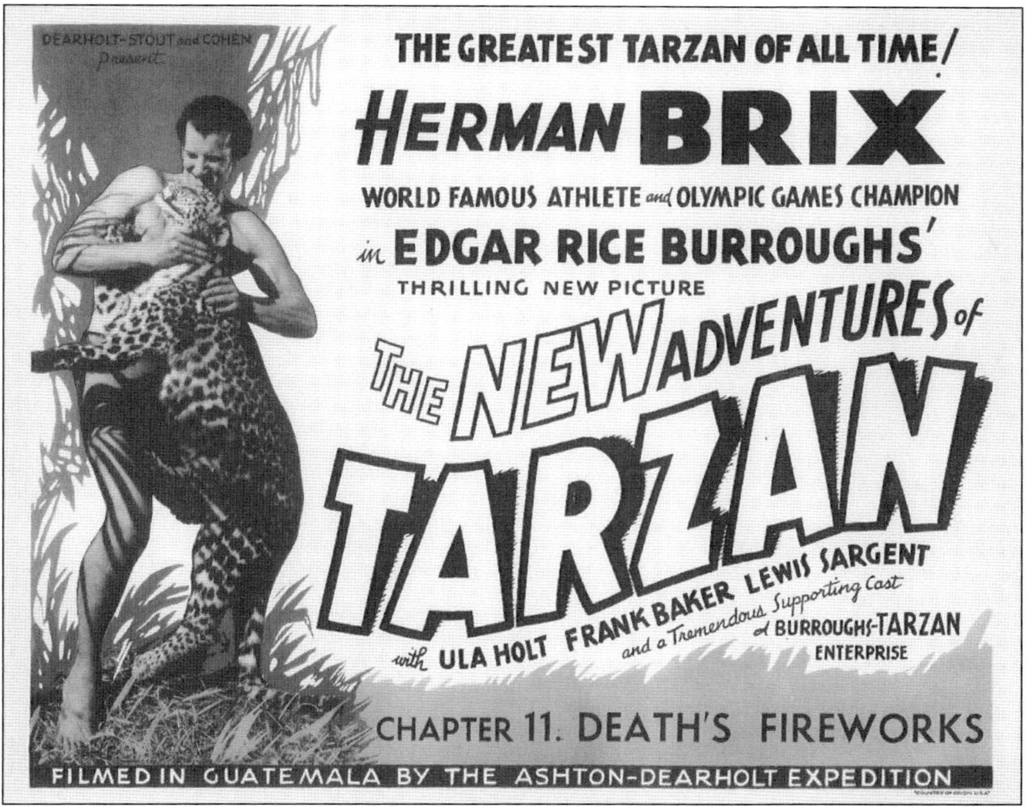

Ashton Dearholt (1894–1942). Silent film actor Ashton Dearholt appeared in 75 films during the silent and early talkie eras. In 1934, he went into partnership with Tarzan creator Edgar Rice Burroughs to make Tarzan movies. During the making of *The New Adventures of Tarzan* (1935) in Guatemala, Dearholt left his wife, Florence Gilbert, who then married Burroughs. (Cathedral Mausoleum, Foyer, East Wall, Tier 7, Niche 8.)

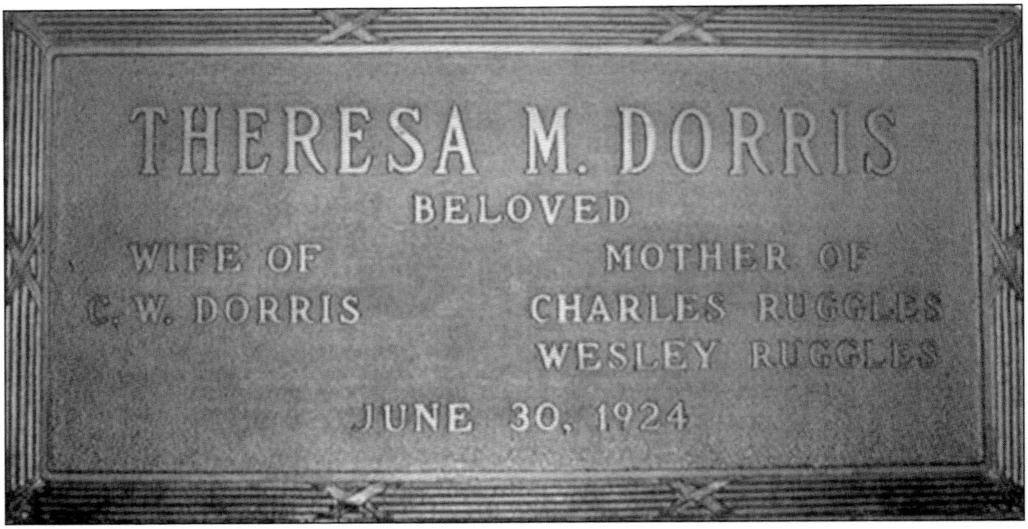

THERESA DORRIS (1875–1924). Theresa Dorris was the mother of actors Charles and Wesley Ruggles. Dorris and Henry D. Meyer, a Pasadena millionaire, were shot and killed in her Los Angeles apartment. Dorris's husband Charles (who is now interred beneath her) was tried for the crime and acquitted. Some speculated at the time that the crime was actually a murder-suicide carried out by Meyer. (Cathedral Mausoleum, Crypt G-4.)

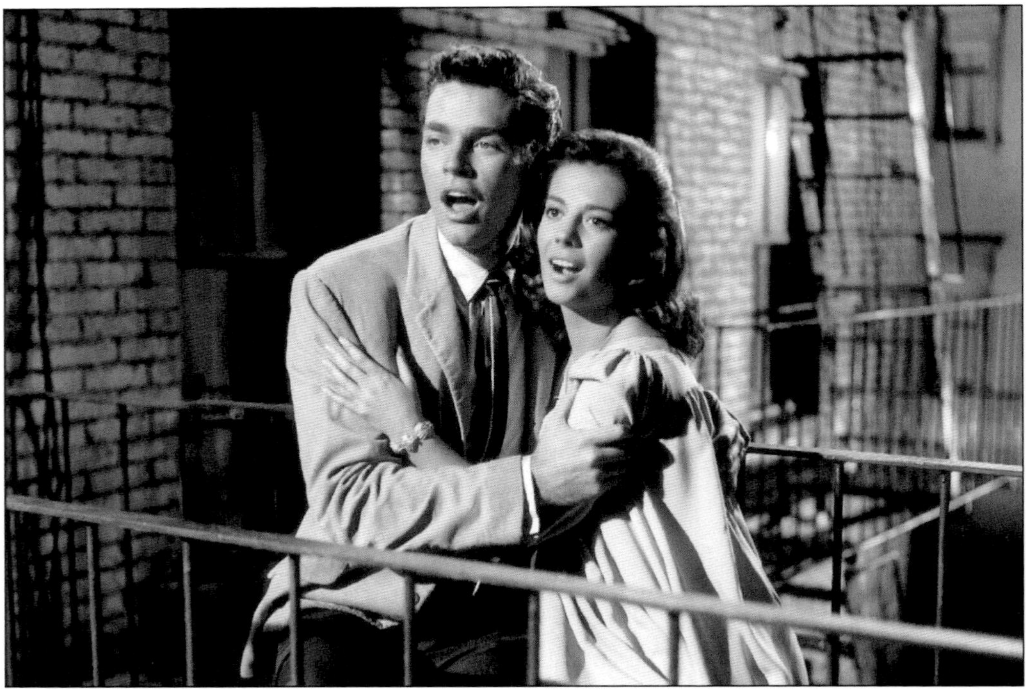

DANIEL FAPP (1904–1986). Daniel Fapp was an Academy Award–winning cinematographer who won an Oscar for *West Side Story* in 1962. A year later, Fapp shot the war film *The Great Escape*, which starred Steve McQueen. He was nominated seven times for Oscars during his career. He is interred in an outside crypt behind the mausoleum. George Chakiris and Natalie Wood are pictured in a scene from *West Side Story*. (Court of the Apostles, Unit 9.)

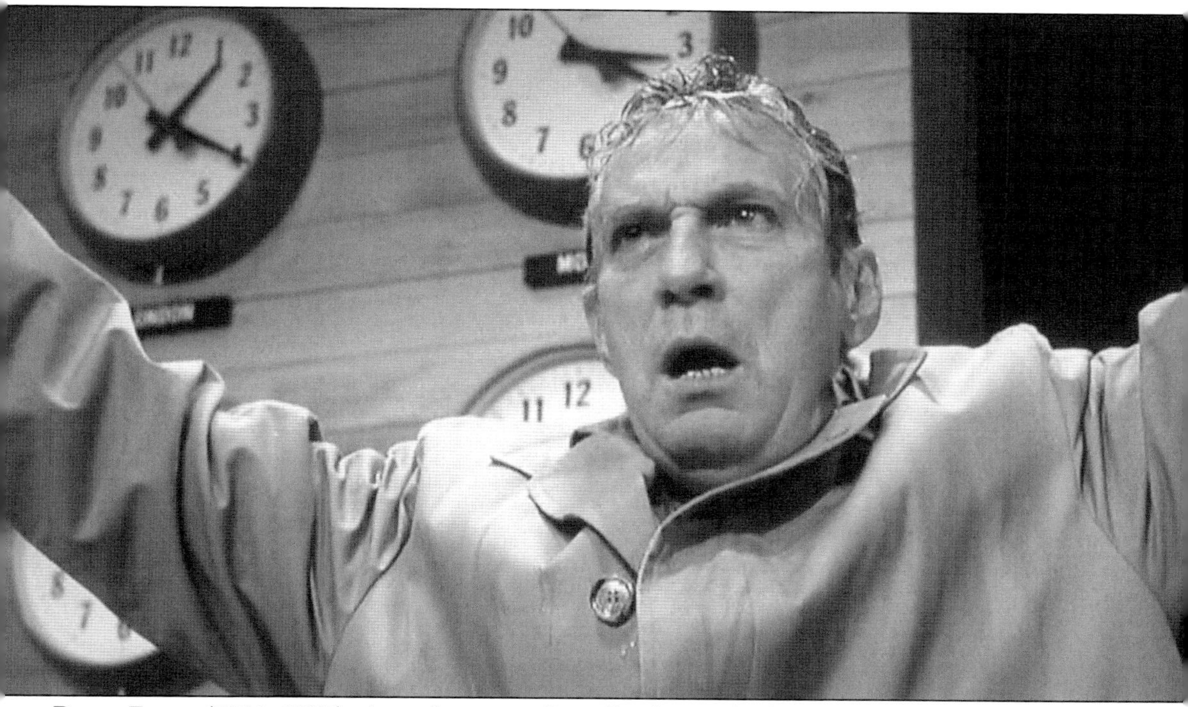

Peter Finch (1916–1977). Australian actor Peter Finch was the first person to win an acting Oscar posthumously. It was awarded for the role of unstable TV anchorman Howard Beale in 1976's *Network*. Beale's signature line, "I'm mad as hell and I'm not going to take this anymore!" has entered the popular lexicon. Finch made films and appeared on radio regularly during the 1930s and 1940s. He caught the attention of Laurence Olivier, who encouraged him to move to London. Despite suffering from stage fright, Finch would make the occasional Hollywood film during this period of his life, but was primarily based in England. Finch first achieved international stardom playing Dr. Fortunati in *The Nun's Story* (1957). He died after suffering a massive heart attack in the lobby of the Beverly Hills Hotel at age 60. (Cathedral Mausoleum, Corridor A, Crypt 1224.)

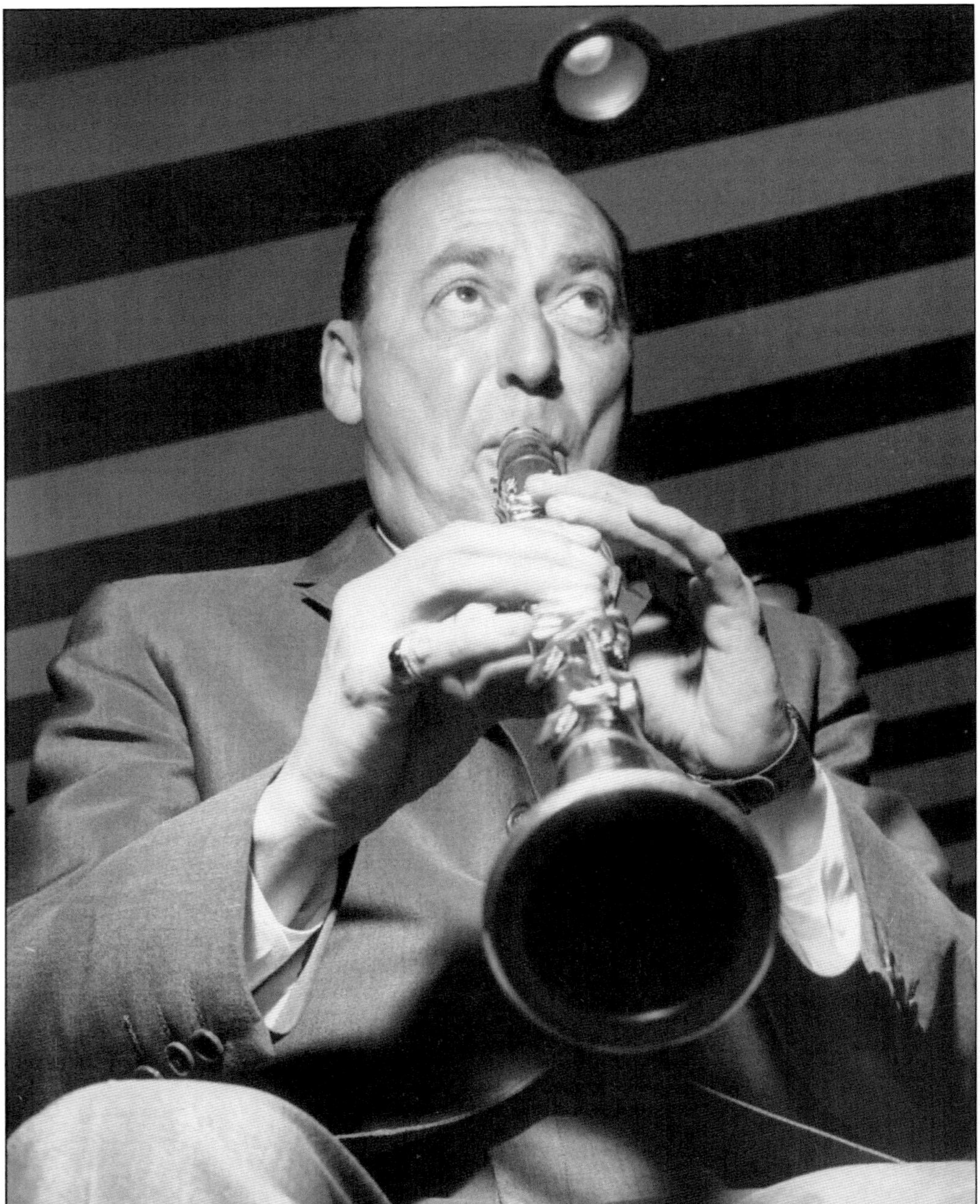

Woody Herman (1913–1987). Woody Herman was one of the most popular big band leaders of the 1930s and 1940s. He led several different bands, each known as The Herd. Herman began his musical career as a clarinet and saxophone player when he was 12. He later played with various big bands, until he became a bandleader himself. Perhaps his biggest hit came in 1939 with the five million–selling song "Woodchopper's Ball." The hits kept coming. By 1946, Herman and his band were the most popular in America, well respected by both his peers and the public. Unfortunately, family issues forced Herman to retire that same year at the height of his popularity. He died at the age of 74 in 1987. As an example of how tastes have changed over the years, Herman was the halftime performer for Super Bowl VII in 1973. (Court of the Apostles, Unit 19, Crypt 6689.)

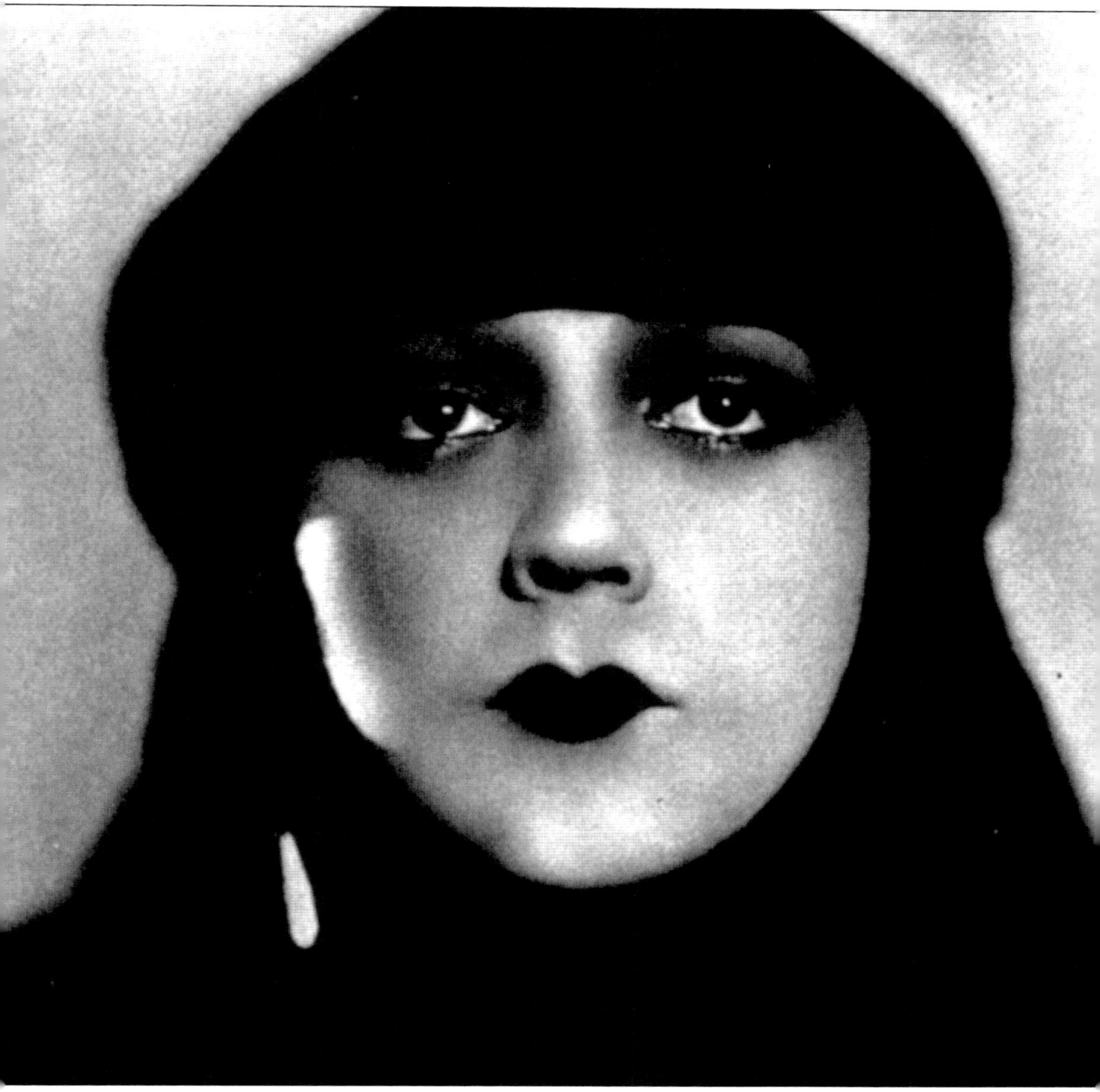

Barbara La Marr (1896–1926). Barbara La Marr was born Reatha Dale Watson in Yakima, Washington. Widely billed as "The Girl Who Was Too Beautiful," La Marr's beauty came with both brains and talent. She first made it in Hollywood as a screenwriter before Mary Pickford suggested that her face best belonged in front of the camera. La Marr appeared in 30 films, and married five times. She also picked up a four-figure-a-week heroin and cocaine habit along the way after studio doctors gave her hard drugs to assuage the pain of an ankle injury she sustained on set. La Marr never made it out of her 20s, dying a few months before Valentino from tuberculosis and kidney failure aggravated by anorexia. An estimated 40,000 mourners showed up to view her body. (Cathedral Mausoleum, Corridor A, Crypt 1308.)

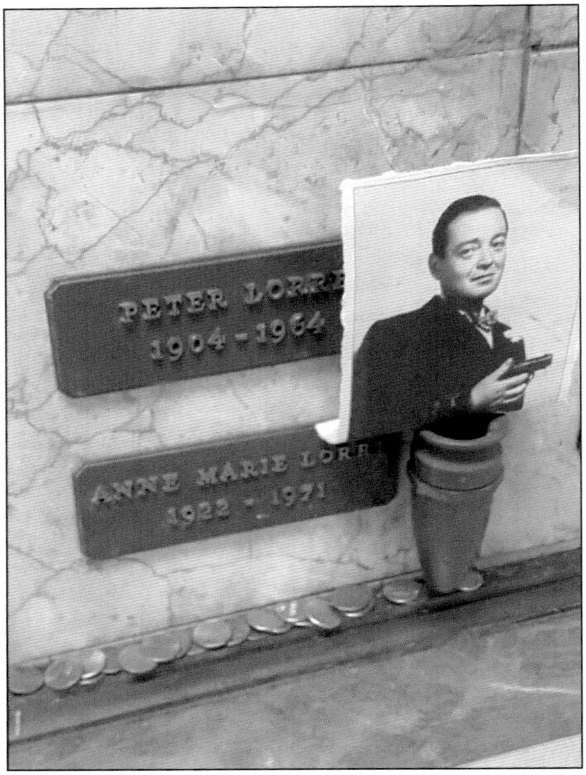

Peter Lorre (1904–1964) Actor Peter Lorre secured his spot as a Hollywood immortal with his portrayals of Joel Cairo in *The Maltese Falcon* and as the black marketeer Ugarte in *Casablanca*. He is buried here with his third and final wife, Anne Marie. His daughter Catherine almost became a victim of the Hillside Strangler serial killer (in fact, two men) but was let go after the killers learned the identity of her father. Both of the killers just happened to be Peter Lorre fans. (Cathedral Mausoleum, Corridor C, Alcove of Reverence, Tier 1, Niche 5.)

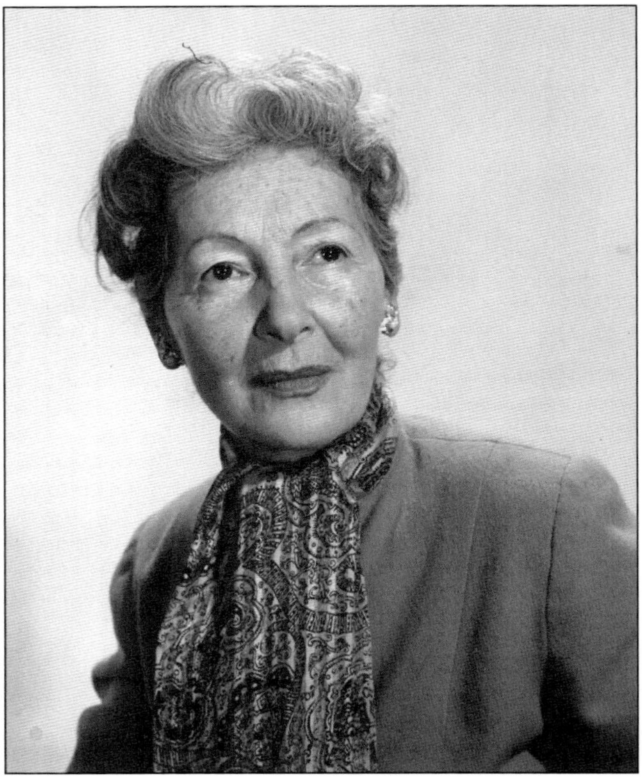

Cilia Lovsky (1897–1979). Actress Celia Lovsky was married to Peter Lorre from 1934 to 1945. They met in Europe and fled from the Nazis together. After her divorce from Lorre, Lovsky became a character actor on television with several credits, including one for an episode of *Star Trek*, where she played the leader of the planet Vulcan. (Cathedral Mausoleum, Corridor C, Alcove of Reverence, Tier 11, as "Cecile Lorre.")

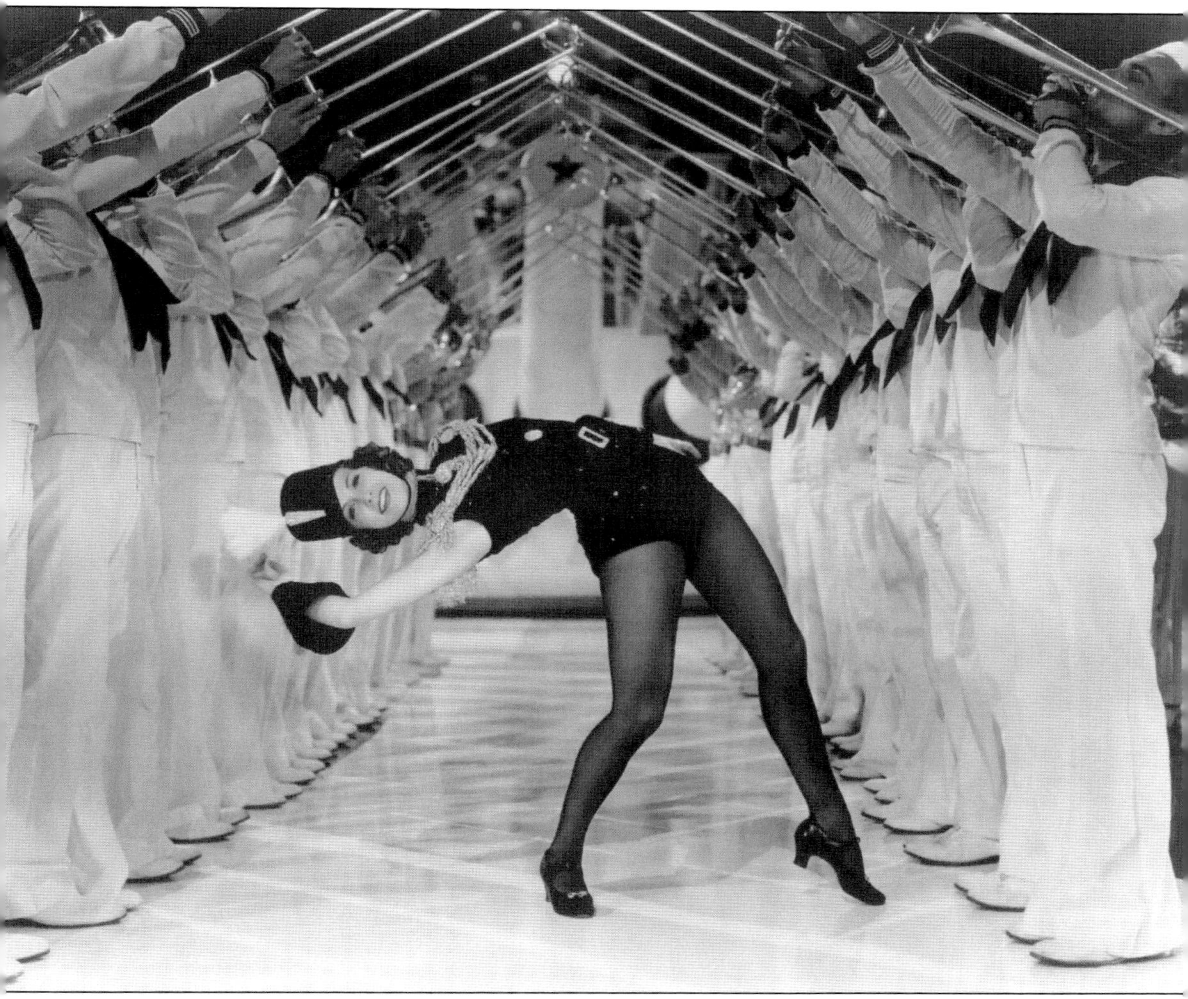

Eleanor Powell (1912–1982). Eleanor Powell was such a great dancer that she was said to have intimidated Fred Astaire. As one of MGM's top dancers in musicals during the 1930s and 1940s, she helped keep the studio profitable during the darkest days of the Depression. She made her film debut in 1935, but was unimpressed with Hollywood and decided not to stay. She was only persuaded to carry on when MGM agreed to outrageous salary demands she made hoping they would turn her down. Powell starred opposite many of the era's top male dancers, including Astaire, who she was paired with in *Broadway Melody of 1940*. Their dancing to "Begin the Beguine" is considered by some to be the finest in film history. Powell was married for a time to actor Glenn Ford. (Cathedral Mausoleum, Foyer, Tier 3, Niche 432.)

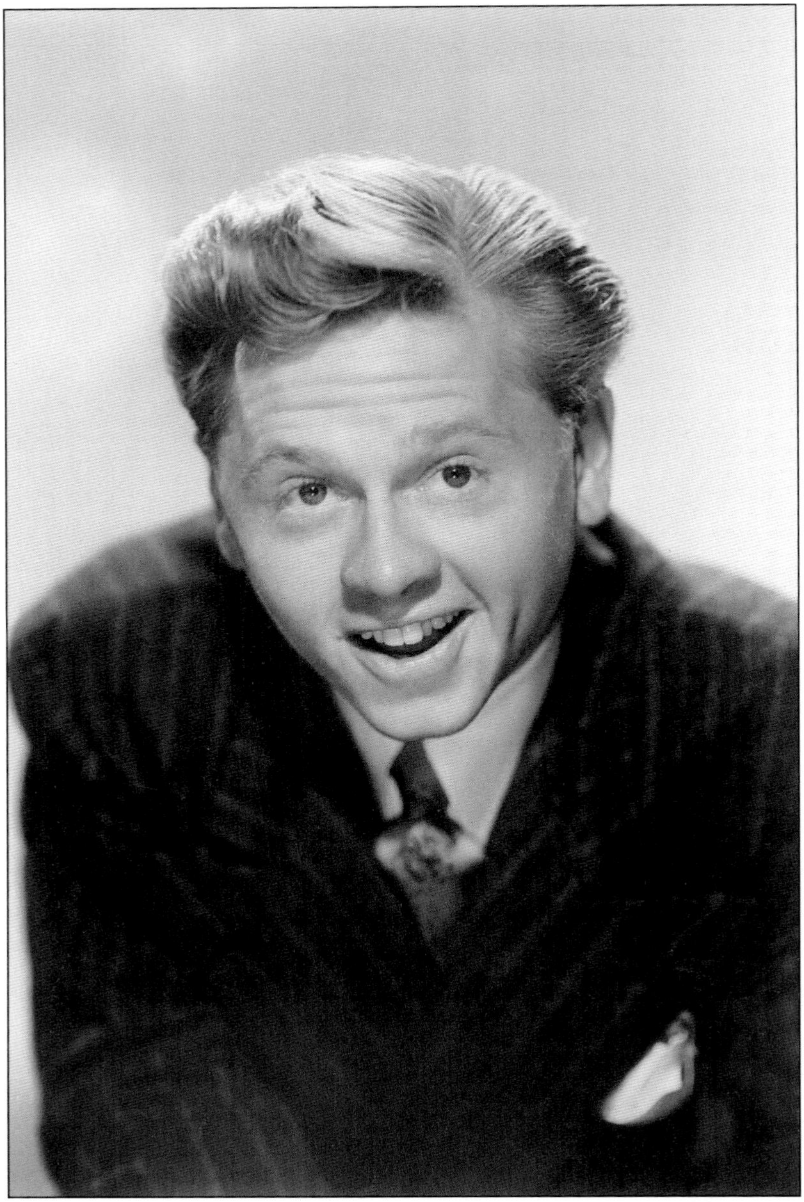

Mickey Rooney (1920–2014). Five-foot two-inch Mickey Rooney is one of the latest luminaries to be added to the H4E ranks. He enjoyed a stellar 90-year Hollywood career. He made over 300 films and was one of the last living actors from the silent era. Rooney began his career in vaudeville and made his first screen appearance at the age of six. He became a star playing the title role in 15 Andy Hardy films in the 1930s and 1940s opposite new H4E mate Judy Garland. He became the first teenager to be nominated for an Academy Award, and by 25 had made over 40 films. Rooney was the top box office draw for the years 1939–1941. Drafted in World War II, Rooney spent two years entertaining troops overseas. He returned to Hollywood in 1945 to find that his services were no longer wanted. He struggled for years to find work but bounced back with several successful film roles in the 1960s. Rooney suffered from addictions to alcohol, pills, gambling, and apparently weddings, marrying eight times. He earned millions during his career but died nearly penniless. (Cathedral Lake View, Elevation 15, Couch B-1501.)

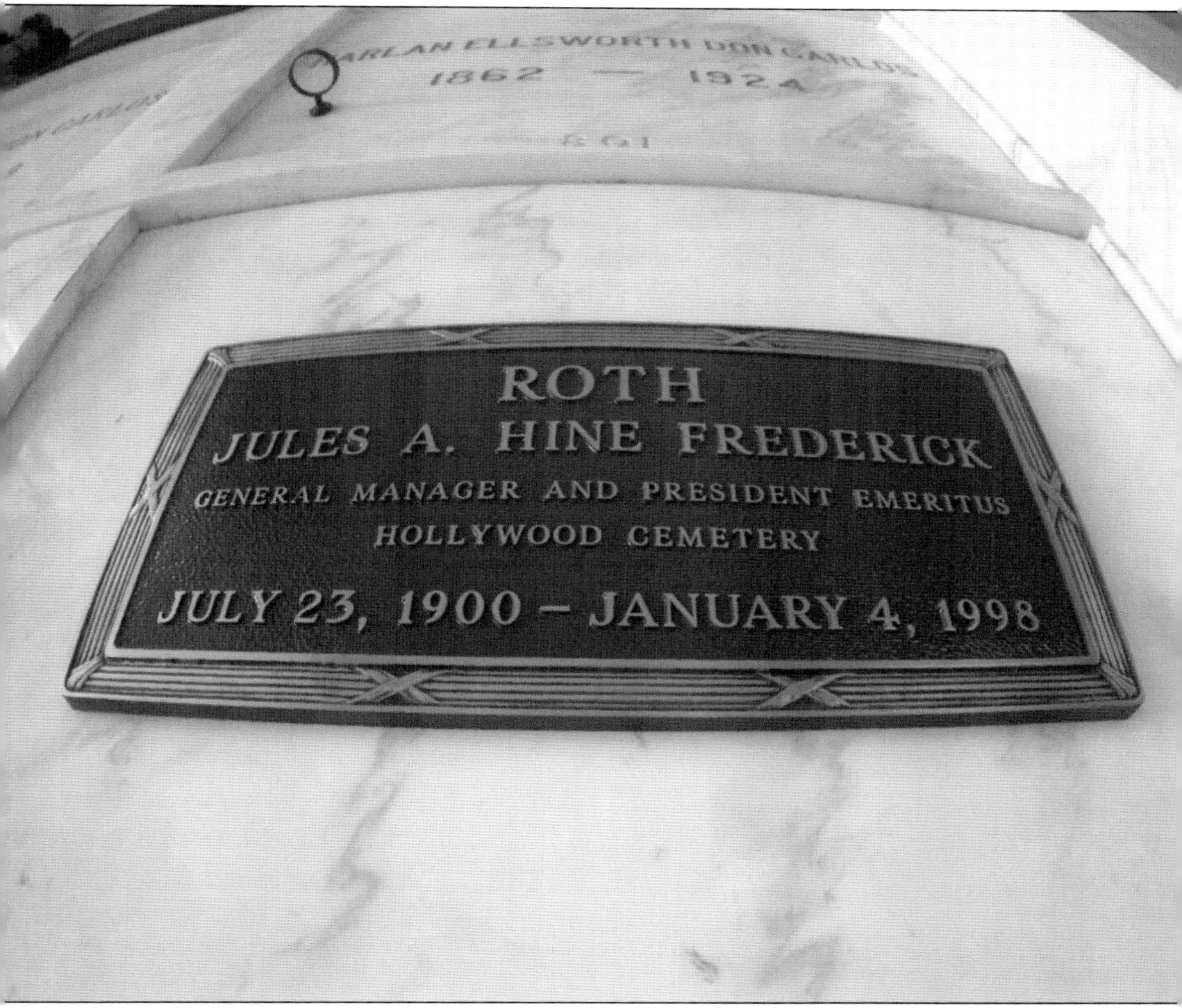

Jules Roth (1900–1998). Once upon a time, conman Jules Roth got out of San Quentin. He had been there for his part in bilking thousands of wide-eyed investors out of millions in what has come to be known as "The Great Los Angeles Swindle." Roth came to visit the graves of his parents in the Cathedral Mausoleum, looked around, liked what he saw, and began buying out shareholders of the privately-held cemetery. For the next 60 years, Roth used the cemetery as his personal ATM, spending lavishly on his wife and multiple mistresses, buying both a mansion in the Hollywood Hills and a 103-foot yacht named the *Queen of Sheba*. Keeping up Roth's luxurious lifestyle required feeding the beast with pitchforks full of money. Cracks began appearing in the cemetery's reputation, as well as in its walls and roofs. Toward the end of Roth's tenure, the only money coming in was the fees paid by family members to remove the bodies of their loved ones for reburial elsewhere. In 1998, Roth died. Three weeks later, Tyler Cassity bought and saved the place. Taphophiles everywhere thank him. (Cathedral Mausoleum, Corridor C, Crypt 802.) (Courtesy Pentax Forums.)

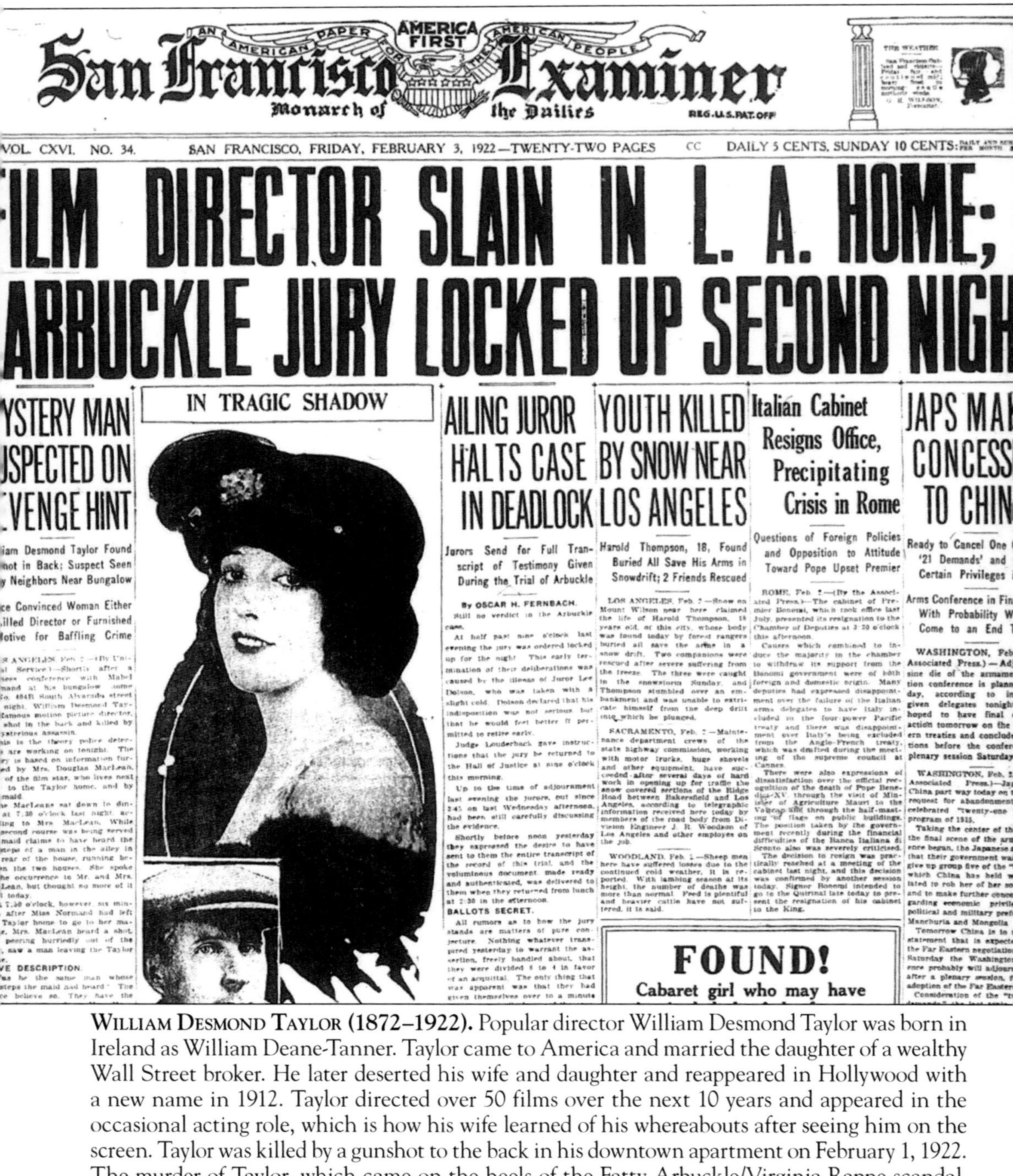
San Francisco Examiner

An American Paper for the American People — America First

Monarch of the Dailies

VOL. CXVI. NO. 34. SAN FRANCISCO, FRIDAY, FEBRUARY 3, 1922—TWENTY-TWO PAGES DAILY 5 CENTS, SUNDAY 10 CENTS

FILM DIRECTOR SLAIN IN L. A. HOME; ARBUCKLE JURY LOCKED UP SECOND NIGHT

MYSTERY MAN SUSPECTED ON REVENGE HINT

William Desmond Taylor Found Shot in Back; Suspect Seen by Neighbors Near Bungalow

Police Convinced Woman Either Killed Director or Furnished Motive for Baffling Crime

IN TRAGIC SHADOW

AILING JUROR HALTS CASE IN DEADLOCK

Jurors Send for Full Transcript of Testimony Given During the Trial of Arbuckle

By OSCAR H. FERNBACH.

YOUTH KILLED BY SNOW NEAR LOS ANGELES

Harold Thompson, 18, Found Buried All Save His Arms in Snowdrift; 2 Friends Rescued

Italian Cabinet Resigns Office, Precipitating Crisis in Rome

Questions of Foreign Policies and Opposition to Attitude Toward Pope Upset Premier

JAPS MAKE CONCESSIONS TO CHINA

Ready to Cancel One of '21 Demands' and Certain Privileges

Arms Conference in Final With Probability Will Come to an End

FOUND!

Cabaret girl who may have

William Desmond Taylor (1872–1922). Popular director William Desmond Taylor was born in Ireland as William Deane-Tanner. Taylor came to America and married the daughter of a wealthy Wall Street broker. He later deserted his wife and daughter and reappeared in Hollywood with a new name in 1912. Taylor directed over 50 films over the next 10 years and appeared in the occasional acting role, which is how his wife learned of his whereabouts after seeing him on the screen. Taylor was killed by a gunshot to the back in his downtown apartment on February 1, 1922. The murder of Taylor, which came on the heels of the Fatty Arbuckle/Virginia Rappe scandal, scared Hollywood studio heads into an era of self-imposed censorship and added "morality clauses" to actors' contracts. Actresses Mabel Normand, Mary Miles Minter, and Edna Purviance each had relationships with Taylor, and the fallout from the murder essentially ended their careers. The murder was never solved, but a recent book speculates that the murderer was in fact a career criminal who was blackmailing Taylor. If this is true, the killer of William Desmond Taylor is also now a permanent resident of Hollywood Forever. (Cathedral Mausoleum, Corridor C, Crypt 594.)

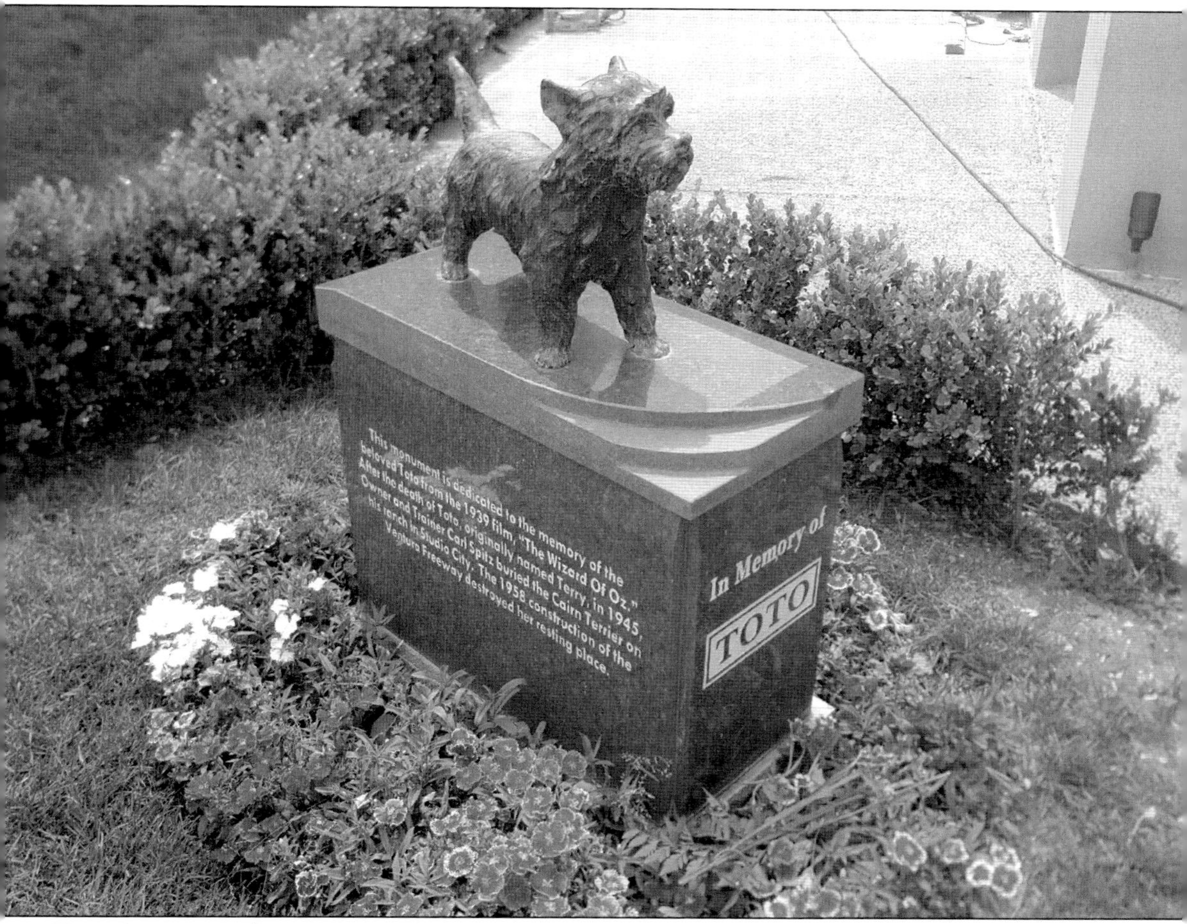

Toto (1933–1945). It is not just humans who have cenotaphs at H4E. No one-hit wonderdog, Cairn Terrier "Terry" appeared in over a dozen films in her career opposite A-listers like Shirley Temple and Spencer Tracy. But it is in the role of Toto for *The Wizard of Oz* (1939) that she is best remembered. Despite reportedly having a higher salary than each of the Munchkins, the film was a difficult experience for Terry, who got her leg broken when stepped on by a Winkie guard. Terry died in 1945 and her trainer, Carl Spitz, chose to bury her outside his dog training school in Studio City. Her eternal rest lasted just over 13 years until CalTrans obliterated the neighborhood to make way for the Ventura Freeway. This monument was placed here due to the efforts of the Toto Memorial Committee, which was headed up by FixNation, J.P. Myers, and Steve Goldstein. The monument is intended to honor all of Hollywood's film animals. (Outside Mausoleum.)

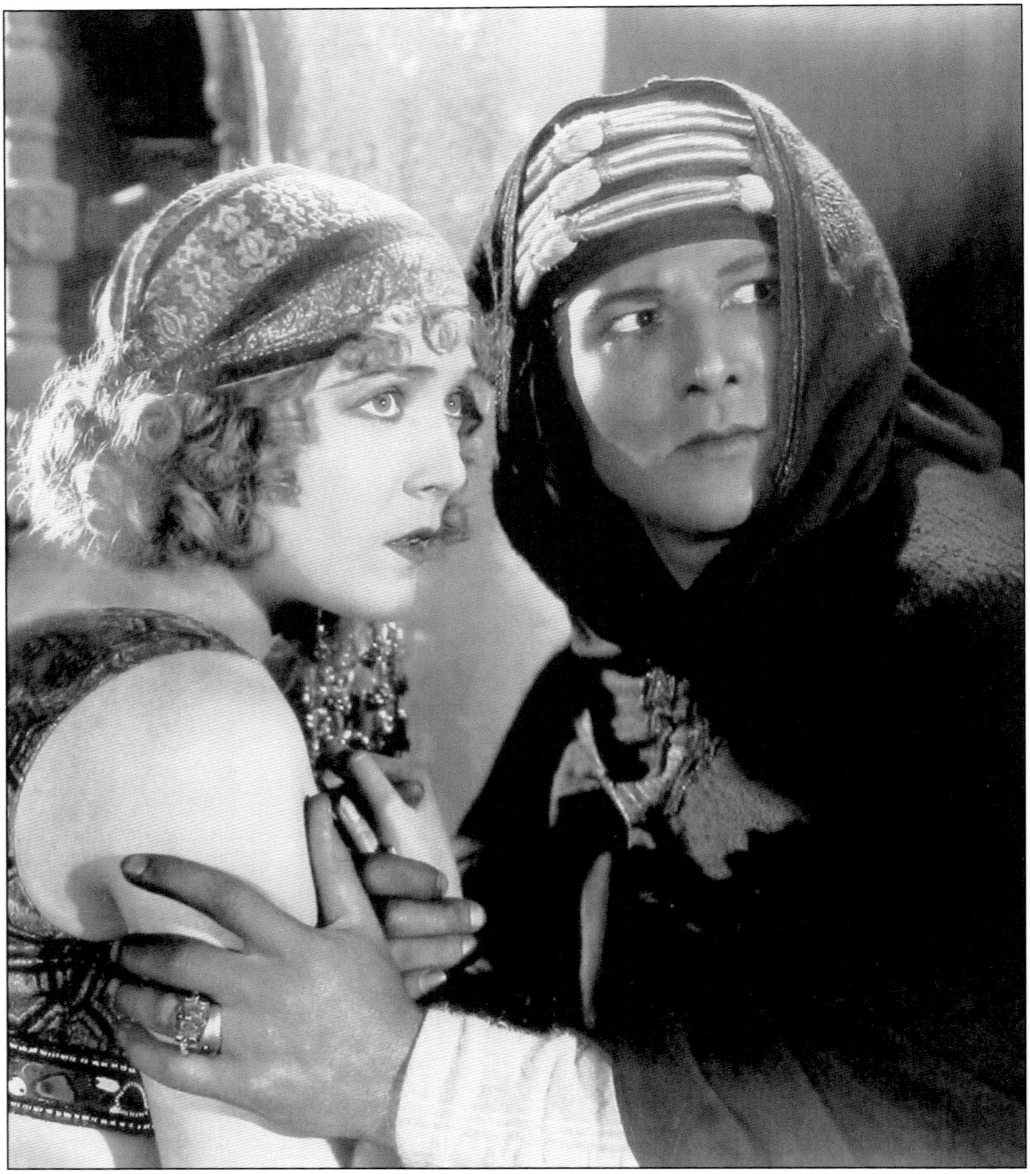

RUDOLPH VALENTINO (1895–1926) AND JUNE MATHIS (1889–1927). Valentino, the great Italian lover of the silent screen, came to America when he was 18. He supported himself in Los Angeles by acting in small roles and teaching the tango to doting older women. He appeared in a film that caught the attention of screenwriter June Mathis, who felt Valentino would be perfect for the starring role in her script for *The Four Horsemen of the Apocalypse*. *Four Horsemen* was released in 1921 and made Valentino an international star. Over the next five years, Valentino had more hits, but was usually on the verge of bankruptcy due to his lavish lifestyle and expensive divorces. He died suddenly at the age of 31 from a ruptured appendix. Mathis offered to house his body temporarily in a family crypt while a permanent resting place was chosen for him. Sadly, Mathis died from a heart attack shortly after Valentino's passing, and was entombed alongside her former friend, who was never moved. Valentino is pictured here in a scene from *Son of the Sheik* with costar Vilma Banky. (Valentino: Cathedral Mausoleum, Corridor A, Crypt 1205; Mathis: Cathedral Mausoleum, Corridor A, Crypt 1199.)

BOBS WATSON (1930–1999). Robert B. "Bobs" Watson was part of the Watson showbiz family of child actors during the 1930s known as "the first family of Hollywood." Bobs played the role of Pee Wee in *Boys Town* (1938) with Spencer Tracy. He was inspired by the film to become a Methodist minister. (Court of the Apostles, Unit 9, Crypt 6593.)

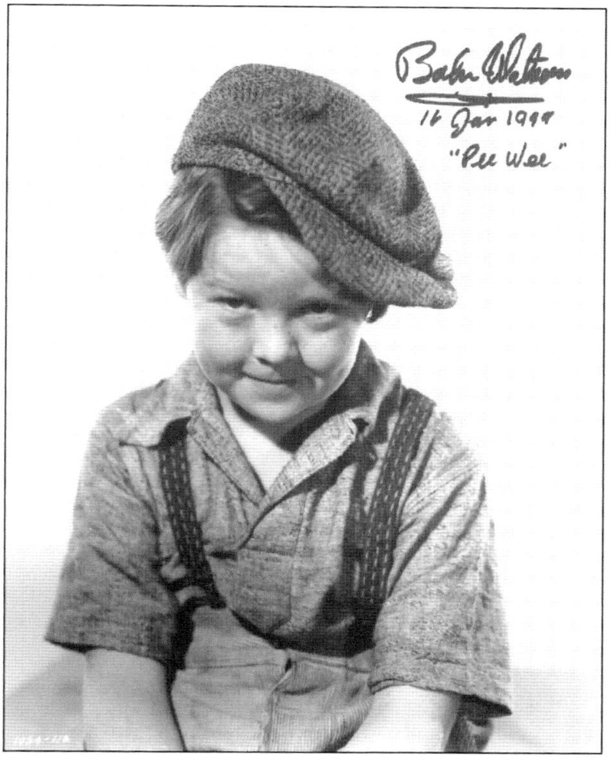

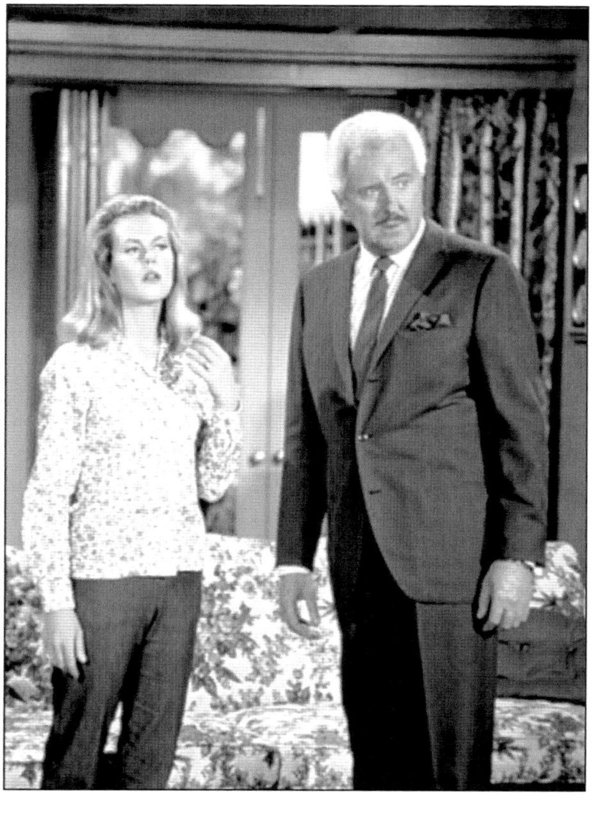

DAVID WHITE (1916–1990). A bronze bust of David White is in a niche near Rudolph Valentino's crypt. White's most famous role was playing Larry Tate, Darrin Stephens's boss on *Bewitched*. His son Jonathan is also here, having died two years before his father as a passenger on the ill-fated Pan Am Flight 103 that was blown up by a terrorist bomb over Lockerbie, Scotland. David White is pictured here with Elizabeth Montgomery. (Cathedral Mausoleum, Valentino Shrine 1, Tier 6, Niche 13.)

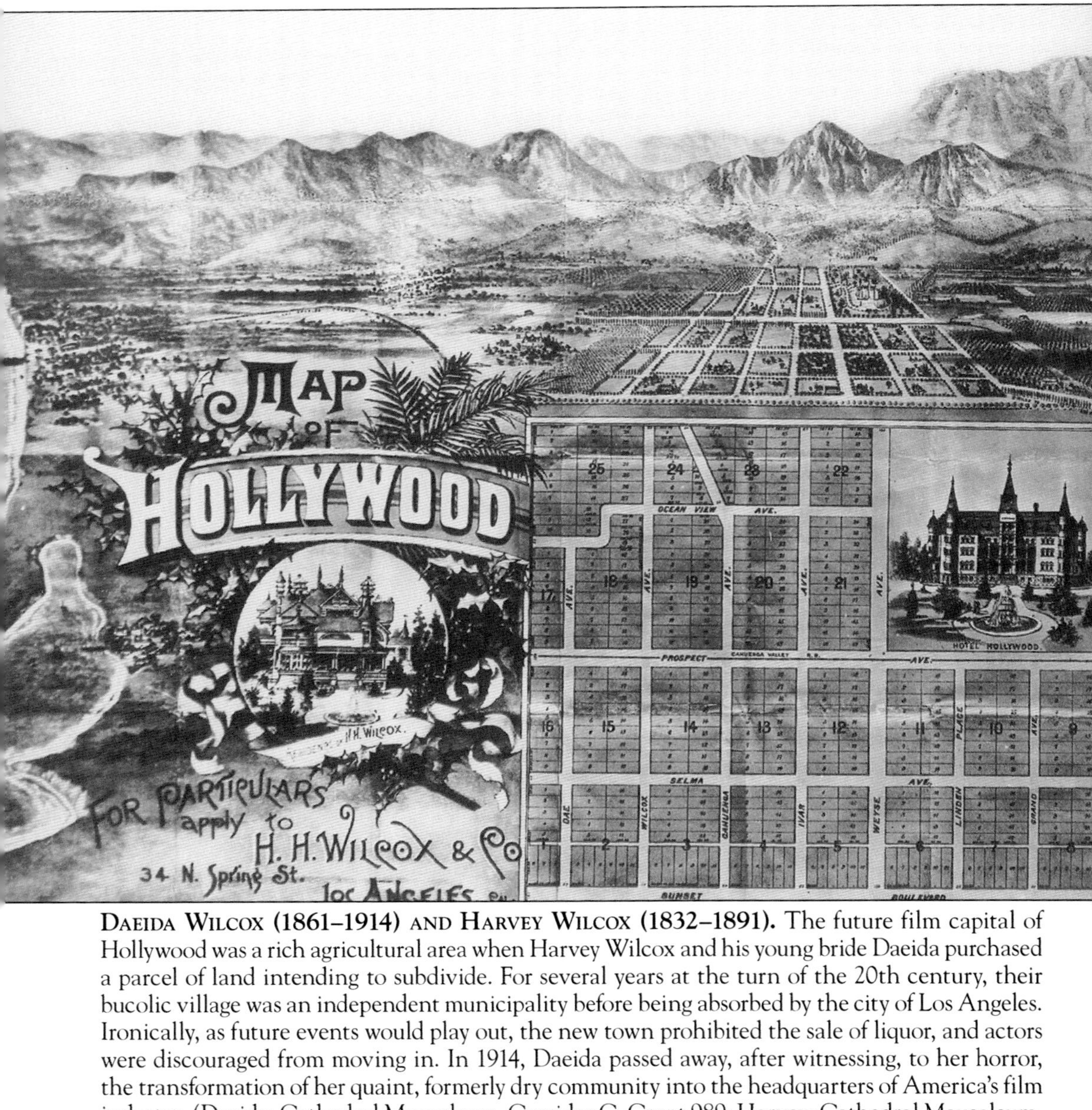

DAEIDA WILCOX (1861–1914) AND HARVEY WILCOX (1832–1891). The future film capital of Hollywood was a rich agricultural area when Harvey Wilcox and his young bride Daeida purchased a parcel of land intending to subdivide. For several years at the turn of the 20th century, their bucolic village was an independent municipality before being absorbed by the city of Los Angeles. Ironically, as future events would play out, the new town prohibited the sale of liquor, and actors were discouraged from moving in. In 1914, Daeida passed away, after witnessing, to her horror, the transformation of her quaint, formerly dry community into the headquarters of America's film industry. (Daeida: Cathedral Mausoleum, Corridor C, Crypt 989; Harvey: Cathedral Mausoleum, Corridor C, Crypt 594.)

AFTERWORD

Hollywood Forever is so rich with interesting residents that for every person featured in this book, another could be inserted in their place. H4E is filled with people who have left their mark on the world, whether for good or bad. Most of these personalities worked in artistic fields, especially in the visual arts. But inside the walls of H4E, some of the graves themselves are works of art.

A fine example is the monument of Carl Morgan Bisby (1898–1959) (Section 13, Space 521), which is shaped like a Pioneer Atlas rocket. Bisby was a graphic designer, not a rocket scientist like H4E resident Theodore Von Karman. He just liked rockets so much he chose to place one on his grave.

Just to the west of Bisby's rocket is a grave shaped like an LP record. And speaking of records, visitors to Section 2 must check out the "grave marker" of DEF Records that was placed here when the label "died" and was given a funeral.

But perhaps the most interesting marker in the entire cemetery can be found in the Secret Garden section, next to Paramount Studio's north wall. The marker is a plain piece of black slate. At its base is a box of chalk embedded into the ground. On this piece of poignant performance art, visitors are encouraged to write their own epitaphs. When you think about it, that is what we do, like it or not, each day of our lives.

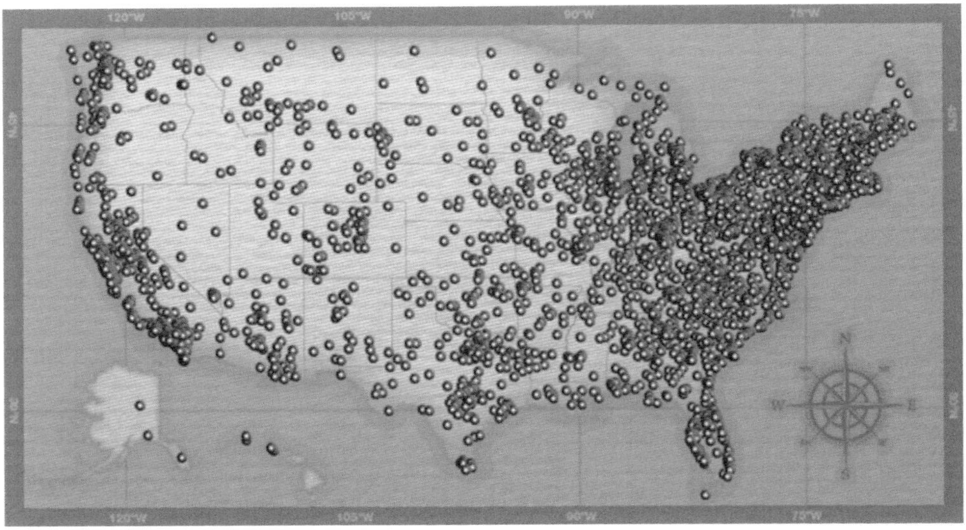